FREEDOM FLYERS

FREEDOM

The Tuskegee Airmen

J. Todd Moye

FLYERS

f World War II

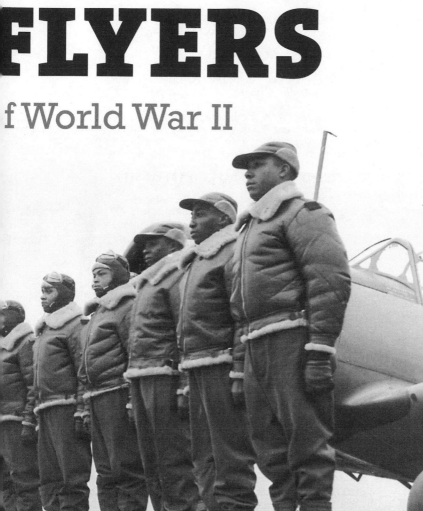

OXFORD
UNIVERSITY PRESS
2010

OXFORD
UNIVERSITY PRESS

Oxford University Press, Inc., publishes works that further
Oxford University's objective of excellence
in research, scholarship, and education.

Oxford   New York
Auckland   Cape Town   Dar es Salaam   Hong Kong   Karachi
Kuala Lumpur   Madrid   Melbourne   Mexico City   Nairobi
New Delhi   Shanghai   Taipei   Toronto

With offices in
Argentina   Austria   Brazil   Chile   Czech Republic   France   Greece
Guatemala   Hungary   Italy   Japan   Poland   Portugal   Singapore
South Korea   Switzerland   Thailand   Turkey   Ukraine   Vietnam

Published by Oxford University Press, Inc.
198 Madison Avenue, New York, NY 10016

www.oup.com

Oxford is a registered trademark of Oxford University Press

Library of Congress Cataloging-in-Publication Data
Moye, J. Todd.
Freedom flyers : the Tuskegee Airmen of World War II / J. Todd Moye.
p.   cm.
Includes bibliographical references and index.
ISBN 978-0-19-538655-4
1. United States. Army Air Forces. Fighter Group, 332nd.
2. United States. Army Air Forces. Fighter Squadron, 99th.
3. United States. Army Air Forces. Composite Group, 477th.
4. World War, 1939–1945—Aerial operations, American.
5. United States. Army Air Forces—African American troops.
6. World War, 1939–1945—Regimental histories—United States
7. World War, 1939–1945—Campaigns—Europe.
8. World War, 1939–1945—Participation, African American.
9. African American air pilots—History. I. Title.
D790.252332nd.M69 2010
940.54'4973—dc22
2009034079

1 3 5 7 9 8 6 4 2

Printed in the United States of America
on acid-free paper

Title page illustration: Maj. James A. Ellison reviews the first class of Tuskegee cadets at
TAAF, returning the salute of Mac Ross. *U.S. Air Force Historical Research Agency.*

For Luke and Henry

Contents

FREEDOM FLYERS

Prologue
"This Is Where You Ride"

John Roach grew up in the South End of Boston, the son of West Indian immigrants. His father, a native of Montserrat, had fought for the British Empire in World War I in a unit composed entirely of dark-skinned men and worked in Boston as a laborer; his mother worked for white families as a domestic. Roach's neighborhood was mixed—"Chinese, Japanese, Italians, Greeks, Russians, all kinds of people." Scraps with kids from the Irish neighborhoods nearby were not uncommon, but Roach cherished his experience growing up in the South End. "I think it was a gratifying experience to live in that area because it was like an international community," he remembered. "You got to know each other and got to realize that no matter where you're born, you're a person. Everybody has likes and dislikes, everybody has quirks that you may or may not like. And you realize that you just take people as they come, and the better you treat them, the better they'll treat you in most cases." He learned something else from his parents: "You can't fight your way up to the top with your fists. You can with your character." Roach developed a keen mind and a strong character, and he expected to rise as high in life as his talents could take him.[1]

As a child, Roach developed a fascination with airplanes. His mother later told him that when she took him for walks in his baby carriage, he would scan the skies for airplanes and point at them excitedly if any should pass overhead. In elementary school he found kindred spirits, two classmates who shared his interest in flying machines. "We found out that you could get to East Boston Airport by going down to Rose Wharf on Atlantic Avenue in Boston, and there was a ferry that went across the bay to the edges of the East Boston neighborhood. We'd walk along in front of where the ferry came in and where you paid your money to go across on the ferry, and we'd beg pennies from the neighbors going by until we had 4¢," enough for ferry fare. From the ferry landing in East Boston they walked a mile or more to the airport.

"You couldn't get out on the airport, but you could hang on the fence. And we would hang on the fence and watch the airplanes take off and land. Once in a while one would taxi by, and we'd just go out of our minds," Roach said. "We'd do that all day on a Saturday after we had done our chores at home, and then we'd head on back, beg pennies again from the people on the sidewalk, come across on the ferry, and then walk home. My mother never knew I did that, or she would have killed me.

"That was my introduction to the aircraft," Roach remembered. "I just watched them take off. I couldn't understand how a huge thing like that could get up in the air and fly so graceful, but that did it. I said, 'Somehow I'm going to fly airplanes.' I didn't know how. I didn't know where or why or when, but I knew somehow I'd do it. My mother said she thought so too when she found out I liked airplanes." Roach could not have known it then, but the nation's armed forces systematically denied African Americans even the opportunity to learn to fly, and civilian institutions were not much more accommodating. At the beginning of 1939, the year Roach turned fourteen, there were only twenty-five licensed African American pilots in the entire country.[2]

Roach attended racially integrated Boston public schools. When he graduated from Mechanic Arts High School, a venerable institution several miles from his home, in 1943, he knew little of the political machinations on the part of the National Association for the Advancement of Colored People (NAACP) and other black institutions that had recently forced the U.S Department of War to open a military flight training facility in Tuskegee, Alabama, for African Americans. He just knew that he wanted to fly. "That's when I found out that there was this unit being established at Tuskegee Army Air Field to train black pilots," he said. Before then it had "never crossed my mind that there were no black military pilots. I figured, you know, airplanes were airplanes" and could be flown by anyone with the desire and ability to learn how to fly them. Roach, who considered himself as patriotic and gung-ho about military service as any other American teenager, began devouring reports from the Tuskegee program that he found in the black newspapers in his neighborhood barbershop. Six months after his seventeenth birthday, in June 1943, Roach gathered up his birth certificate, his diploma, and a letter from his parents giving him permission to join the armed forces, and set off for the recruiting station in downtown Boston to enlist in the Army Air Forces (AAF) for flight training.

"What would you like, sonny?" a white sergeant at the station asked him. Roach answered that he had come to join the AAF. The sergeant explained to him, not unkindly, that the AAF was not accepting black recruits but that he was welcome to sign up for service in the infantry. Roach started to argue with the sergeant based on what he had learned from the newspapers, thought better of it, and left. He went to nine other recruiting stations in greater Boston and was rebuffed at each one. Roach started to wonder if he wasn't being discriminated against. "I was kind of surprised because after reading the African American newspapers and all the other papers,

I thought all of this stuff was south of the Mason-Dixon Line, but here I'm finding it right here in Boston, Massachusetts," he recalled.

Roach convinced himself that all of the military recruiters he had encountered so far were Southerners who had been assigned to Boston, and "they're carrying that thing"—racial prejudice—"with them." On his tenth attempt, at what he believed was the only recruiting station in Boston he had not already tried, he explained his predicament to an Aryan-looking corporal who listened politely to the story. To Roach's unending surprise (he was still chuckling about it in 2001), the corporal agreed to process his papers, scheduled him for physical exams at Fort Devens outside of Boston, and arranged for a staff car and chauffeur to drive him there.

Roach passed the exams, was assigned to a training class at Tuskegee, and received a train ticket to Biloxi, Mississippi, where he would first undergo basic Army training at Keesler Field. Roach got on the train at Boston's South Station, "and I sat down, about the sixth car back, which was fine; it was comfortable, it was away from the coal-driven engine," he said. "I rode all the way down to Washington, D.C. Everything was going fine."

At Washington's Union Station a D.C. police officer stepped onto the train. The lawman scanned Roach's car, noticed the young soldier, and approached him. "I didn't pay any mind, because I had my ticket and military stuff and everything," Roach said. "So the policeman is going by, and he looks at me, and he says, 'What are you doing here?' I had no idea what he was talking about. I said, 'I've enlisted in the Air Force. I'm going to pilot training.' He said, 'No, no, what are you doing sitting here?' I said, 'The seat was empty, so I sat here.' He said, 'Come on with me before I throw you off the train.'"

The policeman "took me down to the first car behind the coal car"—the dirtiest, smokiest, least comfortable car on the train—"and that was where African Americans were." By law, it was the only place black Americans could sit when traveling through the South, a region the nation's capital was culturally very much a part of in 1943. For the very first time in his life, John Roach met Jim Crow. The policeman said, "This is where you ride."

Roach was livid. As the train left Washington, his cheeks burning, still stunned and indignant, Roach caught sight of an American flag waving in front of the U.S. Capitol. He began thinking about the policy makers who worked there. "I wonder if those people know what's going on out here," Roach thought to himself. Even sixty years later, he claimed, "I couldn't believe they did."

Horace Augustus Bohannon required no introduction to Jim Crow. The tenth of ten children born into very poor circumstances in Atlanta, Georgia, he knew all about racial segregation and unequal treatment long before he came of age. "You knew that you didn't go that way because that was white only, and you know that you're supposed to be reserved—or preserved—over here. But that's the way we came up. We had to learn to live with it," Bohannon remembered. "Somewhere early in life, my mother got us to understand that if you live right, you could do well despite the segregation laws and so forth." They could survive, if not thrive, even in the unjust system if they followed her simple piece of advice: "You do right."[3]

Bohannon's family suffered terribly in the Great Depression, so he got the first of many jobs at the age of eight. His favorite childhood assignment was as a helper on a laundry truck, because the laundry service made pickups and deliveries at Candler Field, Atlanta's airport: "Once you got there, there were these pilots standing around talking," Bohannon recalled. "You didn't get to touch the airplanes, but you were at least in the audience, listening to them talk, which I enjoyed." The truck's driver, "a full-fledged Georgia cracker, filled up with all the things that his father had taught him," noted Bohannon's interest, took pity on him, and tried to talk the boy out of what was quickly becoming his life's dream. "Horace, I know you like that stuff, but I think you're wasting your time," Bohannon remembered the man telling him. "There is no chance in the world that you could ever work around them or be one of the pilots."

"I did not argue with him, but I like to look back on it today, and I wish I could see that same man," Bohannon said before he died in 2003. "He didn't mean to be destructive; he just thought he was doing me a favor to say, 'Don't even dream about it.' I never quit dreaming about it."

Bohannon worked his way through Booker T. Washington High School in Atlanta and went on to study at Lincoln University just outside of Philadelphia. When Lincoln began a program to train civilian pilots, Bohannon "wasn't far back in the line of students that went down to sign up. It was so exciting," he recalled, "because there was something new every day. I don't care who you were; there was always something that you didn't know, about flying, about the whole world."

Bohannon dropped out of college after his junior year and returned home to earn money. A friend in Atlanta let him know about Tuskegee Army Air Field (TAAF), the military base under construction about a day's drive away, in Tuskegee, Alabama. Tuskegee Institute had been training civilian pilots for a number of years and had just opened Moton Field, a primary flight training base it operated under contract for the Army Air Corps (AAC). Now the War Department was building TAAF from scratch on the outskirts of town.

The idea of building an air base intrigued Bohannon. He found a job at TAAF as a carpenter's apprentice. Then almost as soon as he got to Tuskegee, he learned of a program in the works to train black instructor pilots for the incoming cadets. Bohannon used the skills he had learned in civilian pilot training to pass the entrance exam for that program, and he began the training course. When the program was unexpectedly interrupted, he found work driving the station wagon that ferried aviation cadets back and forth from their living quarters at Tuskegee Institute to Moton Field and later was hired as the timekeeper in the control tower, tabulating cadets' flight times.

In March 1943, unable to save enough money to allow him to return to Lincoln, Bohannon quit his job at Moton Field and went back to Atlanta to drive a cab. By September he had saved enough money to resume his studies and was back in Pennsylvania. Once there, he found out that he had been drafted into the Army. He turned back around and reported to Fort Benning, Georgia, in October. He applied for transfer and was accepted into the flying corps, transferred to Keesler Field for basic training, and made his way back to Tuskegee as a flight cadet. Bohannon was surprised at how well he took to military life, but he did, mainly because "in the Army Air Corps you got to know just millions of people who had dreams and desires and so forth." He cherished the camaraderie he developed with the cadets he met there, young men like Charles Johnson Jr., whose renowned father was the president of Fisk University in Nashville; Mitch Higginbotham, whose first cousin A. Leon Higginbotham would become a distinguished attorney and federal judge; and "Pokey" Spaulding, whose family managed the North Carolina Mutual Insurance Co. in Durham, North Carolina, one of the most prosperous black businesses in the country. At the outset of the program, the AAC only accepted cadets who had completed at least two years of college, so the Tuskegee training program drew from the black elite. Pilot Roscoe C. Brown Jr. may have been correct when he said, "The Tuskegee Airmen were probably the most talented group of African-American men ever brought together in one place."[4]

Sixty years later Bohannon could still recite the "dodo" verses he was forced to memorize as a cadet. If an upperclassman asked, "What time is it?" he had to stand at attention and say, " 'Sir, the inner workings and hidden mechanisms of my poor chronometer are in such a sad state of discord with the great sidereal movement by which all time is commonly reckoned that I cannot with any degree of accuracy give you the correct time. However, without fear of being too wrong or too far off, I will say that it is fifty-eight minutes, twenty-two seconds, two ticks of a tock past the hour of four, sir!' Oh, we had a good time," he recalled.

Bohannon remembered December 20, 1944, the day he graduated from the cadet program, as one of the proudest of his life, because he got to show his family around TAAF. "Papa came, and of course on guard at the gate were a black sergeant, a black corporal, a black private. The whole military is black," Bohannon said. "As he drives up through there, they find some other men doing their work—all over the place, except for the very top cadre of officers, we're all black. And that place was clean, orderly. I wish you could have seen it." His family was impressed.

But Bohannon's best day came soon after the war ended, when he was an officer in the all-black 332nd Fighter Group stationed at Godman Field in Kentucky. Officer-pilots who needed to log a certain number of hours per month were allowed to fly almost anywhere they wanted on weekends, provided aircraft were available. When Bohannon's time came, "Of course the place I wanted to fly was Candler Field."

Bohannon took off from Godman. When he radioed in his location and announced to the tower in Atlanta his intent to land, the flight controller there asked for a fighter pull-up. The maneuver would require Bohannon to fly in at low altitude, abruptly pull his P-47N propeller-driven fighter plane, one of the most powerful in the U.S. military's arsenal, into a straight vertical climb, loop around, and land. This was regular duty for a fighter pilot, but was guaranteed to provide a thrill at a civilian airport. On his initial entry, Bohannon radioed the controller, "Sir, what is the minimum altitude?" The response: "My grass needs cutting."

According to Bohannon, he barreled full-speed into Candler Field about 3 feet off the ground and pulled his aircraft straight into the air. When he reached the top of his loop, he engaged the plane's landing gear and cut the engine. The airplane descended into a perfect landing. "If you do it just right," he said, "you don't have to give it any gas. And that's the best one I ever did." Onlookers at Candler Field, perhaps some of them boys who were as crazy about flying as John Roach and Horace Bohannon had been, "were cheering and cheering and cheering.

"I figured they might not recognize me because the helmet covers your face, and all you can see [from outside the plane] is the goggles and the helmet," Bohannon said. "I took the helmet off, took the goggles off, raised the seat up so you could see there's an African American flying that brand-new airplane. That was the P-47N, the latest model. And it was pretty. All the way up the taxiway, they're cheering. Especially the black guys: 'Hooray! Hooray! Hooray!' "

Roy Chappell spent the first several years of his life in the small towns of Williamsburg and Pineville, Kentucky, before his parents moved the family to Monroe, Michigan. He learned all about strict systems of racial segregation in Kentucky, but he found an informal system at work in Michigan. Chappell attended integrated schools as one of very few black pupils in Monroe; he excelled as a student, graduating in the top 10 percent of his class, and as an athlete, lettering in football and starring on the track team.

Even so, he said, "in a town like Monroe you sort of knew the places that you shouldn't go. Nobody tells you, they didn't put up any signs, but you sort of know that they don't hardly want us in there, so don't go in that restaurant."[5]

His father died during Chappell's senior year of high school, in the depths of the Great Depression, but his family was able to scrape together enough money to send him off to Kentucky State College for Negroes. Chappell excelled there, too, winning election as president of his sophomore and junior classes. He was drafted into the Army in his junior year and allowed to take the entrance exam for pilot training. Unlike the other men he met in pilot training, he did not "come out of the womb wanting to fly," Chappell said. "All I was trying to do was stay out of the Army. I didn't want to sleep on the ground. I didn't want to carry that big old rifle." He found himself at an immediate disadvantage. A fellow cadet told him, "'I don't know how you're going to learn how to fly. You can't even drive a car.' But I said, 'That's OK.'"

Chappell completed the first two phases of flight training in Tuskegee but proved unable to master the techniques required of the third and last phase, advanced training. He had been learning to fly twin-engine bombers for the newly created 477th Medium Bombardment Group, but "washed out" of the program just short of earning his commission as an officer. Chappell failed to become a pilot, but the all-black 477th needed navigators and bombardiers, too. So Chappell shipped off to Sheppard Field in Wichita Falls, Texas, to attend navigation school. "On the base there must have been close to 1,500 or two thousand cadets," he said. "There were only thirty-five of us that were black. We had our own barracks. We had our own classroom. And we flew together as a unit." There were also other blacks, enlisted men, on the base. "We used to go over there to get haircuts, and we used to go over there sometimes to their little club they had," Chappell said. "And the people, the enlisted personnel on all these bases, they wanted us to succeed so bad you could just feel it." Chappell passed the training program and won his officer's commission. He assumed he would be transferred to the 477th at Godman Field, but instead Chappell's class was sent to Midland Army Air Base in west Texas to achieve dual ratings as navigator-bombardiers.

Having already been commissioned as officers, Chappell and his crew arrived at their new base and went to the officers' mess. The base commander informed them that as officer-cadets they would be expected to eat in the cadets' mess, but they convinced him that they were entitled to all the privileges enjoyed by other officers on the base, all of whom were white. "So that was fun," Chappell deadpanned. His class initially used the Midland Army Air Base officers' club without any trouble. After about two weeks, however, they received notice that they were no longer welcome there because there had been undefined threats of violence from other base personnel. "They said, 'Well, instead of being able to come to the officers' club, we'll give you room service.' So we had room service. We could call up, and they would deliver us a hamburger and a milk shake and all that." They enjoyed this particular luxury—which was of course unavailable to their white counterparts—but began writing letters of complaint to the NAACP, Eleanor Roosevelt, black newspapers, the War Department, and anyone they could think of who might be in a position to help them. "As a result," Chappell said, "about two weeks later we received a notice that the officers' club was now open for the colored officers to come back and use it, and the commanding officer on the base got shipped out to someplace else. So we went to the officers' club for the rest of the time that we were there."

Chappell's group graduated from bombardier training and joined the 477th at Godman just before the group transferred en masse to Freeman Field, Indiana. Immediately upon arrival, Col. Robert Selway, commanding officer at Freeman, designated that base's officers' club for "instructor personnel" and created another for "trainee personnel." "We didn't like this idea," Chappell remembered. "Everybody who was 'trainee personnel' happened to be black, and everybody that was 'instructor personnel' happened to be white. Although we had some guys back from a tour of duty overseas, all these were classified as 'trainees.' "[6]

More than one hundred officers of the 477th refused to obey Selway's designation order, which effectively segregated base facilities for officers in direct contradiction to War Department policy. Selway "started calling us in one at a time, and that thing was almost like a little court martial," Chappell said. "There were a couple of white officers, a couple of black officers, and a stenographer. And they asked us had we seen the order, had we read it?" Chappell answered that he had read the order segregating "instructors" and "trainees" and that he understood it, but under no circumstances would he obey it. "So then they read us the Sixty-fourth Article of War, and they had one of the legal people there to explain it to us: that in time of war when you disobey a direct order by your commanding officer you can be shot and all that kind of thing. Then the commanding officer gave us a direct order to sign the order, and I said, 'No, sir, I will not sign.' And we were sent back to quarters under arrest."

The 477th was transferred back to Godman Field, with 104 of its officers still under arrest. "And when we got back to Godman Field, they put barbed wire around the barracks and put up big poles with lights on top of them and all that shining down on us," Chappell recollected. "And the strange thing was that people that were coming in and out of our barracks were German prisoners of war. See, they all had free range to walk all over everywhere and everything. It seemed so strange to see something like this going on. But that's what happened."

The 477th was ostensibly training to fight in the Pacific. But the unit's numerous base transfers, Selway's poor leadership, and the low morale among the officers who were punished for their skin color left the group perpetually unprepared for combat, and Japan surrendered before the group could be deployed overseas. What Chappell remembered most about his World War II experience was not bitterness over the racial discrimination he and his fellow officers faced, however, but his group's collective determination not to disappoint other black Americans who looked up to them. Chappell, who had a terrific sense of blues humor, found that as disruptive as the transfers may have been, the travel from base to base had its advantages, too. A soldier who knew how to make the most of a situation could even enjoy a ride on a Jim Crow train. "A buddy and I would always say when we got on the train, 'You look for that lady with the shoe box!'" Black travelers could not count on being served in the trains' dining cars, and many of them could not have afforded to eat there anyway, so they invariably traveled with home-cooked fare in a telltale carrying case.

Chappell and his friend scanned each train for the seat next to the good Christian sister they just knew would be onboard with a scrumptious meal: "We know she's got some fried chicken, pound cake, and some deviled eggs!" Chappell recalled, "And she would say, 'Oh, you poor little soldier boy. I know you're hungry. You've had nothing to eat like this in a long time. Come over here and have a piece of my chicken.' We got on the train, man, and we started looking around: 'Look up there... Yeah, that's a shoe box!'" The cumulative effect of those longing looks from the enlisted men who needed the officers of the 477th to excel, the civilian bar patrons who never let Chappell and his mates pay for a drink, the generosity of the traveling church ladies "was really uplifting. It really helped a lot. That's the kind of thing we ran into all the time."

Milton Henry grew up with his ten brothers and sisters as a third-generation Philadelphian in a household where "we were poor, but we didn't know we were poor. We used to always clean our plates because [our parents told us] there were poor people who didn't have something to eat. And yet by any standards, we were just absolutely poor." That did not stop the family from taking advantage of the city's rich cultural offerings and excellent, desegregated public schools. Walter L. Henry Sr., a postal worker, and Vera Robinson Henry, a housewife, centered the family's life in the all-black Union Baptist Church, the sort of place where the congregation included "people who worked in all kinds of jobs and positions, and then you also had people like Marian Anderson and others who were big-time folks on the world scene." Walter Henry taught his sons, "Be patriotic. You cannot disgrace your race, you cannot disgrace your family, you cannot disgrace your nation."[7]

"Philadelphia," Henry said, "was just a great place for me to grow up. I guess the Quaker influence was there in Philly, and even though you could see evidence of discrimination if you really looked for it, we didn't look for it because nobody was all that offensive with this racism thing." Despite the pacifism that pervaded his hometown, when faced with the prospect of Hitler's Final Solution, Henry joined the war effort. "Killing folks because of their nationality [that is, ethnicity] was so foreign to everything that we had learned in church and certainly to the Quaker position," he said.

With his father's encouragement, Henry interrupted his studies at Lincoln University to sign up for the Army Air Corps in April 1941. He was ambivalent from the start. "Frankly," he remembered, "the one reason that I suppose that I went into the Air Corps was because the idea of killing somebody just did not suit me one bit." Flying airplanes, "You didn't have to put a bayonet into anybody. And it was such a nice, clean thought: that you could fight [for your ideals], but at the same time you didn't have to be involved in these brawls with people with bayonets and rifles and all that sort of thing."

Henry initially assumed that everyone in the American military had joined with the common purpose of defeating Adolf Hitler's brand of racism. He was disabused of that notion as soon as he got to Alabama. "I can only say that I was really shocked when I went south and met those people in Alabama. For the first time in my life, I met people who were not civil to me, and that was an extraordinary shock to me, really. That was so extraordinary, to find that racism was so predominantly important to the brass that ran the Air Corps and the Army."

Henry's official introduction to Jim Crow took place in Montgomery, Alabama, 40 miles west of Tuskegee, where he was assigned to a unit at Maxwell Field before beginning flight training. He enjoyed Montgomery. Alabama's capital city was home to Alabama State College for Negroes, and the campus attracted bright students and professors from all over the South and parts of the north. Henry liked getting to know them. With a friend he attended a social function in downtown Montgomery one day in 1942, then boarded a municipal bus headed back to Maxwell Field. "We didn't notice, but at the top of the bus there's a little bead [on a wire] that they were moving back and forth, and that was to signify that whites would sit in front of that and blacks would sit behind." They sat down near the front. "We rode down to the center of Maxwell Field, and at that point we began to see a whole lot of whites getting on the bus,"

Henry said. "The bus driver yells out, 'You niggers get in the back of the bus!' I'm an officer and a gentleman, and I don't think he knew anything about me. So for him to be referring to me as a nigger, I didn't think he was talking to me."

The bus driver again told the pair to move to the back of the bus. Henry's friend complied, leaving him alone in the front. "And then the bus got strangely quiet," he recalled. "I sat there for a second, and then I got up and I walked to the front of the bus, and I told him, 'Give me my nickel back.' I'm not accustomed to using profanity at that point, because old Philadelphians don't curse. It's just not appropriate. But I said to him, 'I ought to punch you in your damned mouth.'"

The driver reached under his seat for a gun. "I grabbed his wrist and held on to him. In the meantime, there are four British cadets on the bus, because at Maxwell Field the Royal Air Force was training there at the same time, and they came to my aid. They said, 'He's done nothing.'" Henry speculated that the British officers' strange accents threw the bus driver off; in any case, he was allowed to exit the bus without further incident. Military policemen arrived almost immediately and whisked him off to the base commander's office.

"You boys don't know how to act in the South," the commander told him. "I'm gonna help you out." The commander, Henry recalled, "got the most ignorant-looking nincompoop you ever saw in your life, and he said to him, 'I want you to instruct him on how to act in the South.' And I'm telling you, I was just so amazed." Henry was used to studying; he had excelled as a student at Lincoln, where he constantly engaged in informal debates with fellow students like Kwame Nkrumah, the future president of Ghana ("I liked Nkrumah because he was such an intense fellow," Henry said), but this new course was something else entirely.

Henry's instructor said, "'Whenever a white man looks at you, you don't look him in the eye. You drop your eye. And don't ever look at a white woman.' He went through a whole litany of junk that I was supposed to do. He was going to remake me into something I wasn't." Henry was baffled, he later said. "I don't want to walk around there with a whole litany of all the things that I'm not supposed to do. Heck, what about the white man. What's he supposed to not do to me?"

Northerners like Henry came to Alabama in such numbers during the war that the military developed a series of what were called "common sense" lectures designed to help the men acclimate to Jim Crow. But Henry refused to go along. "The South was a part of this nation, and I couldn't see where I had to go traipsing around on eggshells," he said. "I just couldn't feel that way. And I guess I just never have been able to understand: Why have I got to turn myself inside out to make somebody else feel better? No."[8]

John Roach, Horace Bohannon, Roy Chappell, and Milton Henry were not among the more than 450 Tuskegee-trained pilots who served the U.S. in overseas combat during World War II. But they and their fellow Tuskegee Airmen fought battles that were just as significant in the larger war to give American ideals meaning. Twelve years after Milton Henry was ejected from a Montgomery bus, the Rev. Martin Luther King Jr. ascended a Montgomery pulpit for the first time as a public figure. King, the newly chosen spokesman for the Montgomery Improvement Association, spoke on December 5, 1955, of his belief that "democracy transformed from thin paper to thick action is the greatest form of government on earth." King may not have known of Milton Henry then, but he had Henry's brand of "thick action" in mind that night, as he helped launch the Montgomery Bus Boycott.[9]

Nearly one thousand young men with similar backgrounds and similar expectations graduated from the Tuskegee Army Flying School between 1941 and 1945. Roughly 14,000 additional men and women worked alongside the pilots in some capacity—as civilian or military flight instructors, as secretaries, parachute-packers, medical doctors and nurses, mechanics, and in dozens of other jobs. Their personal narratives—the stories that describe what it was like to both propel and ride a wave of social change—survive in the archives of the Tuskegee Airmen Oral History Project, an effort on the part of the U.S. National Park Service to record the memories of the men and women who fought Adolf Hitler and Jim Crow simultaneously. Black pilots and black military and civilian support personnel in the Army Air Corps/Air Forces, those who served overseas and those who remained stateside, all shared the experience of fighting what the editors of the *Pittsburgh Courier* first called a "Double Victory" campaign: war against fascism abroad and racial discrimination at home.[10]

1

The Use of Negro Manpower in War

Wilson Vashon Eagleson II was "airplane-nuts" as a child. "I guess I have been interested in aviation all my life," he said. "The first time I got to ride an aircraft I was ten or eleven years old. I think [my family] gave me $5 to go and take an airplane ride from one of the old barnstormers back at the country fair years and years ago. That must have been back about 1930 or '31. It was a biplane with an open cockpit, and for $5 you'd get a couple of circles of the field and land. I got to ride in one of those, and that was the end of it; that's all I wanted to do the rest of my life." He collected airplane trading cards obsessively, covering one wall of his bedroom with them. "Anything I could get my hands on concerning airplanes, I read about it." Vash Eagleson dreamed of becoming a pilot himself, but as he grew older he began to understand that practical barriers would probably prevent him from realizing the ambition. "I guess you dream about something like that even though it seemed to be beyond [the realm of possibility]," he said. For one thing, "I knew that I would never be able to afford to learn to fly." It occurred to him only later that his skin color was the greatest barrier of all.[1]

That obstacle fell in World War II, but only as the result of a concerted effort on the part of African Americans. Even before the United States joined the conflict, they had made full inclusion in the Army Air Corps (AAC) and the field of aviation generally a paramount goal. It would be difficult to exaggerate the wonder and romance Americans of the late 1930s and early 1940s associated with flying, or the importance many blacks placed upon creating opportunities for themselves in the career field of aviation. Pilot Harvey Alexander explained what made flight so attractive for African Americans: "I was aware of discrimination and segregation on the ground, how things were there. But up in the air, I was free as a bird because I was in control. I decided what to do and when to do it and how to do it. Each time I landed, that good feeling left me because I was back on the ground and back into the same old–same old. But I loved to take that plane off and get in the air. It was a different feeling altogether."[2]

Pilots dominated the popular culture of the late Depression era; they were the heroes of boys' books, comic strips, and moving pictures even as Americans thrilled to the real-life exploits of Charles Lindbergh and other record-setting aviators. Flying an airplane required technical skills, quick

13

decision-making abilities, and a daring personality. The script of a Frank Capra–produced wartime propaganda film captured perfectly Americans' understanding of what it took to be a military pilot. The film's narrator, a Hollywood actor named Ronald Reagan, intoned dramatically, "[A] fighter pilot is a combination of a mathematician and an athlete, a scientist and a sharpshooter. He's got to know what goes on inside his plane. The heart of his fighter is steel and copper; its bloodstream is gas and oil. But its brain is the man who flies it." In their leather flight jackets, sunglasses, and scarves, airmen were the masculine ideal of the day. But the leaders of the elite AAC, which had been throughout its history to that point a fighting force of white men only, expected it to remain that way. This was the case as late as 1940, when Gen. Henry H. ("Hap") Arnold, chief of the AAC, wrote to his general staff, "Negro pilots cannot be used in our present Air Force since this would result in having Negro officers serving over white enlisted men. This would create an impossible social problem." Arnold proved mistaken in that belief, because black Americans were able to make a political issue of that "social problem."[3]

Wars inevitably produce unintended consequences for the societies that fight them. The greater the mobilization for war, the greater the scope and speed of the social changes it catalyzes. World War II was total war, and after December 7, 1941, the United States mobilized totally to prosecute it. The underpinnings of its national economy, social relations among its people, expectations about what kinds of people could perform what kinds of jobs: all shifted in some way to enhance the nation's ability to make war. All changed as a result of the national emergency, but Americans considered some changes the results of special cases that would revert to prewar norms when the emergency ended. American women, for instance, revolutionized their place in the workforce in the course of the war, but when their husbands and brothers came home from overseas they were unable to sustain many of the gains they had made. In contrast, no area of American social life underwent greater permanent change as a result of the war than that of race relations, because African Americans were able to force action on the debate over what one military policy statement called "The Use of Negro Manpower in War."

Blacks gained more in relative economic strength and in the civic sphere than any other group of Americans during the course of the war, and social trends that the wartime mobilization unleashed eventually broke down barriers of racial segregation and discrimination in American life. When the United States entered World War II, three-quarters of American blacks lived in the states of the former Confederacy, where fewer than one in twenty eligible black citizens were even allowed to register to vote and Jim Crow segregation was enforced by law. Most southern blacks lived rural lives, working with family members in sharecropping or tenant farming arrangements, which placed them in exceptionally vulnerable economic positions even before the Great Depression struck. They were especially hard-hit during that crisis; nearly 90 percent of all African Americans lived at or below the federal poverty line in 1940, a time when roughly three-quarters of black adults had not finished high school. Systematically denied a quality education, they could expect to live shorter and less healthy lives than whites, working in more dangerous and less rewarding jobs. The average African American worker earned thirty-nine cents in 1940 for every dollar earned by the average white.[4]

Racial segregation may have been enforced by law only in the Southern and border states, but it had a national presence. Jim Crow, moreover, was more than just a social system that divided public spaces between members of the black and white races. It was exactly what its white defenders called it: a "way of life" that included elements of culture, expectations of behavior, and a political economy that mocked the ideals of a democratic republic wherever Jim Crow ruled. Civil rights activists and organizations had begun to confront the system long before the United States entered the war, but they had been unable to leverage their protests into an effective challenge. It appeared unlikely at the time that the one institution the activists would have to move, the federal government, would side with blacks fighting for change. Unlike his wife, President Franklin D. Roosevelt seldom if ever demonstrated a personal concern for the plight of African Americans before 1940. His 1932 election victory and subsequent New Deal coalition relied heavily enough on the votes of Southern white segregationists that David Lilienthal, the administrator of the Tennessee Valley Authority, one of Roosevelt's pet projects, considered the president "a prisoner of the Southern wing of the Democratic party."[5]

The national emergency provided the opportunity the civil rights activists needed to organize forces for change and to force Roosevelt to take their side. For good reason, historians now place the domestic wartime experience within the context of the "long civil rights movement." They see the wartime mobilization as having transformed the racial balance of the political economy not just in the South, but across the United States. According to this school of thought, wartime demographic, economic, and political changes set in motion forces that would eventually doom Jim Crow but would also ignite a backlash against civil rights reforms.[6]

The transformation began as the U.S. economy ramped up for the war effort, even before the Japanese attack on Pearl Harbor. Wartime industrial production pulled southern blacks into the cities of the Midwest, Northeast, and West Coast, and offered new job opportunities. The black populations of Chicago and the self-proclaimed "Arsenal of Democracy,"

Detroit, more than doubled between 1940 and 1950, a decade in which the black population of Los Angeles more than tripled and San Diego's black population grew fourfold. African Americans found residential segregation and hiring discrimination in these cities, to be sure, but Jim Crow segregation was less entrenched outside of the South, and at least blacks could vote outside of Dixie. To a lesser but not insignificant extent they poured into the urban areas of the Sunbelt South, too, changing those cities forever.[7]

Blacks made up approximately 3 percent of the workforce of national defense industries in 1942, but they increased their share to roughly 8 percent of the workforce by 1945, a time when African Americans comprised roughly one-tenth of the nation's total population. The number of black federal employees, a raw measure of African Americans' strength in the national political economy, more than tripled during the war years to roughly 200,000. Even more tellingly, the membership of the National Association for the Advancement of Colored People (NAACP), the nation's pre-eminent black advocacy organization, grew ninefold during the war years. The organization added 170 new local branches (including one in Tuskegee) in the final year of the war alone.[8]

Racial discrimination in wartime industries certainly existed outside the South, but it was haphazard. In March 1941, when North American Aviation built a new plant to manufacture airplanes under a defense contract in Kansas City, the company's president declared that he would hire no Negroes, "regardless of their training as aircraft workers." But three months later the brothers of Local 683 of the United Auto Workers, employees of the Vultee Aircraft Co. in southern California, resolved to work to break down "the anti-labor, racial discrimination policy in the aircraft and national defense industries[,] recognizing that our national defense must rest on the maintenance of our democratic principles."[9]

As Roosevelt admitted in his 1942 Columbus Day fireside chat, "In some communities employers dislike to employ women. In others they are reluctant to hire Negroes." But he also concluded, "We can no longer afford to indulge such prejudices or practices." Black Americans forced the issue. The *Chicago Defender* and *Pittsburgh Courier,* arguably the most influential black newspapers of the day, had demanded Roosevelt take action on job discrimination as early as 1940, and the NAACP had been calling for desegregation of the armed forces since at least 1937. When A. Philip Randolph, leader of the Brotherhood of Sleeping Car Porters, the most powerful black labor union in the country, led a movement that threatened to stage a massive march on Washington to protest racial discrimination in the military and defense industries to take place in July 1941, the White House took notice.

Such agitation on the part of progressive labor union locals, black news-papers, and civil rights organizations forced the federal government to take the side of desegregation even before the United States entered the worldwide conflict. In June 1941 the Council for Democracy, an advocacy group headed by the influential radio broadcaster Raymond Gram Swing, a white liberal, excoriated Roosevelt and his growing war machine for treat-ing black Americans as second-class citizens. The council warned that "a dangerous and stupid policy which compels one-tenth of our population to fight simply for a chance to participate" in the effort to make the world safe for democracy would make Negroes "embittered and disillusioned," creat-ing "fertile ground for subversive propaganda, agitation and unrest." Advo-cacy groups like the Council for Democracy and the NAACP voiced their criticism of federal policies so publicly that Roosevelt was forced eventually to admit they were right and join them. The president was unable to run the risk that black Americans would protest the discrimination they faced in large numbers and thereby jeopardize the all-out war effort.[10]

Randolph addressed his "fellow Negro Americans" that spring to assure them that "You possess power, great power. Our problem is to harness and hitch it up for action on the broadest, daring and most gigantic scale." He laid out a program of action that would allow the black minority to translate what power it had into real, substantive, long-lasting change during the emergency of wartime. "In this period of power politics," he wrote, "noth-ing counts but pressure, more pressure and still more pressure." "March-on-Washington committees are being set up throughout the country," Randolph warned Secretary of War Henry L. Stimson a month before the march was to take place. Randolph sarcastically invited Stimson to address the "great throng of Negroes from all parts of the country" from the steps of the Lincoln Memorial.[11]

The White House was unwilling to risk the damage such a demonstra-tion could inflict on the national image, and the administration moved quickly to compromise with Randolph. Roosevelt refused the demand to desegregate the armed forces, but he did issue Executive Order 8802, which banned racially discriminatory hiring practices in defense industries and created the Fair Employment Practices Commission (FEPC) to investi-gate claims of discrimination. Executive Order 8802 perfectly encapsulated Roosevelt's *modus operandi* when dealing with civil rights issues: he acted under pressure to avert a developing catastrophe and did so in a way that minimized actual change. In a perfect world the FEPC would have been given sufficient staff and budget to enforce the order more vigorously than it did, but its very existence broke new ground. The agency used the power of publicity to force progress in war production industries; aircraft manu-facturers, for example, hired five thousand black Americans between 1940 and 1942 alone. Just as significantly, in return for calling off the march, Randolph had forced Roosevelt to acknowledge the problem of racial discrimination in the workforce and to take meaningful action against it, thereby providing a mobilization model that civil rights activists would follow to great results over the coming decades. For all of these reasons, the year 1941 marks as good a starting point for the history of the modern civil rights movement as any.[12]

World War II was the watershed event for African Americans, as for all Americans, in the twentieth century. The Tuskegee Airmen, the country's first African American military pilots, and the men and women who kept them flying, were far from the only blacks to serve in the Jim Crow-era armed forces. They are the exclusive focus of this book because their collective experience provides a case study for the scope and pace of the social changes that black Americans both shaped and responded to during the war years. During the war blacks forced their way into an institution whose leaders, the evidence shows, if left to their own devices would never have accepted African Americans as equals.[13]

As late as 1940 the U.S. Army Air Corps, which would be renamed the U.S. Army Air Forces the following year and the newly independent military branch U.S. Air Force just after the end of the war, had no plans to include black Americans in any of its activities outside of the most menial labor that was necessary to keep its bases functioning. An August 1940 headline in the *Chicago Defender* accurately described War Department policy at the time when it chided, "Only White Flyers Will Be Shot Down in Next War." The opportunities the Army Air Corps afforded black Americans before the war were not only neither separate from nor equal to those provided to whites, they were practically nonexistent; blacks comprised less than 2 percent of the AAC's personnel. Every branch of the armed services practiced racial segregation, as did nearly every other major institution in American life at the beginning of the war. But of all the branches of the armed services, with the possible exception of the Marine Corps, the prewar AAC went furthest in its denial of opportunities to blacks.[14]

The experience of the Tuskegee Airmen also provides a classic example of how black Americans were able to leverage the limited power they held in the national political economy to force change during the middle decades of the twentieth century. Black newspapers, civil rights organizations, and historically black colleges compelled the AAC to open its training programs to black Americans as the war loomed. The program was never universally popular among blacks, some of whom grudgingly accepted the new Tuskegee program as a half-a-loaf measure but continued to urge the desegregation of existing training programs, and some of whom refused to compromise with Jim Crow for any reason. In response to the War Department's original announcement of the Tuskegee program's creation, the *Pittsburgh Courier* editorialized, "When the cry is for national unity, the increase of segregation based on fallacious theories of race is a mighty poor way to bring it about. Segregation benefits neither the white lads, the colored[,] nor the country."[15]

However, after the door to service in the AAC had been opened a crack, the Tuskegee Airmen's performance combined with wartime exigencies to open that door wider and make further opportunities available. By the end of the war, the Tuskegee Airmen had helped prove that racial segregation of fighting forces was so inefficient as to be counterproductive to the nation's defense. Shortly after the war ended, the U.S. Air Force became one of the very first national institutions to overtly renounce the practice of racial segregation. Remarkably, these radical changes took place in the span of fewer than ten years. The collective experience of the Tuskegee Airmen lay at the heart of them.

The U.S. Army Air Corps was born in the wake of World War I. The Army's Aviation Section, a division of the Signal Corps, did not exactly distinguish itself during the Great War, but air power did win recognition as an important factor in warfare, and military planners came to understand that military aviation could provide a decisive advantage in future combat. Congress authorized the creation of the AAC in 1926, "strengthening the conception of military aviation as an offensive, striking arm rather than an auxiliary service" of the infantry.[16]

In fact, the expansion of an all-white AAC had the practical effect of decreasing opportunities for black Americans in the Army as well. The 1926 legislation authorized an increase in the size of the AAC but not an expansion in the overall size of the armed forces. The War Department managed to enlarge the flying corps by shrinking the Army's 10th Cavalry and 25th Infantry, all-black units that had served capably in World War I. Throughout the 1930s the War Department held steadfast to the notion that its forces had to be segregated by race in order to maintain morale, prohibited blacks from enlisting in the AAC, and transformed all-black cavalry and infantry units into little more than "housekeeping detachments."[17]

The findings of a series of studies on black soldiers' performance in the First World War allowed the War Department to maintain racial segregation in the ranks of the armed forces as a military necessity and to avoid providing separate-but-equal opportunities for black Americans. In 1925 the Army War College, a combination think tank and leadership development school, produced "The Use of Negro Manpower in War," the most influential of these studies and a classic example of the pseudoscience that both characterized and solidified American whites' perceptions of blacks in the interwar years. Narrowly focused on the performance of the black officers and soldiers of the 92nd Infantry Division in the 1918 Meuse-Argonne offensive, it provided ample justification for the War Department to apply racist policies much more broadly throughout the armed services.[18]

"Under the terms of the Constitution the negro [sic, throughout] has the rights of citizenship," the study began, somewhat promisingly. "It is evident that he must bear his share of the burden of war." However, the authors of the study—a committee including a Col. Bishop, a Maj. Drain, and a Maj. Somervel of the Army War College staff—then set out to determine how blacks, which they called "a sub-species of the human family," might best provide their proportionate share of the nation's defense within the limits of their perceived capabilities. The committee considered "research by previous classes [of the War College], by the Faculty, [and] on War Department experiences during the [First] World War," but evidently did not consult academic research on the topic, and clearly did not confer with African Americans. The prominent University of Chicago biologist Julian Lewis would later charge that such "research" (if indeed it could be called that) did little more than "use meaningless scientific verbiage to rationalize a biased attitude based on emotional convictions."[19]

"The negro is physically qualified for combat duty," the committee wrote. But, it reported dejectedly,

The negro is profoundly superstitious.

He is by nature sub-servient [sic] and naturally believes himself to be inferior to the white.

He is jolly, trustable [sic], lively and docile by nature, but through real or supposed harsh or unjust treatment may become sullen and stubborn.

He is very susceptible to the influence of crowd psychology....

The psychology of the negro is such that we may not expect to draw leadership material from his race. The negro has not a lot of confidence in leaders of his own race and it would be an impossibility to place leaders of his race over whites....

He has not the physical courage of the white. He simply cannot control himself in fear of some danger in the degree that the white can....

The negro is unmoral [sic]. He simply does not see that some things are wrong....

The negroes' growing sense of importance will make them more and more of a problem, and racial troubles may be expected to increase.

It is unclear what sources the authors drew on in arriving at these conclusions, but they certainly matched the beliefs most whites held toward black Americans at the time.[20]

Maj. Gen. H. E. Ely, commandant of the War College, urged the War Department's chief of staff to adopt the conclusions of the study as policy. "The negro issue should be met squarely," he argued. Ely reminded readers of the study, who would have included members of the army's general staff and high-ranking civilian and military employees of the department, "The War Department had no pre-determined and sound plan for the use of negro troops in the beginning of the World War. It had no adequate defense against political and racial pressure and was forced to organize negro combat divisions and commission unqualified negro officers." Ely referred here to a concerted effort by black intellectuals and civil rights leaders, most notably W.E.B. DuBois's editorials in *The Crisis*, the NAACP's journal of news and opinion, to force the War Department to allow African Americans to serve their country in meaningful ways during the Great War.[21]

DuBois had argued that if given the opportunity, black Americans would serve their country in wartime as patriotically and as capably as all other Americans and provide an objective demonstration of black competence. In doing so, he hoped, blacks would make it more difficult for whites to deny them the rights they had been guaranteed by Reconstruction-era amendments to the Constitution. DuBois envisioned military service as means to an end. He and other leaders of the NAACP applied political pressure on the Woodrow Wilson administration to open opportunities in the armed forces to African Americans so that they might prove their love of country, their technical skills, and their courage. At the same time, as in "Close Ranks," a 1918 editorial, DuBois advised African Americans to "forget our special grievances and close our ranks shoulder to shoulder with our own white fellow citizens and the allied nations that are fighting for democracy." (DuBois would come to regret this counsel.) At war's end he advised blacks to resume their striving for full civil rights and wrote in another *Crisis* editorial, "We return. We return from fighting. We return fighting. Make way for Democracy! We saved it in France, and by the Great Jehovah, we will save it in the United States of America, or know the reason why."[22]

DuBois's advocacy won for black Americans what the great intellectual's biographer called "the right...to die discriminated against in the war for world democracy," but it did little to alter the image of American blacks in the white mind. More than 350,000 African Americans served in World War I, but fewer than seven hundred of them as officers. Roughly 90 percent of black personnel received no more than minimal training and served in unskilled or semiskilled specializations such as stevedores and Messmen in the U.S. Navy and in service, labor, and engineering battalions in the Army. By many, but by no means all, accounts African American fighting troops performed well in combat. The all-black 92nd Infantry Division of the Army saw action in France as a part of the American Expeditionary Force, and four additional all-black infantry regiments fought under French command. The 369th Regiment, known as "the Harlem Hellfighters," spent 191 days under fire on the front lines of the war—more than any other American regiment—and came home with 171 Croix du Guerre, the French military's highest honor. But according to Gen. Ely of the War College, "The results are well known.... The negro, particularly the officer, failed in the World War." According to the authors of the "The Use of Negro Manpower in War," black troops had proven in the course of the war that their unique biological destiny suited them for service in labor battalions but not combat units. Under no circumstances, they recommended, should the War Department throw good money after bad in an effort to mold them into capable officers.[23]

Policy makers in the War Department proved only too happy to follow these recommendations throughout the 1930s. Though the study made no recommendations specific to the AAC, it was easy to apply its suggestions to the area of military aviation in general. If Negroes were, as the study concluded, "mentally inferior" to whites, "rank cowards" who were afraid of the dark, then they surely could not be trusted with machines as expensive and complex such as aircraft—not as pilots, not even as mechanics. Furthermore, if officer training for blacks was a waste of taxpayer dollars, then military aviation training for blacks was doubly wasteful. Graduates of the flight training program automatically became officers in the AAC.[24]

With an eye toward the next war, in the mid-1930s generals in the AAC began to lobby for an expansion of the service. Training blacks was, to say the very least, not a priority for them. Events in Europe in the latter half of the decade moved expansion plans for the AAC from the realm of the hypothetical to the real. As a January 1940 War Plans Division memorandum put it, "From the point of view of the War Department, the aviation problem passed from the planning stage to the execution phase over a year ago." These plans made no allowances for training anyone from the black tenth of the nation's total population.[25]

By then the war was well under way in Europe, and it seemed increasingly likely that the United States would be drawn into the multi-sided conflict one way or another. In 1939 fascist armies defeated Republican forces in the Spanish Civil War (aided greatly by German air support), Germany annexed parts of Czechoslovakia, and Adolf Hitler unleashed the blitzkrieg on Poland, inciting World War II. Great Britain and France declared war on Germany, but the United States remained officially neutral. President Roosevelt walked a narrow line: public opinion would not allow an all-out declaration of war absent a direct attack on American interests, but Roosevelt recognized American participation in the conflict as unavoidable and encouraged the nation's military forces to prepare accordingly. African Americans followed the developments closely, knowing full well what the possibility of a victory for the forces of fascist racism held in store for people of color around the world. According to some, they had already experienced it firsthand: "What else are jim-crow [sic] laws but Fascist laws?" asked *Courier* columnist J. A. Rogers.[26]

Early in 1939 Roosevelt approved a plan to double the size and strength of the AAC by the summer of 1941. Congress appropriated more than $300 million to the Air Corps Expansion Program in June 1939, and the AAC embarked on a mission to modernize its training facilities, train a new generation of military pilots, and procure new airplanes. As difficult as it would be for the AAC to purchase more than three thousand new airplanes and the equipment it would take to keep them flying (to be added to the 2,468 airplanes then available), the War Plans Division of the War Department foresaw that manpower, not machinery, would prove the deciding factor in the AAC's rapid modernization. In a 1940 update on the expansion program Brig. Gen. George V. Strong of the War Plans Division wrote, "In this country of vast production capacity for any mechanical product, the bottleneck for the rapid expansion of aviation forces will be the training of pilots and skilled aviation mechanics...rather than the procurement of aircraft." Strong predicted that it would take much longer to create the necessary network of training bases for the expanded military aviation program, and he called for a civil aviation training program "a hundred times greater than that which has existed in the past" to create a pool of pilots whose skills could be developed for military aviation when necessary.[27]

While Japan approached achieving total control of mainland China, the Republic of France fell to Nazi Germany, and Great Britain barely maintained the last sovereign democracy on the European continent—thanks almost entirely to the Royal Air Force's ability to defend Britain's skies against the German Luftwaffe. Americans watched and waited. The Air Corps Expansion Program, as dramatic as it was, was intended to bring forces only up to the point where they could successfully defend the borders of the United States, its territorial possessions, and American interests in the Western Hemisphere against the growing threat.[28]

Almost as soon as Roosevelt announced his intention to expand civilian pilot training in late 1938, blacks began deluging him with requests to allow them to enroll. The presidents of the historically black Wilberforce University, Hampton Institute, and Tuskegee Institute offered their campuses as training sites. The *Chicago Defender* initiated an editorial campaign to open training to blacks, and the paper's publisher, Enoch P. Waters, helped bankroll a publicity-generating barnstorming trip designed to show the world that blacks could fly if given the chance.[29]

Chauncey Spencer and Dale White, Chicago-based stunt-show pilots, flew a well-used Lincoln-Paige monoplane from the Second City to Washington, D.C., New York, and back to Chicago to create publicity for the cause of black aviation. While in Washington, they met with the lone black lobbyist on Capitol Hill, Edgar G. Brown, who had been actively lobbying Congress to open the proposed Civilian Pilot Training (CPT) program to African American trainees. According to Spencer, Rep. Everett Dirksen, an Illinois Republican, showed great interest in helping blacks enter CPT, though Spencer later suspected Dirksen only wanted to get his photograph taken with the black pilots for his upcoming re-election campaign. (In fact, Dirksen did successfully add an amendment to the CPT's enabling legislation barring racial discrimination in the program.) Again according to Spencer—the story has not been corroborated—he, White, and Brown were touring the Capitol one morning when a man stopped Brown and said, "Hello, Edgar. How are you?" Brown introduced the man, Sen. Harry Truman (D-Mo.), to the two pilots, who must have cut quite a figure in their pilots' garb, and explained the purpose of their visit. According to Spencer, Truman was impressed by the pair and agreed to go out to the airfield to see their plane. "You flew this thing from Chicago?" he said of the jalopy. "If you've got guts enough to do that, I've got guts enough to help you through."[30]

In the summer of 1939 Congress passed the Civilian Pilot Training Act authorizing the creation of hundreds of flight training facilities at colleges and vocational schools throughout the country and appropriated $4 million for its operation. The effectiveness of the lobbying campaign resulted in allowances for the training of black pilots on a large scale for the first time. The effort to make civilian pilot training available to blacks therefore became a critical first step in the process of opening the AAC to African Americans. By the end of 1939, nearly ten thousand students were enrolled in CPT programs at 437 colleges and seventy vocational education institutions throughout the country. A handful of black students enrolled in CPT programs at predominantly white colleges in the Northeast and Midwest, and dozens more enrolled in CPT at historically black Hampton Institute in Virginia, Howard University in Washington, D.C., North Carolina A&T, Delaware State College for Colored Students, Tuskegee Institute, and West Virginia State College.[31]

Black Americans were as enamored of flight as anyone else in the country, but to this point they had been systematically prevented from pursuing aviation careers, military or otherwise. A 1940 Bureau of the Census publication listed exactly 124 licensed Negro pilots in the entire United States (out of a total population of more than 12 million African Americans), only seven of whom held commercial pilot ratings. Of course, there was not a single pilot of color in the AAC. There was a general consensus among military thinkers throughout the world, not just in the United States, that the balance of power in the worldwide conflict would be determined in the air, which made the stakes for opening opportunities in the service even higher. Blacks knew that racial discrimination in the world of civil and military aviation was unlikely to lessen on its own, so they had to force their way in via the political process. This generation of African Americans would have to break down the doors of discrimination to prove themselves as military pilots, the cream of the aviation crop. They would need to establish their patriotism beyond all possible question, demonstrate technical competence, and create opportunities for people of color in the field of aviation.[32]

Black newspapers embarked on a journalistic crusade to open the skies to African Americans, now focusing their efforts on the AAC. David Ward Howe, a columnist for the *Chicago Defender*, advised his readers in 1940, "We must immediately direct our attention to the field of aviation and make every effort to become integrated into all phases of this increasingly important industry." When Britain's Royal Air Force and the Canadian Air Force announced plans to accept cadets of African ancestry, Howe demanded that the U.S. Army Air Corps do the same. Robert L. Vann, publisher of the *Pittsburgh Courier*, led the effort on grounds that "taxation without representation is tyranny": if African Americans were to be taxed at the same rate as their fellow citizens, the federal government should afford them the same opportunities to serve their country and the same job prospects in defense industries. As the Roosevelt administration asked for larger and larger appropriations for the nation's defense in 1939 and 1940, Vann's ideas gained currency. The labor leader Randolph, the NAACP and other black advocacy organizations, and the presidents of historically black colleges and universities—most notably Tuskegee Institute's president, Frederick D. Patterson—joined the newspapers' struggle.[33]

The lobbying campaign to open opportunities for blacks in the armed forces was so closely associated with the Pittsburgh newspaper's editorial advocacy that the various bills and amendments introduced in the U.S. Congress to these ends were known collectively as "the Courier Bills." The *Courier* expanded the effort and came to call it the "Double-V Campaign." James G. Thompson, a *Courier* reader and cafeteria worker at a Cessna Aircraft manufacturing plant, explained the term in a 1942 letter to the newspaper: "The first V [is] for victory over our enemies from without, the second V for victory over our enemies from within. For surely those who perpetuate these ugly prejudices here are seeking to destroy our democratic form of government just as surely as the Axis forces." The Double-V is a useful metaphor for the way that African Americans used their service in the war to force social change, but the concept has limitations. Individual blacks who fought for the United States did so with a complex mixture of individual aspiration, collective pride in the "race," patriotism, and other motivations.[34]

Military brass resisted the civil rights coalition's efforts. In late 1941 a spokesman for Gen. George C. Marshall, the War Department chief of staff, complained that desegregating the armed forces would require generals to solve "a social problem that has perplexed the American people throughout the history of this nation." He harkened back to Gen. Ely's complaint about the way black Americans had been forced upon the military in World War I when he declared, "The Army is not a sociological laboratory." Few people knew it at the time, but Marshall's spokesman was exactly wrong. The Army *was* a sociological laboratory because it operated under civilian control and the civilians were susceptible to political pressure. In any case, given Marshall's reluctance to make the military more racially egalitarian and with no shortage of "scientific" studies such as "The Use of Negro Manpower in War" at their disposal, generals in the AAC would have been comfortable denying blacks any but the most menial positions. Had the coalition not forced the decision into the political arena, the U. S. military would not have trained black pilots in World War II.[35]

Walter White, the executive director of the NAACP, was especially masterful in his use of personal diplomacy to introduce Roosevelt to the idea of training black aviators and then pushing it through to completion. Fighting segregation and job discrimination in the armed forces and defense industries were priorities for the NAACP long before the attack on Pearl Harbor. At the association's 1937 and 1938 annual conferences, members passed resolutions condemning racial discrimination in the armed services, which they called "contrary to the spirit of democracy for which our country is supposed to stand." White forwarded these resolutions to the White House with the note: "We urge the president to use his broad powers of authority to stop such grossly unfair policy." In 1939 White asked FDR "to use the utmost powers of your high office to remove the barriers to full participation by qualified Negroes in every branch of the defense forces of government."[36]

Black voters had broken with the party of Lincoln to support Roosevelt in the 1932 election and had voted overwhelmingly to re-elect him in 1936. But as the president contemplated an unprecedented third term, White assured him that he would have to do more for black citizens if he wanted to keep African American votes permanently in the Democratic column. "I have found deep affection for you and Mrs. Roosevelt among colored Americans of all walks of life," he wrote Roosevelt in a 1939 personal letter. "But over and above this personal regard for yourselves is a widespread and growing feeling of despair, distrust, and even bitterness because of the apparently increasing control of party policy, so far as Negroes are concerned, by southern congressmen, senators, and others who are bitterly anti-Negro." White warned the president, "It is my conviction that it would be a serious mistake to believe that the Negro vote is irrevocably fixed in the Democratic ranks." This was not an idle threat. The Republican nominee for president, Wendell Wilkie, was working hard to entice black voters back to his party. Robert Vann, the *Pittsburgh Courier* publisher who supported Republican candidates generally, threw his weight wholeheartedly behind Wilkie three months before the election, disgusted by what he perceived as Roosevelt's indifference toward striking down racial discrimination in the armed forces and defense industries.[37]

"Negroes . . . [are] naturally disturbed about the many things which could have been done but which have not been done by the present administration," White cautioned the president. He continued:

> One of the sorest points among Negroes which I have encountered is the flagrant discrimination against Negroes in all the armed forces of the United States. Forthright action on your part to lessen discrimination and segregation and particularly in affording opportunities for the training of Negro pilots for the air corps [sic] would gain tremendous good will, perhaps even out of proportion to the significance of such action.

The president sent the letter (apparently unread), along with two others from Negro leaders, to White House assistant James H. Rowe Jr., one of his most trusted political advisors, with a request for Rowe's opinion on the problem of black votes. Rowe reminded the president of an idea they had already considered and tabled—appointing prominent blacks to advisory positions in the War Department and Selective Service system as a way of shoring up black votes—and suggested, "Walter White's letter is unusual in its clarity and thoroughness. If you could find time, it would be worth reading."[38]

As the election approached and the White House continued to stall on desegregation of the armed forces and job discrimination in defense industries, the NAACP official struck again. White was fielding requests from prominent Republicans to throw his personal support behind Wilkie and would in fact come to consider his relationship with Wilkie "one of the three or four closest and richest friendships of my life." He wrote Jacob Billikopf, a former labor leader who was now director of the Federation of Jewish Charities and a major Democratic party figure in Philadelphia, knowing full well that Billikopf had the ears of higher-ups in the party and would share White's concerns with them. "The Negro vote...clearly holds the balance of power in any election as close as this," White wrote, expressing concern that "resentment against...discrimination against Negroes in the armed forces and in employment in plants fulfilling national defense contracts" might cause black voters to return to the GOP fold. Billikopf dutifully forwarded White's concerns to U.S. Attorney Gen. Francis Biddle, who in turn passed them along to Rowe.[39]

The wheels began turning in the White House with only weeks remaining before the election. In a September 16, 1940, briefing, White House Press Secretary Stephen Early announced that the AAC would soon begin training Negro pilots. On September 27 the president met with White, A. Philip Randolph, and T. Arnold Hill, executive secretary of the Urban League, at the White House. Early then announced that all the branches of the armed services would increase the number of positions open to blacks, but not in a way that would challenge the norms of segregation. He implied that White, Randolph, and Hill had blessed the president's decision; the civil rights leaders demanded a retraction. A week after that, Early was arrested for kneeing a black New York City police officer, James Sloan, in the groin. The combination of Early's words and actions did nothing to improve blacks' opinion of the president.[40]

Now Rowe went to work. In late October the White House issued a hastily organized press release in which the War Department announced somewhat more forcefully the creation of a training program for black pilots. At the same time, Secretary of War Henry L. Stimson hired Judge William Hastie, an NAACP insider, as his civilian aide and promoted Col. Benjamin O. Davis Sr. to the rank of brigadier general, making him the first African American general officer in the history of the U.S. Army. Rowe timed the announcements precisely so that they would hit the teletypes at the last possible moment before black weekly newspapers met the deadlines for their last editions before the November election.[41]

In the press release Secretary Stimson stated, "Negro organizations will be established in each major branch of the service...Negroes are [now] being given aviation training as pilots, mechanics, and technical specialists. This training will be accelerated." Stimson did not mention that the only aviation training available to black Americans in 1940 was offered by civilian institutions, not the AAC. Nonetheless, the Air Command dutifully began planning to create what were called "Aviation Squadrons (Separate)" for African American pilots with all-black support units and started searching for a site where it could train the pilots and support crews under racially segregated conditions. The squadrons could incorporate approximately

2,300 blacks into the AAC in various job categories, most of them service-oriented. In March 1941 the AAC would begin accepting applications from prospective aviation cadets for a proposed all-black pursuit squadron. In the meantime, the AAC would decide where to locate the facility to train them.[42]

Building on the momentum that the civil rights coalition created to force black entry to the CPT program, African Americans agreed that all blacks should have an equal opportunity to serve in any capacity their talents suited them for in the AAC. All concurred that it was imperative to force the AAC to develop a training system for black pilots. But within that consensus strong factions developed and disagreements raged over where pilot training should take place. Nearly all preferred the creation of integrated training units, but it seemed clear that the War Department would hold strong to its policy not to train blacks alongside whites at existing bases, even though that arrangement would have saved American taxpayers millions of dollars. The debate therefore turned on where a separate-but-truly-equal base should be built.

The influential *Chicago Defender* argued that the initial AAC facility for Negro flyers should be sited in that city, the home of the Coffey School for Aeronautics, a privately operated school for black pilots. By 1940 Chicago had earned its reputation as a black Mecca, and that perception would only grow through the following decades. Majority-black neighborhoods on the west and south sides of Chicago contained every kind of black-owned business one could imagine; their entertainment districts were unparalleled, and African Americans wielded political power on city, state, and national levels. Oscar De Priest, a black Republican, had represented the South Side in the U.S. House of Representatives from 1928—the first time a black had been elected to the body in the twentieth century—until 1934, when voters replaced him with Arthur W. Mitchell, the House's first black Democrat. Cornelius Coffey and Willa Brown, pioneering black aviators, had built the Coffey School, located at Harlem Airport on the west side of the city, into what was arguably the nation's center of black aviation. Pilots associated with the Coffey School, Brown especially, were instrumental in opening the doors of the Civilian Pilot Training program to blacks, and the school was already administering training programs under contract with the Civil Aviation Authority. Even more importantly, black cadets at a Chicago training base would be treated as something like full and equal citizens by the surrounding, relatively integrated community. Others in the NAACP faction supported a West Coast location for similar reasons and added that the region's climate made it an even better site for year-round flying. William H. Hastie, a former federal judge, stalwart NAACP attorney, dean of Howard University Law School, and now a civilian aide to the secretary of war, advocated a California location because black trainees would be less likely to face indignities there than they would be in the Jim Crow South.[43]

Frederick D. Patterson, the president of Tuskegee Institute, lobbied to have the program placed near his school. Tuskegee too had established itself as a hub of black aviation. The institute had been one of the first historically black colleges to participate in CPT, and its students had excelled in the program. Patterson advertised the region's ideal climate for flying—more than three hundred days of flying weather per year—and the school's success in training civilian pilots. What AAC officials perceived as Patterson's "cooperative attitude" also influenced the decision. Tuskegee Institute officials "furnishe[d] many precepts and examples in conduct and attitude" that made whites in the AAC more comfortable, according to a contemporary Air Corps report, and the AAC believed that the school's "leaders exert great influence in the affairs of the Negro race." For all of these reasons, early in 1941 the AAC announced its plan to contract with Tuskegee Institute to provide primary training, the first of three phases of military flight instruction, for Negro aviation cadets. The service also announced plans to create a full, separate-but-equal, and (with a price tag of $1,663,057 for its construction) very expensive AAC training base where cadets would receive basic and advanced training, Tuskegee Army Air Field (TAAF). The War Department put out the call for volunteers to fill the full complement of its planned all-black 99th Pursuit Squadron, which would require about three dozen pilots, twice that many administrative officers, and nearly five hundred support personnel. The War Department planned to train the black ground-crew technicians who would support the 99th alongside whites at Chanute Field in Rantoul, Illinois.[44]

But the War Department overestimated Tuskegee Institute's national reputation among blacks, and here the coalition that had fought for the inclusion of blacks in the Air Corps disintegrated. A *Pittsburgh Courier* editorial opposed the decision flatly because it "perpetuate[d] the 'American way' of racial segregation" and promised to expose the elite cadets to racial indignities. The *Chicago Defender* editorialized, "It is the patriotic duty of every Negro, every American, to oppose discrimination or segregation in any form wherever found and especially when found in a government agency." The NAACP officially insisted that blacks be accepted as aviation cadets on the same basis as whites, period, and that all training should take place on a non-segregated basis. When it became clear that the War Department would not budge from its practice of segregating units and training classes, the NAACP did not take an official stance in favor of creating the training program for blacks in one location over another. Yet Judge Hastie, among others associated with the NAACP, refused to accept the decision to place the program in Tuskegee without vigorous protest. His new post in the War Department gave him the chance to push for fair and equal treatment for black Americans from within that agency for the next two years.[45]

The NAACP made clear its objection to the creation of what it called "a Jim Crow air squadron," characterizing the Tuskegee program as "an extension of the undemocratic and un-American practice of segregation of the Negro in the national defense program." Patterson tried to smooth things over with the organization. Soon after War Department officials announced the creation of the base in Tuskegee, he wired Walter White to request a meeting with him and Judge Hastie. "Before attempting to arrange conference," White responded, "[I] wish you to understand I must oppose any proposal for segregated training of Negroes."[46]

Patterson's reply telegram illuminated the different approaches to "racial uplift" that had characterized Tuskegee Institute and the NAACP ever since the association's inception four decades earlier, when the NAACP's DuBois criticized Tuskegee's Booker T. Washington for being too accommodating of white racism. In lobbying the War Department to build a new base in Tuskegee, Patterson cabled, his sole interest had been "making available [the] largest possible opportunity for Negroes in all branches of service." He regarded the "question of segregation as academic and unnecessary to be considered in conference." He would make the same arguments for public consumption, in exactly the spirit of pragmatism that Washington had once championed. Patterson insisted that training Negro pilots even in rigidly segregated conditions gave "colored men a foothold in the air corps and will in time lead to mixed air units." (White might not have known that the NAACP's assistant secretary, Roy Wilkins, sided with Tuskegee in this argument. In a letter to Hastie he confided, "As I see it, the main idea is to train flyers...If it comes to a choice between being trained in Alabama or not being trained at all, I would be for Alabama.") Nonetheless, given the gulf between the two institutions, it would be impossible for Tuskegee and the NAACP to cooperate further to reach what were otherwise shared goals.[47]

Hastie was especially furious over the decision to build the base at Tuskegee. In the first place, he would later write, "I can see no reason whatever for setting up a separate program for Negroes in the Air Corps." If blacks could learn to pilot pursuit aircraft—and the AAC seemed to be assuming that this was within the realm of possibility by this point, because it was committing millions of dollars to create the program—then they could learn how to do so just as well alongside white cadets at existing facilities. Moreover, plans were under way to train the first cadre of black ground crew specialists alongside whites at the AAC's Technical Training School at Chanute Field. What made it possible to train black technicians in an integrated setting, but not black pilots? And would integrated training not benefit both blacks and whites? If they were intended to fly together in combat, would they not do well to learn more about each other in training? Finally, how could the decision to build a brand-new air base to train three dozen pilots possibly be construed as an economical use of the nation's manpower and financial resources during a time of crisis?[48]

"When we find Tuskegee Institute working hand in glove with the Army Air Command to establish, intrench [sic], and extend a Jim Crow air training program at Tuskegee," Hastie later alleged, "such conduct should be exposed and condemned." He continued,

> It is an object lesson of selfish and shortsighted scheming for immediate personal advantage with cynical disregard for the larger interests of the Negro and of the nation. Let there be no mistake. Tuskegee is rendering no valuable service to the war effort in its continuing effort to concentrate a black aviation program on and around the Tuskegee campus. With callous indifference to the best interests of the Negro and to the larger values of democratic practices in the war effort, Tuskegee is looking out for Tuskegee. The school gets its mess of pottage in profitable Army contracts and the promotion of its own private aviation training program, while the Air Forces have a willing and useful accomplice in their design of keeping the Negro strictly segregated.[49]

Patterson was aware of this perception, which existed widely by 1940 and which he deeply resented. He fought behind the scenes to ensure that the developing Tuskegee flight program would not succumb to intra-racial rivalries and open him to further charges of Uncle Tom-ism. As an official history of TAAF dryly noted, "Before the plans for the field were complete, it had already become the subject for considerable controversy and many differences of opinion." In April 1941 the AAC chose a site approximately 7 miles northwest of the Tuskegee Institute campus for the construction of TAAF. According to an August 1941 AAC memorandum, "The project at Tuskegee [was] considered by the War Department as No. 1 priority due to political pressures being brought to bear upon the White House and War Department to provide pilot training for colored applicants." However, AAC engineers vastly underestimated how much it would cost to drain and grade the site, and the construction project had exhausted its initial appropriation by November of that year. With only one paved runway to show for its work and money, the War Department announced the suspension of construction until a new appropriation could be obtained.[50]

President Patterson flew into action, writing a blistering letter to Assistant Secretary of War Robert P. Patterson (no relation). In the first place, he argued, Tuskegee Institute engineering professors had previously warned the War Department that it was underestimating the cost to prepare the site. The completion of Tuskegee Army Air Field should not be delayed just because the War Department had planned poorly, and if there was a shortage of funds to complete the work it was up to the War Department to make up for the shortfall. "[T]his is not just another Air Corps project whose completion may indifferently await the regular appropriation of funds," he lectured Robert Patterson.[51]

"[T]his is the only field which is available to Negro fliers," President Patterson reminded his counterpart, "whereas already established fields are providing a splendid opportunity for the training of white youth." President Patterson understood his reputation to be on the line. "Those of us who have worked diligently for the success of this project are seriously disturbed. In the first place this project has been [m]aligned as a 'Jim-Crow' set-up," he wrote, referencing the very public criticism the NAACP faction was directing at him personally. "[Y]et there were some members of the Negro group who, in an effort to serve the best interests of the nation in this period of emergency and at the same time who wanted to see progress by evolution rather than revolution, stood out for the development of this as a separate project." If the War Department approached the construction of TAAF with anything less than total and urgent determination, Patterson warned, his critics would have a field day. Such a failure would not only be "a source of embarrassment to those who have supported the above position, but it also constitutes just the sort of argument which will be used in the future to contribute to the evidence indicating the undemocratic behavior of the federal government in the treatment of its Negro citizens." Even before it was fully constructed, TAAF was a chess piece in a propaganda war. Patterson closed his urgent plea with language that would have placated whites in the War Department but caused his detractors in the NAACP to grind their teeth. "I am convinced that if the proper opportunity is provided," he wrote, "this project will be a source of pride to the Army Air Corps and an asset to the nation, as well as an opportunity for *sensible expression on the part of the Negro people* [emphasis added]."[52]

Alabama's Sen. Lister Hill, known as the "Godfather of Maxwell Field" for his interest in military aviation and ability to procure appropriations for the nearby Montgomery air base that housed the Southeastern Air Training Command, assured Dr. Patterson that he was "making every effort to get increased appropriations so as to insure uninterrupted construction." Hill was as good as his word, and construction of TAAF continued more or less on schedule. Hill was in fact remarkably effective at steering War Department contracts to his home state. Between July 1, 1940, and April 30, 1941—months before the United States had declared war on Germany and Japan—the U.S. government spent just short of $200 million on defense-related contracts in Alabama. This figure was more than three times the amount spent in Georgia, nearly three times as much as in Tennessee, and more than eight times the amount spent in Mississippi. Defense dollars modernized Alabama and brought it out of the Great Depression.[53]

As Dr. Patterson was fending off critics in the NAACP and black press, he and his allies also had to defend the project from the whites of Tuskegee. Tuskegee was of course residentially segregated, with African Americans living closer to Tuskegee Institute on the west side of the town and whites concentrated on the east. When a rumor spread that the AAC was going to build Tuskegee Army Air Field on the east side of the town, whites revolted. Local whites decided that the prospect of bringing millions of dollars worth of construction and hundreds of jobs into the economically depressed area was apparently not worth the damage the base might cause to their customs. William Varner, probate judge of Macon County and scion of one of its wealthiest and most distinguished families, forwarded a petition signed by ninety-five Tuskegee whites protesting the rumored location of the "colored aviation camp."[54]

Addressed to Senators Hill and John H. Bankhead, the petition read, "The undersigned, having regard for the welfare of the white citizenship of Tuskegee and Macon County, urgently request your prompt action in protesting...against the location of a colored aviation camp on the East, or Southeast boundary of Tuskegee." Such a location, the citizens warned, "would destroy the usefulness of this part of Tuskegee...for a white residence section" and constrain the expansion of white neighborhoods. Varner worried that the base would be sited within 2 miles of the town's elementary and high schools for whites, placing black cadets dangerously close to white schoolgirls. He also reported, "The persons who carried these petitions around stated that ninety-five of the one hundred people who were approached gladly signed."[55]

When Hill took the matter up with Maj. Gen. George H. Brett, acting chief of the AAC, Brett expressed his wish to have nothing whatsoever to do with the program. According to a revealing series of transcribed telephone conversations with Hill and his staff, Brett complained, "You are putting me between the devil and the deep blue sea." "[G]osh—I get pounded on that thing," he said of the "Negro airport." "Oh hell," Hill responded, acknowledging the sting of the NAACP's publicity campaign against the creation of the Jim Crow flight facility. "I know what your trouble is—God almighty I know what it is. Don't you think I don't get some of your troubles." Brett promised to investigate the matter and get back to the senator.[56]

Brett discovered that the airport was being built, as he had suspected, at a site several miles north of the town of Tuskegee; the rumor of a facility on the east side of town had no basis in fact. In reporting this news to Hill's secretary, Brett added, "[N]ow you might tell the Senator that I just read a long letter from our Special Assistant Secretary of War [sic] Mr. Hastie[,] who is intensely interested in the colored people, who claims that he notes that they are building separate barricks [sic] for white and...for colored people and separate barricks for white officers[,] and he objects most strenuously—says that the whites must live with the blacks." "Good night!" the secretary responded. Brett clearly misunderstood the cleavages that had already developed between Tuskegee Institute and the NAACP on the issue: "Now you might tell Senator Hill that this little thing he is talking about [the site of the airport] is only just one small phase of the whole problem. Oh yes...they are demanding non-segregation." The secretary replied, "Well, I don't think that is going to work in the South." Gen. Brett agreed. Not only would it not work in the South, but "I don't know why it should work in the North [either]," he opined. "I happen to be from Cleveland, and I'm sure I don't want to live with a nigger."[57]

Brett could take some comfort in the contemporaneous reports he received from the officer at the Southeast Air Corps Training Center in charge of overseeing construction at Tuskegee, which told him that the project was proceeding splendidly. The construction project was never divorced from racial politics, however. "The negro [sic] race is taking a tremendous amount of interest in this development, especially, of course, the faculty of Tuskegee Institute," reported Brig. Gen. Walter R. Weaver. "These negroes are wonderfully well educated and as smart as they can be, and politically they have back of them their race composed of some eleven million people in this country." Brett was somewhat more careful with his words in his written reply than he had been on the telephone: "I...am delighted to hear that you are progressing satisfactorily with the Negro School proposition at Tuskegee."[58]

In February 1941 the War Department awarded multi-million-dollar contracts to the firms of Hilyard R. Robinson, an architect from Washington, D.C., and the general contractors McKissack & McKissack of Nashville, Tennessee, to build the separate-but-equal air base. Robinson had established a reputation in Washington for his Bauhaus-influenced designs of New Deal public housing projects for blacks. McKissack & McKissack was known for its work building black churches and school buildings throughout the South, and the firm boasted a long, proud history. Its principals, Calvin and Moses McKissack III, were the grandsons of a slave whose owner had hired him out as a master builder. They too had benefited from the New Deal's public works building boom in 1930s. The TAAF construction contracts were the first the War Department had ever awarded to black-owned companies. The decision further antagonized local whites, but it did not stop local white-owned companies from subcontracting to construct the base. Because the town of Tuskegee could not provide all of the municipal services necessary for such a large development, the AAC would also have to build its own services into the base, and in the coming years TAAF would grow into a small, nearly all-black city.[59]

The building program accelerated following Pearl Harbor, and TAAF's official history records that many of the buildings on the base were occupied and in use for weeks before they were completed and the AAC certified the construction as having met specifications. In the winter of 1941–42, cadets moved into dormitory buildings before heating systems had been installed. Enlisted men lived for several weeks in TAAF's "Tent City" while they waited for the construction of their barracks. The men in the first cadre of enlisted support personnel transferred to TAAF "got a lot of enjoyment," one of them remembered, out of pulling down the "colored" and "white" signs on the temporary toilets that still dotted the airfield.[60]

As construction of TAAF continued and the flight instruction program started to take shape, the NAACP applied consistent, relentless pressure on the War Department to treat black Americans equitably in every decision it made. The campaign began more than a year before the Japanese attack on Pearl Harbor and would continue past the end of the war. The NAACP did not act alone in this regard, but the organization was at the forefront of efforts to pressure the AAC into accepting as many black pilot cadets into the training program as possible, to ensure them fair treatment while in training, to offer them the opportunity to demonstrate their prowess in combat after graduation, and to admit to their eventual successes. An episode from early in the process epitomizes this effort. Soon after the AAC announced the creation of the Tuskegee training program, at the end of 1940, Walter White wrote to every black man in the United States with a pilot's license, the majority of whom were recent CPT graduates, to see who would be willing to fly for Uncle Sam.[61]

Those who responded to White's call composed a cross-section of young, well-educated black men. In some ways the men represented the elite of black America; they were all college students or graduates, at a time when fewer than 2 percent of African American adults held college diplomas. Yet the majority of them were first-generation college students like Horace Bohannon and Roy Chappell who worked hard to put themselves through school and at least occasionally relied on extended family and community networks to make tuition payments or provide room and board. They were a diverse group, but they held in common an intense patriotism, the confidence that they could serve their country as well as anyone else in whichever roles their talents dictated, and the dream of flight.[62]

Mohamed Shaik was the son of an Indian shaikh-merchant father who had been educated in Great Britain and then migrated from Calcutta to New Orleans; his mother was a New Orleans Creole with Native American ancestry. ("I'm Indian on both sides," he joked about his background; but as far the War Department was concerned, he was black.) Shaik had just graduated from Xavier University in New Orleans, and in the summer of 1940 he and two other New Orleans men of color, Adolph Moret and Octave Rainey, had attended the CPT program at West Virginia State and earned their civilian licenses. In response to White's letter, Shaik assured him, "The question of discrimination of Negroes in the Air Corps is one which touches me deeply since I am capable of meeting all of its requirements." He volunteered his services.[63]

Mac Ross, a graduate of the CPT program at West Virginia State, responded, "I would be more than too glad to join the Air Corps of the United States Army if I was given the opportunity." Given the opportunity, Ross shortly thereafter graduated in the first class of the Tuskegee aviation program. Louis R. Purnell wrote from Lincoln University, "I would like to enlist as a flying cadet in the army. I've passed all examinations successfully with high grades.... I hope you will do all in your power to help me." He too was accepted into the Tuskegee program, graduated, and flew in combat.[64]

Yancey Williams, a senior studying mechanical engineering at Howard University and a member of the NAACP, responded to White with news that the AAC had just instructed him to prepare for a new physical exam. Williams had recently filed suit against the War Department and Air Corps, alleging that he was being denied the opportunity to join the cadet training program based only on his race. Williams had completed Howard's CPT program and a secondary course at Tuskegee Institute, and earned his civilian pilot's license. He passed an Army physical in July 1940, met all of the AAC's requirements for flying cadets, and applied for the program. According to Williams' affidavit, Maj. Gen. Walter S. Grant, commanding general of the Third Corps area of the AAC, flatly refused to consider Williams's application because Williams was black. Williams appealed to the adjutant general of the Army and Secretary of War Stimson, and on December 13, 1940, the appeal was refused solely on the basis of Williams's race. At the same time, the suit alleged, the War Department had begun advertising in newspapers and on the radio, asking more citizens to enlist as flying cadets.[65]

The NAACP's National Legal Committee, precursor to its Legal Defense and Education Fund, led by Thurgood Marshall, accepted the case and assisted Williams' attorneys. Marshall publicized the case aggressively, and NAACP youth councils began raising a national defense fund. Black newspapers covered the case widely, and the publicity deeply embarrassed the Roosevelt administration. As much as any other initiative, the suit forced the War Department to follow through on Stimson's promise to open training facilities for black Americans in the AAC. In a pattern that would replay itself over and again through the following decades, the NAACP's strategy of winning redress through the courts combined in this case with individual initiative, mobilization of younger blacks, and pressure brought by coverage from national media to dismantle a vestige of white supremacy. When the War Department initiated the Tuskegee program, Williams dropped the suit and entered the cadet corps.[66]

Like Williams, Charles W. Dryden received a letter from White, and he responded with an assurance that he would leap at the chance to volunteer for the AAC. The son of Jamaican immigrants who had lived all his life in New York City, Dryden "was born wanting to fly," he would later say. Dryden claimed that even before he could talk, he "used to take little bits of paper and tear them into tiny bits, throw them into the air, and try to say, 'Airplane! Airplane!'" Dryden was a junior majoring in mechanical engineering at the City College of New York when White's letter reached him; he had wanted to study aeronautical engineering at New York University, but his family could not afford the tuition. He had recently completed the college's CPT program and had already tried to volunteer for pilot training in the AAC several times without success. He replied: "[Y]ou ask if I would be willing to enroll in the U.S. Army Air Corps if offered an opportunity. The answer is—Yes, definitely! I would not only enroll but would pursue a lifetime career of service in the Corps." "I shall keep in touch with you," Dryden promised in a subsequent letter to White, "and let you know if Uncle Sam gives our boys a raw deal or a square deal."[67]

Vash Eagleson was among those who responded immediately to White. A transfer student at Indiana University who had graduated from the first CPT class at West Virginia State College, Eagleson had deep roots in the "Talented Tenth" of black Americans, the educated elite that W.E.B. DuBois believed would lead the race to equal treatment in the United States. His mother, Frances Marshall Eagleson, was the first black woman to earn a degree at Indiana University and at the time was employed as the registrar of historically black North Carolina College for Negroes, now North Carolina Central University, in Durham. (Both campuses now have buildings named for her.) His father taught chemistry and coached the football team in Durham while he completed a doctorate in chemistry from Cornell University. Eagleson's paternal grandfather, Preston E. Eagleson, was one of the first two black men to graduate from Indiana University, where he earned bachelor's and master's degrees in philosophy and starred on the football team in the 1890s. Preston Eagleson won the university's 1894 oratorical contest, and he demanded to stay in the same hotels that served his white teammates when the football team played away games; that same year he won $50 in a settlement against a hotel in Crawfordville, Indiana, after its elevator operator tried to deny him service based on his race.[68]

Frustrated by the AAC's multiple rejections, Eagleson joined the Army after Pearl Harbor. He was in Officer Candidate School at Fort Benning, Georgia, when his letter of acceptance to the Air Corps finally arrived, and he traveled to Tuskegee in 1942. In the early years of the war the AAC accepted only applicants who had completed at least two years of college, so its first black aviation cadets—men like Shaik, Custis, Ross, Williams, Dryden, and Eagleson—were Talented Tenth all the way. Full of pride, conscious of the expectations that had been placed upon them, they were determined to succeed once they received the opportunity.[69]

Of the first eighty-one cadets accepted to the program, forty-four were from the South, twenty-six were from the north, and eleven hailed from the Midwest or far west. Thousands more young men came from every part of the country—at least thirty-nine of the forty-eight states, plus Washington, D.C.—to enter the pilot training program at Tuskegee, which expanded in 1943 to train multi-engine bomber pilots in addition to fighter pilots. Just short of one thousand of them graduated from the program, and nearly one-half of that number flew in combat, where collectively they flew more than 15,000 sorties and destroyed more than two hundred German aircraft. Thirty-two of the pilots were shot down and spent time in German prisoner of war camps; sixty-six others gave their lives for their country.[70]

These statistics are important, but they only begin to describe the importance of this historical experience to the history of the American people or the difference it made in the lives of the more than 15,000 men and women who were a part of it, either as pilots or as support personnel. Roy Chappell came closer to describing the experience's significance for African Americans than numbers ever could. When Chappell went off-base and mingled among black civilians, he said, he found that "the folks really would do anything they could for you."[71]

Twiley Barker interrupted his studies at Tuskegee Institute in 1944 to serve in the war effort. After training at TAAF and a brief career as an Air Forces cryptographer, he returned to school under the GI Bill and eventually earned a PhD in political science and fashioned for himself a distinguished career teaching constitutional law and political science. Placing the Tuskegee Airmen experience in a larger context, Barker said, "This is one of the big surprising, untold stories. Those black kids proved to the world that we were as capable of flying an aircraft as anybody else. We were as capable of providing the necessary support services to make certain that missions were accomplished." The lesson of the Tuskegee Airmen experience, he said, was: "We could do the same kinds of things—at the level expected by the military—even though our skin color may have been different. The talent is there, and if it is allowed to reach its maximum potential, any goal can be accomplished." The Tuskegee Airmen were among the first Americans to imagine the kind of racially integrated society that most Americans now take for granted. They worked and sacrificed and proved that such a society could exist and thrive.[72]

That many Americans at the dawn of the twenty-first century would accept this as a given is a measurement of the significant changes the Tuskegee Airmen helped bring about. Few, if any, Americans could have expected in 1941 that this would be one of the major outcomes of the war. Not all black Americans at the time appreciated the Tuskegee program; many considered it an embarrassing symbol of Jim Crow inequality. But blacks did show a remarkable unanimity in forcing the fight for equality and democracy within the borders of the United States to the forefront of American war aims. They proved that a racially segregated military assembled to fight fascism was, to use Walter White's term, an "anachronism," and they pushed the armed forces into the future. By forcing action on the question of "The Use of Negro Manpower in War," they proved their patriotism and their capabilities beyond doubt and kick-started the modern black freedom struggle in the process.[73]

But the Tuskegee Airmen did not defeat white supremacy in the United States once and for all. They did not by themselves end racial segregation in the armed forces. It would take the renewed commitment of thousands of individuals and the creation of new institutions to accomplish these goals in the decades following World War II. The Tuskegee Airmen did, however, prove beyond any conceivable question that black Americans could fly and maintain some of the world's most sophisticated killing machines, lead and staff complicated bureaucratic systems, and excel under tremendous pressure. Above all, they proved to the U.S. War Department that racial segregation of troops was inefficient and not cost-effective, and that it therefore hindered national defense.

It was on this basis that the military, under orders of Commander-in-Chief Harry Truman, would abandon Jim Crow immediately after the war, making it one of the first institutions in the United States to do so. The military, which had been arguably the most racially intransigent national institution in 1940, was transformed in the course of the war and, contrary to all expectations, led desegregation efforts within the national government soon after the war ended. Once the armed forces had thrown their collective weight behind desegregation, the momentum would be impossible to reverse.

The Black Eagles Take Flight

Lemuel R. Custis, a Connecticut native and a recent graduate of Howard University, was a member of the first class of pilot cadets accepted for training at Tuskegee in 1941. He made his first trip by train into the Deep South with "mixed feelings," he said. "It was the first time they pulled a curtain on the old boy," Custis recalled, referring to the practice of drawing a curtain around African Americans to segregate them from white patrons in the dining cars of trains south of the Mason-Dixon Line. "Even when I went up to get the food, which Uncle Sam was providing, they pulled the curtain on me in the dining car. I really then understood I was black," he said with a rueful chuckle. "I just thought I was before, but I knew I was after that." By the same token, however, Custis never forgot "how nice the porters were to me, how they helped me survive that trip. Having that curtain pulled on you, you feel—you wonder how to handle it. But they said, 'If you want to go up [to the dining car], we'll take care of you. If you don't, you can stay in the compartment, and we'll bring the food back.'" Thousands of the men and women who congregated at Tuskegee during the war had a similar experience. They cultivated an atmosphere of camaraderie, individual and collective pride, and high achievement in the midst of a social system that attempted to define them as inferior.[1]

The community the AAC selected for its separate but equal training facilities was a bi-racial, majority-black, and thoroughly segregated town in central Alabama. Tuskegee, the home of Booker T. Washington's Tuskegee Institute, had already established itself as a center of black flying. The institute's president from 1935 to 1953, Dr. Frederick Douglass Patterson, embraced aviation as a field of study in the same way that Washington had promoted masonry, tailoring, and other "industrial arts" for the sons and daughters of freed slaves: he recognized it as a potential source of well-paying jobs for African Americans.

The town of Tuskegee, seat of Macon County, had been an important trading center in the Black Belt cotton economy of the first half of the nineteenth century, but the soils in its vicinity had been exhausted by over-cultivation even before the Civil War, and by 1880 the county was losing population. White Democrats had "redeemed" the county with violence and voting fraud, taking control from a Republican coalition of freedmen and liberal whites by 1874. The conservative white Democrats found that they could not reverse Macon County's economic fortunes by themselves, however, and searched for ways to cooperate with blacks for the common good of economic development without ceding political power to the majority group. Local whites had deep reservations about offering even a decent education to their black neighbors, but elites considered the creation of a school for blacks a worthwhile compromise if it could keep black workers in the area. In 1880 former slaves led by a tinsmith named Lewis Adams and former slaveholders from Macon County successfully lobbied the state legislature for a $2,000 appropriation to create a "normal" school for African Americans, and by 1881 they had raised enough funds to hire a principal.[2]

The man they hired, Booker T. Washington, was the son of an enslaved West Virginia woman and a white man he never met. Washington had internalized from powerful whites in his life the ideals of self-discipline and hard work, a zealot's faith in the value of education, and Victorian-era standards of morality. For better or worse, by the time he reached Tuskegee Washington had already decided that whites with power could help him do the things he wanted to do. In building Tuskegee Institute, Washington would ingratiate himself with white conservatives, both locally and, as his and the institute's reputation grew, on the national level. Washington's black supporters considered this approach pragmatism at work; his critics, of whom there were many by the first decades of the twentieth century, saw the elevation of Washington's personal interests above those of his race. That Tuskegee Institute under his guidance taught the industrial arts, preparing its graduates to be skilled artisans or modern yeomen farmers, and not a liberal arts curriculum, enraged his elite critics further. Those elites founded the NAACP in 1909 as an explicit alternative to Washington's version of what both camps called "racial uplift."[3]

Washington built the institute into a school with regional prominence within a short period of time. In 1895 he captured national attention with a speech he delivered at the Cotton States and International Exposition in Atlanta. Presented to a mainly white audience, Washington's "Atlanta Compromise" speech (as his critics came to call it) was widely praised by white and black Americans at the time. "In all things that are purely social we can be as separate as the fingers, yet one as the hand in all things essential to mutual progress," he advised, in what seemed to some an acceptance of segregation, and he recommended that white employers "cast down your bucket where you are" to encourage them to hire more blacks. Initially, African Americans congratulated Washington with one voice for his bold call for increased economic opportunities for blacks and for reminding Southern whites that they would never progress so long as they excluded their black neighbors from opportunities for economic progress. Later, his critics would chide Washington for playing to whites' stereotypes of Southern blacks in the address and for seeming to accept the social and political inequalities engrained in the Jim Crow system. The speech elevated Washington to national celebrity; by the early years of the new century he was dining at the White House with Theodore Roosevelt and advising the Republican Party on patronage appointments for offices throughout the South.[4]

Washington also encouraged white philanthropists to build schools for black schoolchildren, but his efforts to improve the region's educational system and develop its economy had no more than a marginal effect on its African American residents. As late as 1934 Macon County spent nearly ten times more on the education of whites than it spent on black students, and a study by the prominent Fisk University sociologist Charles S. Johnson Sr. published that year found that material conditions for local black farmers had improved little since emancipation. However, Washington's approach did succeed fabulously in enlarging the town of Tuskegee's black middle class. In the first decades of the twentieth century the institute campus and its adjoining neighborhoods became showcases of black progress. Small, black-owned businesses catered to the black bourgeoisie, and the campus and surrounding community were nearly self-sufficient. Washington's plan for racial uplift made it possible for well-to-do black Tuskegeeans to cushion themselves from the worst aspects of Jim Crow segregation.[5]

Robert Russa Moton, a graduate of Hampton Institute and a Washington protégé, assumed the presidency of Tuskegee Institute after Washington died in 1915. Moton continued to develop the institute under the great man's philosophies of education and economic development, and he capitalized on the relationships Washington had developed with Republicans on the national level. In the early 1920s he shepherded through to completion a plan to build a federally funded hospital for black World War I veterans on the outskirts of town. Tuskegee Institute and a handful of white landowners donated land for the project, and Moton used his considerable lobbying skills in Washington to convince the U.S. Veterans Bureau to choose the site. Moton established a model for the sort of effort that would later result in the AAC's choice of Tuskegee as the site of its training facility. He threw Tuskegee Institute's considerable national political influence and local economic power behind the project, drew on the good relations the institute had nurtured with conservative whites in Washington, and cooperated with local whites to bring the project to fruition.[6]

In return for Tuskegee Institute's gift of several hundred acres for the project, Moton insisted that the hospital be staffed only by African Americans. He was forced to accept a white chief administrator, the staunchly segregationist Alabamian Col. Robert H. Stanley, but held firm in his insistence that the rest of the staff be black, even in the face of resistance from the local Ku Klux Klan. When Stanley tried to hire an all-white crew of doctors and nurses (and the Klan paraded through Tuskegee Institute to demonstrate support for the decision), Moton went over Stanley's head and met in Washington with President Warren G. Harding. Harding froze appropriations for the facility's construction until Stanley could find a full black complement for the hospital. The $2 million complex opened in 1923, and the professionals who staffed the hospital added to Tuskegee's black middle class.[7]

Moton retired from the presidency of Tuskegee Institute in 1935, and Dr. Frederick Douglass Patterson, a veterinary scientist and head of the college's School of Agriculture, took over. On paper, Patterson's background differed greatly from those of Washington and Moton; he held advanced degrees in veterinary medicine and science from Iowa State University and a PhD in bacteriology from Cornell University. Even Dr. Patterson's given names seemed to augur that he was cut from a different cloth than Booker T. Washington. Tuskegee's trustees had surprised the college community by tapping him as the college's president at the age of thirty-four. Patterson's academic credentials spoke for themselves, and he had already improved the veterinary school's academic reputation. But he also held fast to his predecessors' emphasis on education in the trades and pragmatic acceptance of racial segregation as a necessary evil to be worked around. Patterson urged African Americans to seek greater opportunities in vocational education, as he, like Moton and Washington before him, believed that the trades offered the best possibility for "the realization of economic competence by the Negro people." If black Americans had to endure the inevitable indignities of segregation to obtain these equal opportunities, well, that was the price of progress. "[W]e shall need to be careful," he argued, "that our wise insistence upon the elimination of undemocratic practices does not lead us to a point of stupid insistence upon unsegregated opportunity in such a way as to defeat the chance for the employment of specialists through failure to attain the ultimate in one fell swoop."[8]

Patterson championed aviation at Tuskegee on these pragmatic, vocational-education grounds. He wanted African Americans to have access to the technologically advanced, high-paying jobs that the growing field would create; he wanted to prepare Tuskegee graduates for careers as pilots, but also as aviation mechanics, air traffic controllers, and flight instructors. Patterson was not a nationally recognized "race leader" in the way that Washington and, to a lesser extent, Moton had been, but he seldom missed a chance to elevate his and his school's reputation. For instance, when Tuskegee prepared to add aviation to its curriculum in 1935, making it the first historically black college to do so, Patterson asked Claude Barnett, the director of the Associated Negro Press (and, later, a trustee of the institute), to focus his attention on the exclusion of blacks from the AAC. Such stories in the black press, he believed, would highlight the school's efforts to open doors for African Americans in the world of aviation.[9]

The insitute's director of mechanical industries, G. L. Washington, proved indispensable to the efforts to establish the school's aviation program. The engineer may have lacked the technical expertise needed to create an aviation program from scratch, but he showed the dogged determination, attention to detail, and unabashed enthusiasm that would be necessary to get one up and running. An enthusiastic, personable man, Washington also knew to surround himself with well-trained experts and naturally gifted pilots.[10]

Chief among these was Charles Alfred Anderson, a natural-born flyer. When he was an infant, Anderson's parents sent him from their home in Bryn Mawr, Pennsylvania, to live with a grandmother in Staunton, Virginia. She sent him back to his parents at the age of eight, according to family lore, because every time she turned her back he ran off to look for airplanes. As a young man in Pennsylvania, he tried for a long time to find a plane he could rent and a white pilot he could hire to train him to fly, but the common response even in the Quaker State was, he said, "We don't carry colored people." In 1927 or 1928 Anderson did finally find one licensed white pilot who was willing to train Anderson in the pilot's own personal plane, at the princely rate of $30 per hour. But that pilot apparently was not gifted; soon after he took Anderson up for his first lesson, the white man crashed his airplane into a forest and destroyed it. Anderson could not find another instructor willing to offer him lessons, so he borrowed $2,500 and bought his own Monocoupe. According to Anderson, he so wanted to fly that he taught himself to operate the plane by allowing licensed pilots to borrow the aircraft and then observing them from the co-pilot's seat as they flew, and then through the ultimate trial and error. He cracked up at least two planes while teaching himself to be a pilot.[11]

Anderson taught himself to fly well enough to earn his pilot's license in 1929, making him the second African American to hold one, but he found that he loved flying so much that what he really wanted to do was teach others. To do that, he needed a transport license, and to earn a transport license he needed to find another licensed pilot willing to give him advanced instruction. Again the white pilots he approached turned him down. He finally found a willing instructor with an unlikely background. Ernest Buehl had flown fighter aircraft for the German army in World War I and, according to Anderson, he proved in his dealings with the young pilot that "he was always in favor of white supremacy." But it did not take Buehl long to decide that Anderson knew what he was doing. When Buehl accompanied Anderson to his test for the transport license in July 1932, the federal inspector told the German immigrant, "You know, I have never given the flight test to a colored person. I don't know if I will." According to Anderson, Buehl responded, "Well, he can fly as well as anybody. There is no reason why you shouldn't give him the test." Anderson later claimed that he answered every question on the written examination correctly and passed the flight check. The inspector decided that he could not in good conscience fail the black pilot but could not bring himself to award Anderson the perfect score he earned, either. He gave Anderson a score of eighty out of one hundred.[12]

Hungry for anything he could learn about airplanes, Anderson joined the Pennsylvania National Guard with hopes of transferring into an aviation unit. Because the guard did not accept blacks, he tried to pass as white. Anderson was light-skinned, but his true racial heritage was soon discovered, and he was kicked out of the service. He tried again to pass as white to enter Pets Aviation School in Philadelphia, but he was asked to leave that program also. With no job prospects in aviation, he dug sewer lines for a time on a Works Progress Administration project.[13]

After news of Anderson's success in earning a transport license spread through the African American community, Anderson met Dr. Albert E. Forsythe, a black surgeon working in Atlantic City, and agreed to give him flying lessons. Anderson was working for a wealthy white family in Bryn Mawr as a chauffeur and gardener at the time; it was too expensive for him to store and operate an airplane on his own. Forsythe became Anderson's student and friend, but more importantly for the history of black aviation, his patron. Anderson remembered Forsythe as "a very, very aggressive and determined man, and an ambitious person [who] wanted to advance aviation among the blacks." He suggested the idea of a transcontinental flight to publicize the cause of black aviation. With Forsythe bankrolling the flight, the pair flew an airplane with no more than a 65- or 70-horsepower engine and a maximum cruising speed of 130 miles an hour from Atlantic City to Los Angeles and back in 1933, making them the first black pilots to execute a round-trip transcontinental flight.[14]

Forsythe and Anderson had plans for international flights, to Canada, the West Indies, and South America. They needed an airplane with a stronger motor for these flights, so they visited the Lambert Co. in Saint Louis, chatted with local aviator Charles Lindbergh, and purchased a Monocoupe with a stronger Warner engine. Anderson thought Lindbergh was "tops and supreme in aviation," but beyond that had "never been much impressed with Lindbergh, because I always considered Lindbergh to be a racist." The men named their aircraft the *Booker T. Washington* because both men honored the Tuskegee founder's work ethic and Forsythe had attended the institute before graduating from McGill University in Canada. In 1934, with financial support from Tuskegee Institute, Forsythe and Anderson toured the islands of the Caribbean. They flew to the Bahamas; to Cuba, where President Fulgencio Batista gave the pair a heroes' welcome; through a tropical storm to Jamaica; and to Haiti. Their engine threw a piston over the mountains of the Dominican Republic, but Anderson was able to land the plane safely on the shores of a lake. They waited in a Dominican Army jungle camp for more than two weeks until replacement parts could be flown in from the United States.[15]

When Forsythe and Anderson returned home, they were the toast of Atlantic City. Forsythe wanted to continue the publicity-generating trips, even dreamed of organizing a round-the-world flight with Anderson, but he found that his surgical practice demanded too much of his time. Anderson returned to barnstorming, renting planes from others and flying them in front of paying crowds. Anderson eventually found his way to Washington, D.C., where he and two others instituted an aviation ground school curriculum for the black public high schools. When Howard University won a CPT contract, Anderson was hired as an instructor.[16]

The Civil Aviation Administration (CAA) awarded Tuskegee a CPT contract for the 1939–40 school year at the last possible moment, and the school scrambled to find operators who could manage the program. Fortunately, Joseph Wren Allen, the white owner-operator of Alabama Air Service in Montgomery, an hour's drive from campus, agreed to make his facilities available. Washington found two professors in Tuskegee Institute's mechanical industries department who were willing to try to teach the program's ground school courses. He later wrote that he never doubted the pair "would do their best and put everything they had in the instruction. But I was frankly interested in [Tuskegee's aviation students] making the best record possible on the examination and felt teachers with considerable training and experience in aeronautics would make the difference in the results of the examination." True to the Tuskegee tradition, he placed pragmatism above racial solidarity and contracted with two experienced white instructors from the aeronautics department of nearby Alabama Polytechnic Institute (now Auburn University) to provide the required ninety hours of instruction in navigation, meteorology, civil air regulations, and aircraft operations. They proved entirely cooperative, and Washington gave the men a large share of the credit for the remarkable success of the first class of students.[17]

The cost of transporting the students to and from Montgomery for flight instruction became prohibitive, so Washington approached the owners of an airfield closer to campus. Kennedy Field, roughly 7 miles south of campus, had been built by three local white amateur aviators—Forrest Shelton,

Joe Wright Wilkerson, and Stanley Kennedy—for their own use and had not been certified by the CAA. Washington estimated that it would cost less to bring Kennedy Field into compliance with federal regulations than it would to transport CPT students to Montgomery and Auburn, and he convinced the white pilots to transfer their lease of the field to the college in exchange for free storage of their shared airplane. In the tradition of Booker T. Washington's self-help philosophy, the Tuskegee students who enrolled in CPT provided the manual labor necessary to improve the field to CAA standards, and the program moved to Kennedy Field in the spring semester of 1940.[18]

Remarkably, when the first class of students took their written exams that March, every single one of them passed. They were apparently the first class in the history of the CAA Southeast Region's college aviation program (which included classes from such institutions as Georgia Tech, Auburn, and the University of North Carolina) to pass unanimously, and student Charles Foxx's score of 97 was the highest individual score ever recorded in the region to that point. These accomplishments won heavy attention for Tuskegee in regional newspapers and national aviation magazines. As a result of the publicity, young black men throughout the country began writing Tuskegee for information about military flight training—so many, in fact, that Washington remembered that the time it took to answer them all became a burden on the clerical staff. Military aviation training was, of course, unavailable for blacks in 1940, but Tuskegee had already distinguished itself as the natural place to inquire.[19]

Tuskegee administrators were so encouraged by the class's success that they began pressing the CAA to award the program a contract to offer advanced training classes. In 1940 the CAA initiated plans to offer the students throughout the United States who passed the basic CPT program a secondary course that included additional ground school classes and more advanced instruction in the air at a handful of schools that had distinguished themselves as basic CPT sites. (The CAA considered its advanced coursework equal to the primary flight training that cadets were required to complete in the AAC.) Patterson and Washington wanted Tuskegee Institute to become the first African American institution to offer the training when the CAA began the program in 1941; its only competition for the honor was the Coffey School in Chicago.[20]

G. L. Washington was surprised to learn in June 1940 that the CAA had stepped up its plans and wanted contractors to initiate the program the following month, rather than in the fall of 1941 as originally announced. The advanced program would require equipment and instructors that Tuskegee did not yet have, and Tuskegee had promised to build a new facility to replace Kennedy Field on land it owned as part of the original application.

Tuskegee had not yet begun construction of the new facility, but the CAA chose the institute over the Coffey School anyway. Washington knew exactly why his school won the contract: Tuskegee, he later wrote, had established

a reputation for cooperating with state and Federal Governments; an excellent tradition and setting for training; a name known throughout the world; widespread national publicity at the time for achievement of Civilian Pilot Training students on CAA examinations and in flying; the Goodwill of people of the south and north in key positions...whose opinions could be determinative; a geographical setting favorable to flying training; a favorable impression with CAA-Washington for overcoming obstacles; and possibly other attributes which cause decisions in [its] favor. Further, it could, as a partner in a segregated project, be quite relieving and comforting.[21]

Immediately after Tuskegee finalized the contract, Patterson flew to Washington, D.C., and hired Anderson away from Howard. Washington gave him the title of chief flight instructor soon thereafter; Anderson would be known affectionately as "Chief" for the rest of his life. Kennedy Field could not accommodate the larger Waco aircraft necessary for advanced instruction, so Washington again arranged to use the airfield at Auburn. Lewis Jackson, whom Anderson would remember as "a brain, a very brilliant young man," soon arrived at Tuskegee and worked as Anderson's counterpart in flight instruction. A product of the Coffey School, Jackson later earned a PhD and served as president of Central State University in Ohio.[22]

Again Alabama Polytechnic professors agreed to teach ground school courses, and Washington managed to hire Joseph T. Camillieri, an Italian American pilot instructor, and Frank Rosenberg, an instructor and mechanic, through a classified ad placed in a New York newspaper. Students who had distinguished themselves at historically black colleges' CPT programs were selected for the course; many of them would either remain in or return to Tuskegee later as instructors themselves. All ten of the students in the first advanced class—which Washington had managed to organize in a matter of days—would pass the CAA's examinations in October 1940. By the end of that year, Washington could boast with more than a little justification that "Tuskegee Institute stood out, possibly alone among universities and colleges of the nation participating in the CPT program"— not just black universities and colleges, but all universities and colleges.[23]

That same month the War Department announced its plans to create the 99th Pursuit Squadron and the training base for black aviation cadets at Tuskegee. The creation of the AAC program required the construction of another airfield for primary military training, which the college had hoped to build anyway for the CAA. Rather than continue to expand and make improvements to its "Airport No. 1," which it was still leasing from Stanley Kennedy, the institute would need to construct a new airdrome, which it could then operate under contract for the AAC. All of its instructors would be civilian employees of Tuskegee Institute, but they would be expected to teach cadets to fly according to AAC standards. First Tuskegee Institute had to construct the facility.[24]

Tuskegee had already invested roughly $15,000 in its aviation program, but it had been reimbursed by the CAA for less than $500 of its expenditures. If it were to create the new program, the school faced costs of at least $10,000 for additional aircraft and salaries, in addition to the price of construction. "While there were many supporters of the aviation activities among the faculty, administration, and staff of the institute," Washington recalled, "nevertheless rumblings grew on the campus, and persisted, because of spending on aviation. There were those who viewed flying training as nothing more than an avocation or luxury instruction." The free spending at an institution that perennially operated on a shoestring budget seemed to some a betrayal of Tuskegee Institute's philosophy. The institute's leaders had made similarly large investments on many occasions in the past, but always with an eye toward creating practical programs for students that would launch them into careers. In this case, the critics charged, "Badly needed money for instructional purposes was going freely into something that would not enable the student to make a living." The critics did not sway Patterson and Washington, who did expect that the training would launch their students into aviation careers. But before the institute could construct the new Moton Field facility, it had to find financing for it. The effort to secure a loan brought prominent visitors to Tuskegee.[25]

In March 1941 the board of trustees of the Chicago-based Julius Rosenwald Fund, a charitable foundation endowed with Rosenwald's profits from the Sears Roebuck Co. he had founded, held its regular board meeting on the campus of Tuskegee Institute. The site may have seemed an unlikely one for the gathering of distinguished academics, captains of industry, and politically prominent men and women, all of them white, but the fund had by this point a long-standing relationship with the institute, having supported its efforts to train teachers for the surrounding rural areas (the special focus of the fund's philanthropy), and the trustees were to consider Patterson's request to provide financing for the field. The fund's newest and most renowned trustee, First Lady Eleanor Roosevelt, attended her first board meeting there. She was familiar with Tuskegee because of the institute's infantile paralysis hospital, a special interest of the first couple. Already an aviation enthusiast—"[F]lying is the nearest thing to heaven most of us are likely to experience during our mortal lives," she had written in a 1939 article for *Collier's Magazine* titled "Flying is Fun," in which she also encouraged parents to allow their children to take flying lessons—Roosevelt decided she could do some good by visiting Kennedy Field.[26]

She met there with Chief Anderson, informed him that everybody had told her that black people could not fly airplanes, and asked if he would mind taking her for an aerial tour of the vicinity. "We had a delightful flight," Anderson remembered. "She enjoyed it very much. We came back and she said, 'Well, you can fly all right.'" Of course, Roosevelt knew full well about the program that had been in existence for more than a year by that point, and she would not have believed for a second the folklore that African Americans as a race were incapable of flying airplanes. She made the flight with Anderson purely for publicity purposes, and her plan worked. The photograph of the first lady sitting behind Anderson in a Waco biplane appeared in newspapers across the country, and Roosevelt described the flight glowingly in her widely read newspaper column, "My Day."[27]

Roosevelt's report reflected her wide-ranging interests. Calling Tuskegee "a very fine institution which has always interested me very much," she also commented on the school's poor surroundings. The conditions of the black schools the trustees visited were deplorable; those of even of the white schools were such, the first lady assured her readers, that they "would hardly satisfy you if you believed education was necessary for participation in our democratic form of government." The Rosenwald Fund trustees also visited the Tuskegee hospital while in the area. Roosevelt praised the work of Dr. John Chenault, "almost the only Negro doctor in the country, I think, who has had full training as an orthopaedic surgeon and has specialized in infantile paralysis" and looked forward to sharing photographs of Chenault's poliomyelitis unit with the president. (She did not mention in her column that the National Foundation for Infantile Paralysis had to finance Chenault's work in Tuskegee—and would continue to fund the facility to the tune of more than $1 million in the decade of the 1940s alone—because the Roosevelts' nearby Warm Springs Foundation served white patients only.)[28]

"Finally," she reported for her national readership, "we went out to the aviation field, where a Civil Aeronautics unit for the teaching of colored pilots is in full swing.... These boys are good pilots. I had the fun of going up in one of the tiny training planes with the head instructor, and seeing this interesting countryside from the air." For millions of newspaper readers throughout the country, this would be the first they had heard of black aviators, and Roosevelt was careful to place the program in larger context. "The days at Tuskegee have given me much to think about," she concluded. "To see a group of people working together for the improvement of undesirable conditions is very heartening. The problems seem great, but at least they are understood and people are working on them."[29]

The trustees of the Rosenwald Fund expressed the belief that the cost of the facility should ideally be borne by Tuskegee Institute's board of trustees, but in the end voted to lend up to $175,000 to the school for "the purchase of a suitable site, development of an airfield, construction and installation of facilities and purchase of equipment." A month later the institute purchased 650 acres of the S.M. Eich plantation 3 miles northeast of campus, and Moton Field, named for the institute's second president, Robert Russa Moton, was born.[30]

The Eleanor Roosevelt connection took on a life of its own in the folklore of the Tuskegee Airmen. Eventually, collective memory gave her full credit for the creation of the military's Tuskegee flight program. Anderson himself remembered in an oral history interview that Roosevelt just happened to be in town to visit the infantile paralysis center when she made an impromptu flight with him, and that two or three weeks later the AAC announced it was creating a flight program at Tuskegee. A Tuskegee cadet recalled that Eleanor Roosevelt, in the vicinity because she was on the Tuskegee Institute Board of Trustees in this version of the story, had flown with Anderson out of sheer curiosity and "as a result of that, she convinced her husband that blacks could fly, and six months later there was a program at Tuskegee." A student journalist for the college newspaper who accompanied Roosevelt on her tour of the campus and witnessed the historic flight said, "Shortly after [the flight], word came down that it had been officially ordered by the president and obeyed by the generals, that [blacks] were going to be immediately taken in for the flying corps. And the training was going to take place at Tuskegee."[31]

In reality, the War Department had announced the creation of the program five months before Roosevelt's flight with Anderson, and it was the AAC that had asked Tuskegee Institute to find a suitable location for a primary flight training facility. Gen. Walter R. Weaver, commander of the Southeastern Air Corps Training Command, informed Patterson and Washington in February 1941 that the school would need to build the primary facility from scratch and that it would have to be "fully equipped and staffed and ready for receiving cadets [by] July 15, 1941."[32] This meeting led to Tuskegee's request of the Rosenwald Fund, which in turn led to the trustees' meeting at Tuskegee and Eleanor Roosevelt's visit. Yet many Tuskegee Airmen remembered the first lady as the catalyst and main party responsible for the program as a whole.

They were not alone in this belief. There was no question among the general public at the time (and can be no question now) that the first lady held more liberal racial views than did the president and that she pushed him to guarantee the civil rights of black Americans. Americans who liked FDR personally but disagreed with his policies found his wife to be a convenient figure to blame when the administration veered too far left for their tastes. The public plainly ascribed to the first lady much more influence with various federal agencies on these matters than she wielded in reality, and military men were especially quick to blame her for what they perceived as the War Department's cowardly kowtowing to bellyaching special interest groups who had Mrs. Roosevelt's ear. Gen. Frank O'Driscoll Hunter, who would clash with blacks in the Air Forces in the course of the war, described his branch's chain of command this way, beginning with his superior officer: "General Arnold got his orders from General Marshall, and he got his from Secretary of War Stimson, and he got his from Mrs. Roosevelt."[33]

Having secured the necessary loan from the Rosenwald Fund, Tuskegee Institute moved ahead quickly, contracting with the civil engineering firm of Alexander and Repass of Iowa to prepare the Moton Field site and construct the necessary buildings to AAC specifications. Archie Alexander, the firm's co-owner and one of the nation's premier black engineers, hired several white subcontractors from the area, and Tuskegee Institute made available several of its master craftsmen, facilities, and student laborers for the urgent project. Heavy rains delayed construction through much of the summer, but the facility was ready to open by late August.[34]

G. L. Washington assigned Anderson, a man whose purpose in life, he recalled, "was flying and teaching others to fly," as Moton Field's chief instructor pilot, made Lewis Jackson his director of training, and hired Austin ("Butch") Humbles, a West Virginia State CPT graduate, as the field's chief mechanic. Chief Anderson's wife, Gertrude, oversaw administrative operations at the field as Washington's secretary, Katie Whitney (who would soon marry instructor Linkwood Williams) served as Washington's secretary at the field, and Gracie Perry handled administrative duties for Humbles. Perry was a native of Selma, the home of the Air Corps's Craig Field, so she had seen air operations before. But when she saw Moton for the first time, she later recalled, "I was just in awe. It was just fascinating, and I was so proud of those guys. The guys looked good! And the cadets were just so erect. They had to march to meals, they had to march to the bus, they had to march this way. It was just interesting."[35]

The military training program at Moton fell under the responsibilities of Capt. Noel Parrish, a white liberal and the newly arrived director of training for the 66th Army Air Corps Primary Flight School. Parrish was a rather unlikely AAC officer, but his personal experiences and unique set of values made him the perfect man for the job. There literally was not a better-qualified individual for the position in the entire service.

Parrish's father, a Disciples of Christ minister who held a series of teaching jobs and pastorships throughout the Deep South and border states, moved the family to Houston, Texas, when Noel, the oldest of four children, was fourteen. As a teenager, Noel Parrish might have been considered a racial radical. He organized Christian Endeavor Societies in his father's and uncle's congregations in Houston, through which he worked to pass resolutions opposing war and racial segregation. He challenged congregants to accept Negro parishioners and as a result of his activism, Parrish recalled, "I got to be such a pest that my uncle asked me to move to some other church where it wouldn't deplete the family income by getting somebody fired, namely the pastor."[36]

Parrish enrolled at Rice Institute (now Rice University) at the age of fourteen and graduated in 1928. He found that precious few employers were willing to hire an eighteen-year-old college graduate (and a 120-pound one at that), so he returned to Rice in 1929 to take education courses with the goal of becoming a teacher. But schools superintendents proved no more likely to hire a man little older than their high school students, so Parrish became a low-wage white-collar worker at the Texas Co. (later Texaco) just as the Great Depression hit the state. Without a family to support and the last man hired, Parrish was the first fired, and he again found himself unable to find work. He moved to San Francisco but found job prospects even worse there. Unable to think of a better alternative, he responded to a recruiting pitch from the U.S. Army in 1930.[37]

Parrish volunteered for the Eleventh U.S. Cavalry based in Monterey, California. "Since you did cavalry drill in the morning," he reasoned, "[along with] infantry drill in the afternoon and worked in the stables at night, I thought that would help my physical condition, which was rather poor." Parrish put on 40 pounds of muscle in a matter of months, which made him an attractive candidate for flight training when that opportunity arose six months after he enlisted. It was fortunate that a position in the AAC presented itself, because while in the cavalry Parrish found out the hard way that he was afraid of horses. The cavalry's training, he remembered, "was calculated either to kill you or make a man out of you, no middle ground in there," and the riding "was about as physically disturbing as anything that [later] happened in the Air Force."[38]

Parrish was scared of airplanes, too, he candidly admitted later. But anything had to be better than the soul-deadening boredom of the cavalry, so he asked for a transfer to the AAC. He supposed that at least his better-educated comrades in the flight cadets would have more interesting vocabularies than the riffraff of the cavalry. He graduated from the first class of basic aviation training at Randolph Field in San Antonio and earned his second lieutenant's commission in 1932. The AAC was a terribly dangerous place in the early 1930s; fifteen of the ninety-six members of Parrish's class died in flying accidents within a year after graduation, mostly from pilot error, and the service's overall casualty rate for pilots was worse then than it would be during World War II.[39]

Even so, competition for flying jobs in the Depression-era AAC was fierce. After a year as a flying officer, Parrish lost his commission in a reduction-in-force, but he re-enlisted, flew transport planes as a private first-class pilot, and was reappointed as a reserve officer when the AAC began expanding under President Roosevelt's steady military buildup. He earned an active commission soon thereafter. Parrish became a career officer in 1936, but perhaps because he had also been an enlisted man, Parrish thought he "had some rather non-elitist and leveling philosophies of human behavior." Those philosophies would serve him well during the war.[40]

Always an independent thinker, Parrish got interested in the concept of flight training. What combination of physical and mental abilities did a man need to become a capable pilot? What tests could the service devise to determine with any degree of predictability who possessed those qualities? Could they be taught? He rejected what he called the "mysticism" inherent in the conventional wisdom of the time, the belief that a would-be pilot either "had it" or didn't, because no one could define "it" to Parrish's satisfaction. He gravitated instead to what he called "pragmatic testing," a good example of which he learned in parachute training, where jumpers had to fold their own parachutes. It was pretty easy there to figure out which trainees were and were not proficient. "This is my idea of the most realistic final exam anybody could have," he said. His evolving ideas on the subject at the time might be called "Darwinian"—the parachute test, at least, involved heavy doses of natural selection—but not "social Darwinist," as was most of the thinking regarding race in the AAC between the wars. Parrish's practical approach required instructors to ignore any prejudices they may have held toward the groups from which their trainees came, and to trust their flyin' eyes. Could the trainee pass the flight tests or not? Throughout the war whites would ask Parrish, "How do Negroes fly?" His answer was consistent: "Negroes fly very much like everyone else flies."[41]

Parrish returned to Randolph Field as a flight instructor, and by the late 1930s he was working as the AAC supervisor of a civilian flight school at Glenview, Illinois, with additional supervisory responsibility for the CPT program being operated by the Coffey School in Chicago. In the summer of 1941, because (he believed) he was "the only Air Force officer who had any direct contact with the blacks," Parrish transferred to Maxwell Field to develop plans for the new school at Tuskegee under the direction of Maj. Luke S. Smith, director of training at the Southeast Army Air Forces

Training Center at Maxwell Field. Washington considered Smith an exceptionally fair-minded advocate for the Tuskegee program and apportioned a great deal of credit for the training program's eventual success to Smith and Parrish.[42]

When he transferred to Tuskegee, Parrish observed, as he wrote in a letter to his mother, that local whites were obsessed with "trying to convince themselves and everybody else that they are better than the Negroes and have little interest in anything else.... Being sensible in this kind of situation really puts you in the middle." Parrish acknowledged the complexity of the assignment, which was a result of all of the attention the black press was paying to it, the very public advocacy of the NAACP, the high hopes black Americans had for the program, and the nearly complete reluctance to train black pilots on the part of the AAF brass. He later understood that most officers in his position would have regarded the assignment as a dead end, but, he said, the "goal seemed important enough to justify going ahead with it without worrying too much about my personal career at the time. I thought all of that would take care of itself later." In fact, Parrish's superiors promised him that if he did a good job with the development of the controversial Tuskegee program he would be given command of a P-51 combat squadron in the European Theater within a year.[43]

Parrish understood exactly how complicated and difficult his assignment at Tuskegee would be. "It became a matter of setting up, at least for training, a new air training force," he wrote. "You would have inside the white Air Force a miniature...black Air Force which would, of course, be serviced and supplied, commanded, led, and everything by the Air Force itself." The proposed program "would be a separate training unit and a separate combat unit and, in a sense, a separate training command under the regular Air Force command. All of this was so complex that it was a wonder it ever worked at all."[44]

There was, of course, an alternative. "[I]ntegration would have been a simpler thing all the way around," he later said, but "there was no chance of that happening at the time for a number of reasons." The idea that the AAF could implement integrated training, especially in the South, without eliciting intense and noisy opposition from Southern elected officials, Parrish believed at the time, "was just visionary. How long that would take, nobody could predict at that time. [But] wars changed things, and they do change things. World War II changed things more rapidly than anyone had reason to predict before the war."[45]

To Parrish's unending dismay, his superiors in the AAF insisted on referring to the flight school at Tuskegee as an "experiment" and continued to do so throughout the war. The concept turned out "not to be fatal, but it was a handicap," in his judgment, particularly when Parrish attempted to cherry-pick the most academically accomplished and experienced black flyers for the first classes of pilot cadets at Tuskegee. That was not the way other cadet applicants were classified and placed in training courses in the regular AAF, but Parrish recognized that this group had a better chance of succeeding with a cadre that would "graduate first and be leaders, automatically, and be senior in military rank." "[F]rom somewhere in the depths of the classification department of the Air Staff" came the answer that such skimming would "invalidate the experiment," which, he gathered, "was designed to find out something about blacks" rather than train black pilots for the war effort.[46]

Parrish took command of the primary school at Moton Field in August 1941. The instructors there were all civilian employees of Tuskegee Institute, most of them African American. There was a popular saying in the wartime AAF: "There are three ways to fly. There's the right way, the wrong way, and the Army way." Parrish was responsible for enforcing the standards of the third way. Soon after the first class graduated from primary training, Parrish, now a major, transferred with them to TAAF in December 1941 and became responsible for the basic and advanced phases of flight school under commanding officer Maj. James A. Ellison. Lt. William T. Smith, a 1939 West Point graduate, replaced Parrish at Moton. Ellison, an AAC man with more than thirty years of service, saw the construction of TAAF and the creation of the flight school through to completion but did not last long in the command; he was replaced less than a year later by Col. Frederick von Kimble. Within a year Parrish would replace Kimble.

The thirteen men of the first class of flight cadets at Tuskegee, Class 42-C (so named because they were scheduled to graduate in the third month of 1942; a class scheduled to graduate in January 1942 would have been designated 42-A), officially entered the U.S. Army Air Corps in July 1941. At the same time, a cadre of 271 enlisted men entered training schools at Chanute Field in Rantoul, Illinois, under more or less desegregated conditions. The trainees at Chanute lived in separate barracks and ate in a separate mess, but trained with white instructors in mechanics, welding, armoring, parachute rigging, communications, weather observation and forecasting, and clerk and supply courses. In some cases they interacted with white trainees. Upon completion of training these men would transfer to TAAF as the 99th Pursuit Squadron's ground crew. There had been internal discussions within the Southeastern Training Command over possibly creating a stand-alone training complex on the campus of Tuskegee Institute for this purpose, but it was generally agreed that it would be impossible to duplicate the facilities and expertise Chanute could offer, especially on short notice. Five of the men were being trained as non-flying officers for the ground contingent of the 99th; two of them, Elmer D. Jones and Elcan R. Ward, had graduated from Tuskegee Institute's advanced CPT programs.[47]

African Americans' pride in the cadets and technicians in training was tempered by the knowledge that the 99th would need thirty-three trained pilots to fill out its full complement. With a typical "washout" rate of at least 40 percent, if the Tuskegee program could only admit twelve or thirteen cadets a month, it would take at least a year to train and graduate the full squadron of pilots—and this at a time when the outcome of the war was very much in doubt. The cadets entered ground school training on the Tuskegee Institute campus and took their first preflight and flight lessons at the CPT program's facilities at Kennedy Field. Flight instruction began at brand-new Moton Field in September. The class of 42-C included John C. Anderson Jr. of Toledo, Ohio; Charles D. Brown of Abbeville, S.C.; Theodore E. Brown of New York, N.Y.; Marion A. Carter of Chicago; Lemuel R. Custis of Hartford, Conn.; Charles H. DeBow Jr. of Indianapolis; Frederick H. Moore of Sommerville, N.J.; Ulysses S. Pannell of Reagan, Texas; George S. "Spanky" Roberts of Fairmount, W.V.; Mac Ross of Dayton, Ohio; William H. Slade of Raleigh, N.C.; Roderick C. Williams of Chicago; and Capt. Benjamin O. Davis Jr., originally of Washington, D.C.[48]

When the aviation cadets began training in July 1941, the entire U.S. military had exactly two black officers other than chaplains on active duty. Brig. Gen. Benjamin O. Davis Sr., a veteran of a "Buffalo Soldier" cavalry regiment, the Philippine occupation, and several ROTC assignments at historically black colleges including Tuskegee (which he abhorred because of its sharply segregated atmosphere), was working at the War Department as an assistant to the inspector general. Davis had been promoted to the rank of general officer by Franklin Roosevelt as part of the October surprise that accompanied the announcement of the 99th's creation when Roosevelt needed black votes to ensure a third term as president. His son, Capt. Benjamin O. Davis Jr., was every bit as remarkable a figure. A 1936 graduate of West Point, Davis had endured four years of the silent treatment from his classmates. He entered the academy firm in the belief that "I was better than anybody else in the things I was interested in doing. No doubt in my mind whatsoever." But on his third day as a plebe (a freshman at the academy), the only African American on campus, he had "the biggest disappointment in my life." Sitting in his room by himself, Davis heard a knock on the door announcing a meeting to take place in the basement of his dormitory in five minutes. By the time he arrived the meeting had started. "The first thing I heard was a question from one of the BCT [Basic Cadet Training] detail, that was the detail that ran the plebes: 'What are we going to do about this nigger?' "[49]

Davis never had a roommate at the U.S. Military Academy, always ate alone in the mess hall, never shared a word with fellow cadets except in the line of duty. He knew that the practice of silencing "had been applied in the past to certain cadets who were considered to have violated the honor code and refused to resign." But Davis had committed no such violation; he "was to be silenced solely because cadets did not want blacks at West Point." What his fellow cadets failed to realize, he later wrote, "was that I was stubborn enough to put up with their treatment to reach the goal I had come to attain.... I refused to buckle in any way. I maintained my self-respect." In fact, he emerged from the experience feeling "a hell of a lot superior, morally," to his classmates.[50]

Davis Jr. had requested assignment to the AAC and passed the service's physical entrance examination in his senior year at West Point, but he received the same answer that all black Americans received in those years: The AAC is not accepting Negroes at this time. Upon graduation Davis, then a second lieutenant, married Agatha Scott, a teacher from New Haven, Connecticut. They reported to the 24th Infantry Regiment at Fort Benning, Georgia, where they found that "[s]egregation was complete and absolute" and received the silent treatment all over again. In 1938 Davis Jr. was transferred to Tuskegee, where he replaced his father as professor of military science and tactics with responsibility for the ROTC program. Davis received quick promotions while at Tuskegee; he was a captain by 1940. But, he remembered, "My job at Tuskegee was as close to nothing as it could be and still be called a job." Agatha Davis helped fill the hours of what Benjamin Davis called "the essentially nonproductive, even useless existence we lived at Tuskegee" by organizing under-the-radar boycotts of white merchants who mistreated blacks in town. When his father was promoted to brigadier general and given command of a cavalry brigade at Fort Riley, Kansas, Davis Jr. jumped at the chance to transfer out of Tuskegee as the general's aide.[51]

Davis Jr. had been at Fort Riley for a short time when he received the surprising word that the chief of the AAC, Maj. Gen. George Brett, wanted him to transfer into the branch. Brett expected that Davis would take command of the newly created 99th after completing pilot training. The AAC brass thereby acceded to requests from Parrish and from Tuskegee's Patterson for at least one handpicked leader in the first class of cadets; once again, the planners could not possibly have chosen a better leader for the cadets. Davis relished the chance to realize his Air Corps dream but looked to returning to Tuskegee with ambivalence.[52]

Davis turned out not to have a natural aptitude for flying. To Parrish's frustration, instructors must have reported that Davis did not "have it" as a pilot cadet, because Parrish assigned him extra instruction from Chief

Anderson. Davis's problems, Parrish recalled, stemmed from the same attributes that made him an exemplary West Point cadet and infantry officer. Parrish found Davis "overly conscientious in everything he did...cautiously precise in everything he did in the air." In this particular case, military discipline may have proved a hindrance: "If you told him to make a right turn, instead of feeling it out, he would just walk the stick over and make a right turn as though he was maneuvering on a parade ground to a precision of a specific angle." West Pointers who undertook flight training "did have a rather surprisingly high elimination rate" for this reason, according to Parrish, but Davis was able to develop the skills and attitude he needed to become a successful pilot.[53]

Davis was surrounded at Tuskegee by a small handful of accomplished pilots. George S. "Spanky" Roberts, another of the 42-C class, was a graduate of the first CPT class at West Virginia State College who, like Parrish, had also graduated from college at the age of eighteen; he distinguished himself as the best flyer of the group. Lemuel R. Custis graduated from Howard University before it initiated the CPT program. Cadets like Roberts and Custis who were assigned to Tuskegee typically attended basic Army training at Keesler Field near Biloxi, Mississippi, or at a handful of other bases in Dixie first. The pilots and ground crew members came from every corner of the country and for many, the trip was their first to the strictly segregated South. Maurice Thomas, a native New Yorker who had never before been south, recalled, "I'll tell you the God's honest truth: When I got into the South, I thought I was in a loony bin."[54] Alexander Jefferson, a pilot cadet who had grown up in Detroit in a Great Migration family, had a slightly different perspective on the experience. "I have run up against racism," he said.

> A lot of the Tuskegee Airmen from New York and other places say that on their first trip to the South, they were completely afraid, completely bamboozled. Me, I knew about the South. I'd been going down there every summer all my life, and I spent four years [as a college student] in Atlanta. I knew racism. Never went downtown to Atlanta to a department store. Get on the streetcar, you go to the back, automatically. This is something that I just took for granted as the way of doing things. It didn't mean that I acquiesced to it; I hated it. But understand the system, which means that we were part of the change. I lived to be part of the fantastic system that helped to change it.[55]

Tuskegee did not have a train station on the Western Railway of Alabama line, the main line between Montgomery and Atlanta, so cadets disembarked at the small Macon County community of Chehaw. The train station was unremarkable and the surrounding vicinity even less so.

Nonetheless, Chehaw made an impression on nearly everyone who passed through Tuskegee in the course of the war—apparently because the train's conductor had an unforgettable way of announcing the upcoming stop. Jefferson mused, "I can remember the conductor: 'Cheee-haw!' Oh my God." There was nothing to see from the Chehaw platform save cotton fields and scrubby pine trees, and many arrived when it was pitch-black anyway, so the cadets, enlisted men, and others who traveled to Tuskegee with such high hopes had to have experienced an anticlimax when they arrived.[56]

In July 1941, TAAF's living facilities were still months away from being completed, so Custis and the other cadets in the inaugural class bunked in a renovated bathhouse on the Tuskegee campus. (B.O. and Agatha Davis lived in cramped quarters in a campus building next door.) Custis found it difficult to adjust to military discipline, but the instruction was comparatively easy—in part, he believed, because the civilian instructors, including the white ground school instructors, were so helpful and eager to see the cadets succeed. "My understanding was that most of the white personnel that was involved in this had volunteered, so they wanted this thing to succeed," he said. "It wasn't a bunch of white guys being sent there to do something they didn't want to do." His fellow cadets, nearly all of whom had completed CPT, helped Custis overcome the difficulties he faced in learning to fly.[57]

Lewis J. Lynch was "elated" to be accepted into the cadet corps. "Going to Tuskegee was the culmination of my aspirations. I thought, 'Boy, this is it. I'm going to go down there, and I'm going to learn how to fly, and I'm going to be a big hero, and I'm going to come back with a Distinguished Flying Cross and girls are all going to fall at my feet.'" But he realized almost from the beginning of his training at Moton that he was not grasping something basic. Lynch "damn near killed my instructor" and himself in one lesson; the instructor scheduled him for a check ride with Director of Training Lewis Jackson.[58]

"I knew the procedures. I knew all that. But I was doing [everything] by rote," Lynch said. "After we'd been up maybe ten minutes, Jackson said, 'OK, I've got it. You follow me through,' which means get on the controls with him and feel everything he does with the controls; so I did that." To teach Lynch to fly, Jackson would have to help him develop an experiential understanding, not just textbook knowledge, of how to operate the Stearman trainer aircraft. "One of the first things he did was roll the airplane upside down, and we were hanging on our seatbelts, and he's pushing the stick way up in the corner; he's pushing the rudders; and I can see how far you have to push this thing, and how you can manhandle that airplane," Lynch said. "It's not a nice, smooth, comfortable ride. [Jackson] said, 'Now, follow me through. Look at the wings.' I could see, 'Shoot, you push the rudder all the way in. You do this with the stick. It's not comfortable, but you do it.' I could see how you could kick this airplane around. Finally I'm flying the airplane. Now I know that I can throw this airplane around and that I really have to be in charge." (Lynch graduated from TAFS and flew forty-two missions in the war.)[59]

There were originally four civilian instructors at Moton Field, all of them with deep Tuskegee connections. Milton Crenchaw, a Little Rock native, had graduated from Dunbar Junior College in that city and transferred to Tuskegee Institute to study auto mechanics. He entered the first CPT class there and helped build the facilities at Kennedy Field, walking the 7 miles to the airfield every day from his dormitory. Crenchaw hitchhiked to Birmingham and passed the CAA examination that allowed him to instruct pilot cadets on Dec. 8, 1941. As a flight instructor in the college's CPT program, he earned $250 a month, roughly double what professors who had been at Tuskegee for decades were paid at the time. He soon transferred into the program at Moton Field where the course of instruction differed little from that of the CPT program.[60]

Crenchaw compared the process of teaching a cadet to fly to breaking a wild horse:

> You size a guy up.... The Indians had a certain technique, and it wasn't beating them, but trying to be the horse's friend: cultivate friendship and an understanding between the wild horse and you. Well, we would do the same thing. We would cultivate a friendship with the cadet, and you kind of cool him down and tell him about so and so. And then we're going to take a ride.
>
> We go through the different steps. And the steps are the same whether you're teaching a fellow in the first grade or whether you're teaching a horse to stay in the corral or whether you are teaching a cadet. All of them are the same. So you teach basic things: How to fly straight and level. How to make turns, left and right. How to go up and come down. And you give him a little easy training in those four elements: what controls are in charge at certain positions. And as you graduate from one to the other, then you start combining maneuvers—like a chandelle; it's where you make a dive, make a turn and then make a pullout. There are three different controls you have to operate to perform this maneuver. All of the maneuvers are basically the same, and they all [start] from straight and level turns, either diving or climbing. That's all aviation is about, those four things.[61]

Alongside Crenchaw as instructors at Moton were Chief Anderson; Charles Foxx, generally regarded as the most gifted graduate of the Tuskegee CPT program; and Forrest Shelton, one of the three local white pilots who had constructed Kennedy Field.

Herb Flowers became the fifth instructor at Moton. The son of a North Carolina farmer, he had attended North Carolina A&T as a pre-med major for two years, but when his scholarship ran out in the midst of the Great Depression he left school, migrated to Baltimore, and found work as a chauffeur. Flowers read about the campaign to pressure the AAC to admit blacks in Baltimore's venerable black newspaper, *The Afro-American*, in 1941 and volunteered. He was ordered to report to Tuskegee that September as one of ten members of the third training class, 42-E.[62]

Flowers excelled under Crenchaw's instruction and was the first of his class to solo. Five of Flowers's ten original classmates graduated with him from the ten-week primary program at Moton to basic training at TAAF. All six graduated from the basic to advanced phase of training. Flowers did not speak of it, but according to several other sources he progressed so far into the advanced program that he had already bought his second lieutenant's uniform and mailed invitations for his graduation ceremony to his family when he was informed that he would not graduate. Others saw in this event proof of a quota system at Tuskegee: if the AAC washed out a great pilot like Flowers for no good reason, it could only have been because racists there wanted to keep the number of black pilot graduates in a given month arbitrarily low. Flowers, on the other hand, suggested that he was reassigned to the corps of civilian instructors simply because the primary program was ramping up and needed additional instructors. In any case, he was eliminated from the military program and sent to a civilian instructor's course soon before he was scheduled to graduate; he began working at Moton late in 1943. Yet he betrayed no bitterness about the experience. "I enjoyed it tremendously," he said.[63]

The corps of civilian instructors at Moton did expand dramatically after 1942 as outside pressure forced the Air Forces to increase the number of black pilots in training. Philip Lee, a graduate of the Hampton Institute CPT program who had been employed as a CPT instructor at Kennedy Field since 1940, was one of the next civilian instructors to arrive. His college sweetheart, Theophia Hicks, worked at Moton as the secretary to Tuskegee Institute's physical plant engineer, G. A. Reed; they were married in the historic chapel on Tuskegee's campus in 1943. The civilian instructor corps continued to add members from the tiny elite of black aviators. From Pennsylvania came Roscoe Draper, who had left Chief Anderson's hometown of Bryn Mawr for the CPT program at Hampton, and James Plinton, a graduate of Lincoln University who would go on to organize airlines in Ecuador and Haiti and become the first and for many years only black executive of a major American airline.[64] "These guys were like little gods for us as cadets," one of their pupils remembered.[65]

The Tuskegee CPT program contributed James "Muscles" Wright, a Georgian; Claude Platte, a Texan; and Linkwood Williams of Louisiana to the Moton Field instructor corps. Alexander Wilkerson, another Hampton man, joined Wendell Lipscomb, a native Californian, and Jack Johnson from Chicago. Matthew Plummer, a primary flight instructor from Houston, Texas, who would later become an attorney, on at least one occasion organized several of the Moton Field civilian workers to attempt to register to vote at the Macon County courthouse in the town of Tuskegee. (None of them succeeded in registering.) Charles Johnson Jr. was the son of one of the most important American sociologists of the twentieth century. Johnson Jr. graduated from Fisk University in 1942 and volunteered for the Air Forces. A hearing problem kept him from entering the cadet corps, and military disorganization ended the training program for service pilots that he did enter midway through his training. He ended up at Moton as a civilian instructor in 1943 and trained cadets there through the end of the war.[66]

As the training program at Moton expanded during the course of the war, the pool of available men dwindled, and Washington hired an increasing number of women to run the maintenance operations at Moton Field—jobs that women had been denied before the war emergency. Mildred Hanson, one of two female graduates of Tuskegee's CPT program, and Alice Dungey Gray rigged the cadets' and instructors' parachutes. Ruby Washington maintained flight logs. At least three wives of flight instructors worked as secretaries at Moton. There was little turnover at Moton among either AAC personnel, civilians, or Tuskegee Institute administrators.[67]

More significantly, Washington hired a number of women as mechanics. Somewhat to his surprise, they did excellent work. Fannie R. Gunn was representative of the women who responded to the openings created by the crisis. "During World War II, I imagine they took most of the able men and carried them to the Army," she said. "They were short of manpower down at Moton Field. So they announced that they would like to have as many women to come and take a test and have about three months of training at the field." Gunn was one of seven children in a farming family in Hickory Grove, a Macon County community, and completed the twelfth grade at Tuskegee Institute. She was twenty-five years old in 1941.[68]

As a girl, Gunn had been interested in the automotive mechanical work she saw her brothers doing—especially when they built the family's first automobile, a Model-T Ford, out of parts scavenged from other cars—but never had a chance to do it herself before the war came. "Mr. Austin H. Humbles, the head of the maintenance department, wanted some women to go into aircraft maintenance," she recalled. "I [studied] under him for about three months of training. They gave us classes every day, and we graduated after we had those classes. Then they gave us a test, and I passed and I was selected one of the ones to work at Moton Field. I was there for three years. I worked there until the base closed."[69]

Gunn and the other women mechanics performed routine maintenance on dozens of Stearman PT-17s, the workhorse open-cockpit biplanes trainers used at Moton. "We used to do a checkup on the airplanes before the cadets would fly. Then we'd have what you called a twenty-five-hour check, a fifty-hour check and a one hundred-hour check on each airplane. Then Mr. Humbles would have to come in behind us and check them to see that we had done the type of work that needed to be done." Given the local manpower shortage, operations at Moton Field could not have continued without female labor. Every morning Gunn and her crew "would have to take [the trainers] out on the field for the cadets to fly. All the ladies would take them out on the field, warm them up, and have them ready for the cadets to fly." Gunn was let go soon after V-J Day and married a returning soldier. They purchased and ran a convenience store, and she provided day care for local children for years afterward, so she was never again able to use the wartime training she received from Humbles. But she cherished her service. "It was quite an experience for the women," she recalled. "This was really the first time that I have heard of women being connected with this type of work."[70]

Tuskegee Institute's original contract with the War Department called for the college to provide primary instruction at Moton Field for a class of ten students every five weeks. With an estimated washout rate of 40 to 60 percent, Washington expected to have an average of sixteen cadets in training at a given time. Moton Field was built to accommodate this number, and the institute provided mess and barracks facilities for that many cadets, plus transportation between the campus and the field. However, class sizes far exceeded initial estimates from the actual start of the program; the average incoming class had nineteen members during the program's first nine months. The Air Force's training program expanded across the board after Pearl Harbor and African Americans' lobbying campaign pressured the force to admit ever more cadets. By 1944 incoming classes were as large as eighty in number. Tuskegee had to expand Moton Field beginning in 1942, adding a second hangar with needed office and meeting space, additional landing space on the increasingly crowded field, and a lunchroom serving what was now a large civilian workforce, all of which were in place by 1943.[71]

The co-educational campus of Tuskegee Institute provided an unusually rich social life for the cadets. "The preponderance of women students at the institute, because of the war, met important social needs of the cadets during their off-hours and on occasions when dances or other social events we scheduled for them," Washington noted. "This was a feature that cadets at our Army Primary enjoyed that was not in the contract or provided at other primary schools [for whites] so handily."[72] Women students were attracted to flying cadets in uniform, and there were fewer male students on campus during the war, so the cadets faced comparatively little competition from Tuskegee men. (According to two observers, however, there were still as many as four or five college-aged men on campus during the war for every college-aged woman.) Cadets did not have the luxury of free time, and the institute's "matrons" kept close watch over their charges in any case, so there was little opportunity for untoward behavior. It was, in fact, against regulations for cadets to be seen speaking unsupervised with women on campus. But the atmosphere was nurturing, and the cadets did have an unusual variety of cultural and social outlets available to them.[73]

After Pearl Harbor the massive expansion of training programs necessitated less restrictive entrance standards for aviation cadets, and the Air Forces soon opened the programs to men with a high school education who could pass a rigorous entrance exam. Black cadets who entered the Air Forces without college diplomas first attended the College Training Detachment (CTD) at Tuskegee Institute. For hundreds of cadets, CTD provided them their first opportunity to set foot on a college campus, and it put them on the eventual road to college degrees, wider horizons, and better paying careers. Herbert Thorpe, a high school graduate, was accepted into cadet training in 1944 and entered the CTD program. The experience was formative for him: "It was really an eye-opener to me to see how things went on a college campus. I was really impressed to be on a college campus and go to college classes and take instruction from college professors," he remembered, "particularly black college professors. I was proud to be there. I was impressed that there was such a thing, and I was really proud to be in that kind of an environment. I guess the other thing I was impressed with was the level of expertise and education of some of my fellow cadets. It was both intimidating and humbling."[74]

As supportive as the atmosphere of the Moton Field program was for cadets, it was at the end of the day a military training program. Cadets might find that Tuskegee Institute students wanted desperately for them to succeed, that their classmates stayed up late at night to help laggards learn their lessons, and that civilian instructors were willing to do anything they could to help the cadets learn to fly. But if cadets could not learn to fly to military specifications such that they could "solo" within twenty hours of flight time, instructors eliminated them from the program. "Washing out" was of course the overriding fear of every cadet, a terror tied up in a complicated web of race pride, self-esteem, and patriotism. "It was a devastating experience to be washed out," Custis said. "I know if I had been washed out, I guess I would have jumped off a bridge somewhere or something." The cadets dealt with and remembered the fear in interesting ways.[75]

Maj. Harold C. ("Scottie") Magoon, one of the original AAC officers at the Moton Field facility, rose to the position of Army supervisor of the Primary Flying School, the job first held by Noel Parrish, in 1942. As such he was responsible for eliminating the cadets who could not demonstrate flying proficiency within a short period of time, and the cadets did not remember him fondly. Magoon occupied a difficult historical position. In the Tuskegee Airmen oral histories he is remembered as the personification of the AAF's institutional racism, the point of the spear at which blacks were driven from flight training.[76]

The reality of flight training in wartime was that some cadets who could have been taught to be perfectly competent pilots, if instructors had possessed the luxury of time to get through to them, were not afforded the chance. Students in CPT programs had that luxury, but the military was a less forgiving environment. The responsibility for washing out cadets fell to officers like Magoon. And because of the history behind the establishment of the Tuskegee program, it was all too easy for the cadets, both those who were eliminated and those who remained in the program, to attribute eliminations to blatant racism. The War Department had limited black opportunities in military aviation by creating a single all-black pursuit squadron in 1941 (and three additional squadrons in 1942), confining trainees to the comparatively small facility at Tuskegee, and prohibiting integrated units.

These decisions and the accumulation of institutionalized racism that undergirded them, along with the reality of flight training in wartime, limited the number of available slots for black pilots and ensured that the elimination rate at Tuskegee would remain higher than that of white training facilities throughout the war. (Several former cadets recalled Parrish telling them that Tuskegee washed out better pilots than graduated from the all-white programs he had been part of at Randolph and Kelly fields.) There can be no doubt that individual officers in the Air Forces considered blacks to be naturally inferior and that the institution as a whole limited their opportunities, but personalized racism was not responsible for the quota system at Tuskegee.[77]

G.L. Washington remembered Magoon, a native of Buffalo, N.Y., as "a fine officer and person to work with," but the Tuskegee Airmen recalled him via doggerel that attributed racism to his elimination practices. It seemed to them that Magoon spent as much time as possible alone in his office in Hangar One at Moton Field, and they whispered that he did so because he was afraid of black people. To the tune of a popular song of the day, "The Sleepy Lagoon," they crooned, "Major Magoon will get him a coon by noon." Magoon certainly made an impression on the cadets by eliminating many of them, but the endurance of his place in collective memory is surely due in part to the major's exotic surname. No one wrote songs about his predecessor in the position, Maj. William T. Smith.[78]

The Air Force's paper trail indicates that this collective memory of Magoon may have been unwarranted. In a foreword to the official history of the 66th AAF Flying Training Detachment, Magoon expressed evident pride in having participated in a program that had "surpassed the hopes of even its most enthusiastic supporters." Noting that civilian and military observers had considered the program "experimental…at best" when it was conceived, Magoon credited his predecessors Parrish and Smith with having put systems in place that allowed for the program's rapid expansion without sacrificing high standards, and civilian employees and enlisted men for keeping the program on course. In fact, the annual number of trainees accommodated by the training program at Moton Field expanded by 700 percent between 1941 and 1944. Managing the expansion would have been a daunting task for anyone; it could perhaps account for why Magoon spent so much time in his office.[79]

For some, washing out from the program was crushing. For others, it provided relief. In this respect Crawford Dowdell, a pilot cadet from Georgia in the class of 43-F, may have been representative of more airmen than one might expect. "I wasn't a gung-ho pilot person," he candidly admitted later, confessing that he had volunteered for the AAF because a pilot cadet's monthly pay was $25 higher than an infantryman's: "Not ever having had much money, I thought it would be a good boost." But he found that he enjoyed flying. Dowdell had nearly completed primary and looked forward to graduation when he received the call to fly a check ride with Maj. Magoon. Unfortunately, it was obvious even to Dowdell that he could not put the airplane through the necessary maneuvers to military specifications, and he held no ill will toward the supervisor of the flying school for eliminating him from the program. "Some of the guys got upset if they washed out," he recalled, "but I figured if I wasn't going to be a good pilot, I didn't want to be out there. I said, 'Well, if I'm not supposed to fly, I guess I'm not supposed to fly.'"[80]

Dowdell was among the fortunate. In the early months of the Tuskegee program washouts went back to the Army, and many ended up in labor or infantry units. After the War Department announced the creation of the 100th, 301st, and 302nd pursuit squadrons and the 477th Bombardment Group beginning in 1942, however, hundreds of specialist spots opened up for blacks in the AAF. Cadets who were eliminated from the flight program after this point had the opportunity to train as radio operators, bombardiers, navigators, or in dozens of other job categories. After he was eliminated, Dowdell trained in desegregated classes in radio communications at Boca Raton, Florida, and Yale University, earned his commission as a second lieutenant, and returned to Tuskegee as an officer in the 477th.[81]

The washout rate at Tuskegee was higher than at comparable all-white institutions, but these statistics were not necessarily indicators of the quality of the program's instruction. According to Washington, roughly forty contract facilities provided primary flight training for the Southeast Training Center. After the center began monthly evaluations of the facilities, Moton Field's operation was "No. 1 on the list more than once, and was generally near the top, but never at the very bottom."[82]

The Moton Field program's triumphs seemed to validate Tuskegee Institute's approach to "racial uplift." Having proved themselves capable of working in partnership with the AAF, the institute's leaders built on a long-standing culture of achievement to create a training program that whites who had previously been indifferent toward blacks' aspirations, at best, had no choice but to consider a success. In so doing they not only burnished their institution's national image, but they also created dozens of remunerative jobs for black professionals in a career field from which they had previously been excluded and brought bright, young, energetic minds to Tuskegee. Wartime changes altered the town of Tuskegee in these important ways, but it did little to upset traditional racial hierarchies. Blacks who could risk their lives training to defend their country at Moton Field and nearby TAAF still could not vote in Macon County or be served in white-owned Tuskegee businesses on an equal basis. Nonetheless, the creation of the Moton Field-TAAF complex itself provided a new model of black achievement and helped to shorten the reign of white supremacy in Alabama and beyond. Between 1941 and 1945 TAAF became something very close to the equivalent of a small, highly functional, all-black city.

3 The Experiment

In 1941 Clarence C. Jamison had finished two years at the University of Chicago majoring in bacteriology, but his family was having a hard time scraping up enough money for him to continue his education. When he saw a War Department advertisement announcing the flight training program for blacks, he thought, "Hell, that's made for me!" He and another African American friend had already completed the university's CPT course. "I remember the ad," he said. "As an aviation cadet, you'd get $75 a month, I think. And you finished, and then if you became a second lieutenant, you got $245 a month base pay, plus an extra half of that, over $100, for flying pay. And then a subsistence [allowance]. That's about $400 a month. I said, 'Nothing wrong with that. I can go back to school later.'" On top of the pay, Jamison relished the thought of responding to "a great opportunity. I knew we were being pioneers."[1]

The War Department built hundreds of new training facilities across the United States between 1940 and 1945, but the base Jamison went to for his training, Tuskegee Army Air Field (TAAF), was unique. No other base attracted nearly the attention from any segment of the population as TAAF did from African Americans. Most white Americans paid little attention to TAAF if they even knew of its existence (and most did not), but planners in the Army Air Forces openly referred to the base and the effort to train black pilots there as "the experiment." They knew the base and the training program it housed were significant, and they knew they were being watched.[2]

"The experiment" would turn on a series of questions. Would the War Department force blacks at TAAF to live and work under segregated conditions, or could integrationists use the experience at the base to convince the department that segregation was incompatible with war aims? Would the War Department devote the necessary resources to the facility for those participating in "the experiment" to succeed and thrive? If it did, could African Americans prove equal to the responsibility of developing and maintaining their own base and training program? Even the staunchest white supremacist had to admit by 1941 that at least some blacks could in fact be taught to fly airplanes. But could they be taught to rebuild airplane engines and operate communications systems? Could they manage complex administrative structures?

If black Americans could make "the experiment" work, they would give the lie to Jim Crow and lend momentum to a growing movement to dismantle segregation and win new opportunities for American blacks. The task at TAAF, as one Tuskegee Airman put it, was "to prove to people around the world and particularly the people in the United States of America that black people could do something besides unload boxes, that we could fly the most sophisticated aircraft and fix the most sophisticated equipment and [perform] all kinds of activities."[3]

The debate played out first in Washington, where William H. Hastie, civilian aide to Secretary of War Henry Stimson, ensured that debates over TAAF's creation and management reached the highest levels of the executive branch of the federal government. He was an auspicious choice as Stimson's aide. Hastie had been educated in the black public schools of Washington, D.C., and graduated first in his class from Amherst College, where he was also president of the campus Phi Beta Kappa chapter. By 1932 he had earned multiple law degrees from Harvard Law School and joined the faculty of Howard University Law School in Washington. At the same time Hastie worked in private practice with the prestigious firm of Houston and Houston in the nation's capital and became increasingly active in the NAACP.[4]

With Franklin Roosevelt's inauguration in 1933, Hastie accepted a government job and joined the new president's "black cabinet," a quasi-official group of African Americans employed by the federal government that advised the president on policy issues. Hastie served as assistant solicitor in the Interior Department—where he personally desegregated the agency's lunchroom—from 1933 until 1937, when Roosevelt appointed him as a judge of the Federal District Court of the U.S. Virgin Islands, making him the first African American federal judge in the history of the United States. He returned to Washington in 1937 to accept the deanship of the Howard Law School, the institution that trained the generation of black attorneys who successfully dismantled Jim Crow's legal underpinnings in the ensuing decades. As a member of the NAACP's National Legal Committee, he argued the suit that forced the state of Virginia to equalize pay for black teachers and played a major advisory role in forming the strategies that later resulted in the landmark *Brown v. Board* victory.[5]

Hastie was an uncompromising integrationist. In his June 1940 commencement address to the students of historically black Morgan State College he contended, "In this present war, we have got to insist as never before that we're anxious to do our part, but only if equal justice is meted out to us during this period with the prospect of the same thing continuing afterward." He continued, "I believe that while training an army to fight Hitler, we should not let up one bit in our effort to prevent discrimination in the army right here." Hastie was also an NAACP insider upon whom Executive Secretary Walter White depended heavily both before and after the judge began his service at the War Department in 1940.[6]

Hastie's appointment as Stimson's civilian aide was a knee-jerk attempt by the Roosevelt administration to deflect attention from an embarrassing situation that befell FDR's unprecedented campaign for a third term in October 1940. Roosevelt's press aide, Stephen Early, objected when a black New York City police officer ordered him away from the protective line the police had set up outside Madison Square Garden during a Roosevelt campaign speech. According to Hastie's biographer, Early "drove his knee into [the] policeman's groin." Roosevelt worried that the resulting publicity could put black votes in play; indeed, the GOP immediately began urging black voters to reward "this kick in the groin [with] a punch in the eye to all New Dealers on election day." Whether or not the embarrassing Early incident was responsible for it, Hastie's appointment was part of the "October surprise" in which Roosevelt also announced the creation of the Tuskegee flight program and Benjamin O. Davis Sr.'s promotion to the general officer ranks. Hastie worried that if he accepted the post he might be seen as appeasing the administration's intention to fight the war against fascism with Jim Crow forces, but he decided to join the battle for full, immediate integration and full opportunity for blacks from within the system.[7]

Hastie chose as his own assistant a young Chicago lawyer, Truman K. Gibson Jr. Gibson was born in Atlanta to a Harvard-educated father who worked in the Alonzo Herndon insurance empire, one of the most profitable black businesses in the South. Gibson grew up in Columbus, Ohio, and Chicago, and then earned a BA in political science and a law degree from the University of Chicago. His family was Talented Tenth and well connected. (For instance, Benjamin Davis Jr. had lived in the Gibsons' Southside Chicago home to establish residency in Rep. Oscar De Priest's congressional district so that De Priest could write his letter of appointment to West Point.) He had originally attracted Hastie's notice when they worked together on *Hansberry v. Lee*, the case in which the U.S. Supreme Court ruled in 1940 that Illinois's racially restrictive housing covenants violated the Constitution.[8]

Hastie did not shrink from the combat he would have to wage against the dominant segregationist culture at the War Department. From the beginning of his service at the Munitions Building he bristled at the generals' argument that the Army in wartime was no time or place to experiment with "social theories." Any changes that could lead to racial integration, were, Chief of Staff Gen. George C. Marshall believed, "fraught with danger to efficiency, discipline, and morale." Of Gen. H. E. Ely, the officer who had approvingly forwarded the infamous 1925 War College report "The

Use of Negro Manpower in War" to the War Department, Hastie sneered, "A man so misinformed and having such convictions about the Negro cannot possibly judge wisely the considerations involved in the issue now in controversy." The military men responded in kind; one complained that the civilian aide was trying "to advance the colored race at the expense of the Army," and no small number of memoranda circulated through War Department channels with the cover note, "Not to be shown to Judge Hastie."[9]

Hastie was the ultimate bureaucratic warrior in these debates, pressing the secretary of war—and every civilian and military official who served beneath Stimson on the organizational chart—at every turn to afford blacks fair opportunities in the armed services. He served as a communications channel from black America to the War Department, which proved especially helpful when Stimson announced the Tuskegee program's creation. It caused an uptick in the number of blacks applying for aviation training that, Hastie warned, was destined to lead to disappointment because the program could accommodate only a small number of cadets at a time. "The narrow and arbitrary limitations upon aviation cadet training for Negroes continue to be a source of widespread complaint and dissatisfaction with hurtful effect upon morale" among African Americans as a whole, he wrote in a 1942 memorandum for the AAF's civilian leaders.[10]

TAAF could never be large or well enough equipped to accommodate all of the training that would be necessary to bring the black fighter squadron to combat readiness. The fact that a truly separate-but-equal air base could not be created placed stresses on the AAF and previously all-white facilities throughout the nation. Hastie and others concentrated their attention on those pressure points. The 332nd needed flight surgeons, for instance, and the only school of aviation medicine in the service was at Randolph Field in San Antonio; it had never admitted black residents before 1943. Qualified black officers at TAAF studied via correspondence courses and trained part-time as their regular duties permitted at a Maxwell Field branch school. White flight surgeons in training faced no such obstacles. Hastie was able to force the Air Forces to create a similar training regime for blacks, which had the practical effect of desegregating the program at Randolph. He succeeded in creating opportunities for blacks in other job categories as well, so that the TAAF program Hastie and those in his camp had initially criticized as incorrigibly Jim-Crowed created a momentum that resulted in at least small-scale integration throughout the Air Forces during the war.[11]

When an early study found that black aviation cadets graduated at a rate lower than white cadets (42 percent against 59 percent), Hastie pointed out that black cadets were permitted only to become pursuit pilots, the most demanding specialization, and a role that could be filled only by pilots of a certain body type. On the other hand, white cadets who might not reach the level demanded of pursuit pilots or might be too large to fit comfortably into a pursuit fighter's cockpit "had an opportunity to qualify for commissions as flying officers in several categories...There is no way of telling how many of the colored cadets who were eliminated would have graduated in another type of flight training."[12]

Assessing the 1942 Troop Basis, the War Department's most fundamental planning document for the calculation of manpower needs, Hastie found that blacks were assigned disproportionately to sanitary companies (janitorial units) in the medical corps, labor units in ammunition companies in the ordinance department, and service battalions in the quartermaster corps. He argued, "Certainly, the Negro soldier should do his full share of manual, unskilled labor, but...[I note the] unreasonable preponderance, in some places the exclusive assignment, of Negroes to functions of this type." Yet even Hastie was forced to admit that the War Department was hamstrung by the quality of Negro draftees as measured by the Army's Intelligence Classification Test. Only .5 percent of blacks inducted into the Army in a three-month period of 1941 tested in the highest intelligence classification, compared with 11.3 percent of whites. More than half of the black inductees tested in the lowest classification, compared with 7.7 percent of whites.[13]

Hastie was patronized at the highest levels of the War Department. When a friend of Stimson wrote the secretary in January 1942 with the complaint that the Army was not treating blacks fairly, Stimson replied candidly. "We are taking Negroes in the Army in exactly the same ratio as they exist in the population," he wrote. "We are also trying to do our best by them after they get in and in this effort I have myself been personally active." But the Army still faced obstacles in managing Negro units—obstacles that had everything to do, Stimson believed, with inherent deficiencies in the Negro character. "The Negro still lacks the particular initiative which a commanding officer of men needs in war," he informed his friend. "Negro troops do infinitely better when officered by white men than they do when officered by their own, and the best Negro soldiers have always admitted this." Stimson went further. "We would be having a much easier time if it were not for a comparatively small group of Negro radical leaders who are agitating for complete social equality," he wrote. "Incidentally," Stimson assured his friend, "I myself have a Negro aide and have appointed a Negro brigadier general. But I have tried to make very careful selections in each."[14]

Some of Hastie's proposals were so grounded in common sense that they overcame resistance in the War Department. When he pointed out that the Army might defuse some of its racial tensions by encouraging members of all-white and all-black units on the same bases to engage in informal discussions that would inevitably have to lead to increased mutual understanding, the Morale Branch initially dismissed his idea. Yet Gen. Dwight D. Eisenhower instituted a more or less identical program in Europe. That was a rare victory for Hastie; the War Department's experts in bureaucratic procedure stonewalled the majority of his suggestions, and its leaders rejected Hastie's overarching arguments. Stimson deemed most of Hastie's complaints "trivial." Assistant Secretary of War John J. McCloy wrote Hastie, "Frankly, I do not think that the basic issues of this war are involved in the question of whether Colored troops serve in segregated or mixed units, and I doubt whether you can convince the people of the United States that the basic issue of freedom are involved in such a question."[15]

Racism took many forms in War Department policies, some of which were merely theoretical and others of which rose to the level of life-and-death. One of the most galling for Hastie was the Army Medical Corps's age-old practice of segregating donated blood. Never one to mince words, he charged in 1942 that the ideology behind it was identical to the one American boys were fighting against in Europe. Why should the Army draw a distinction between blood from whites and blood from "non-Aryans"? Even the army's surgeon general was forced to admit that there was no "biologically convincing" basis for the practice. The Army segregated the blood drawn from white and black soldiers, he said, solely for reasons "commonly recognized as psychologically important in America." Hastie drew on the expertise of an old friend from Washington and Amherst, Dr. Charles Drew, a pioneer in the storage and battlefield use of plasma and a former director of the American Red Cross Blood Bank, in developing his criticism of the program. It was "indefensible from any point of view," Drew said. Drew had resigned from his position with the American Red Cross because he refused to cooperate with the War Department's segregated blood bank. Now Hastie offered his own resignation over the issue. Stimson refused to accept it, and he reversed the War Department's policy.[16]

By far the most vexing issue for Hastie—and the one over which he would eventually break from the War Department—was that of segregation in the nation's flying forces. Hastie "had seen ingrained racism in the Army," his biographer explained, and "'outright fascism' in the Navy, but in the Air Corps he saw some hope for democracy."[17] Hastie hoped that the comparatively new military wing would be open to new ideas, but in 1941 its top ranks were peopled with career Army men who were not in the habit of questioning received wisdom. Many were Southerners and all of course were white. They had what Hastie considered the supremely annoying habit of referring to the Tuskegee training program as an "experiment."

Hastie summed up the attitude of the Air Corps's general officers toward his efforts in a single word: "Hostile!"[18]

If he accomplished nothing else, however, Hastie provided a conduit for black public opinion on the war effort in general and the Air Corps in particular to the Munitions Building. Hastie made it very difficult for Stimson and others at the War Department to ignore African Americans' concerns—not that Stimson, other civilian leaders, and the generals did not try to do just that. "The narrow and arbitrary limitations [placed] upon aviation training for Negroes continue to be a source of widespread complaint and dissatisfaction with hurtful effect upon community morale," he informed the AAC's civilian leadership in March 1942.[19] Hastie's longest-running bureaucratic battle, the issue closest to his heart, was the treatment of blacks in the flying program. He protested vigorously when he first learned that the Air Corps planned to create a separate but equal air base in the first place. "[W]hy in the name of common sense should all of this elaborate special machinery be set up to train Negro flyers?" he asked.[20]

When he learned that not only would the Tuskegee Army Flying School be segregated from the rest of the AAC, but that blacks and whites would be separated from one another when they ate and slept at TAAF, he protested again. "The establishment of a separate training school for colored flying cadets has already evoked widespread criticism...I know that many individuals and groups have withheld protests and criticism which they have felt to be justified, because of their desire to see Negroes obtain an opportunity to become Army flyers," he informed Assistant Secretary of War (Air) Robert Lovett in 1941. Lovett replied that practices at TAAF "conform[ed] to regularly established practice and that there is no departure in the case of Air Corps establishments," but Hastie found that explanation "not persuasive." He wrote, "As I see it, the question is not what is [being done] or has been done in other circumstances, but whether this is the correct thing to do under the peculiar circumstances of the present case. I feel strongly as I indicated before, that the present proposal is a serious mistake." But Hastie's lonely objections could not change plans for or policy at TAAF.[21]

Air Corps construction documents reveal that base facilities built Jim Crow into the fabric of the base. Quartermaster and commissary facilities that employed black and white civilians, male and female, were thoroughly segregated. One such document called for the installation of:

> ...toilets, lavatories, and drinking facilities in each of the four (4) SH-9 type buildings to be used as technical warehouses at [TAAF] as follows:
>
> 1 toilet and lavatory (colored male)
>
> 1 toilet and lavatory (colored female)

1 toilet and lavatory (white male)

1 drinking fountain (colored)

1 drinking fountain (white)[22]

Judge Hastie warned against such construction. "I can assure you," he wrote again to Lovett,

> that if in addition to the segregated training school, the Army insists upon the proposed separation of white and colored personnel attached to the same unit such a nation-wide storm of protest and resentment will arise as to destroy all of the good-will and support of the Negro public with reference to the Army program. No single enterprise is being watched as closely by Negroes as is the Air Corps training program. I cannot over-emphasize the catastrophic effect of the arrangement now proposed upon morale.[23]

Building any airfield from scratch was difficult enough for the Air Forces; the close scrutiny of the War Department and black press made the prospect that much more daunting, even if Hastie's prophesied "storm of protest and resentment" never quite materialized.

Despite the War Department's close attention to the developing air base, TAAF's first year in operation confirmed many of Hastie's and other critics' worst fears. Maj. Edward C. Ambler, TAAF's intelligence officer and author of the airfield's official history, dryly noted in his narrative of the base's development, "The early set up at the Tuskegee Army Air Field could hardly be dignified by the term organization," and wondered at "the fact that it did not fly apart from its own centrifugal force."[24]

TAAF's commanders faced a nearly impossible administrative task. The commanding officer of any other army airfield the size of TAAF, even in the midst of chaotic wartime expansion, could expect to be responsible for one, perhaps two, phases of pilot training. TAAF, in contrast, housed preflight, basic, and advanced fighter training programs and an artillery liaison pilot training program. Whereas most other bases of its size either taught pilots to fly or trained pilots for combat—an important distinction—in the first two years of its existence TAAF would be responsible for organizing a fighter squadron and sending it directly into combat. After late 1942, when the War Department created the all-black 100th, 301st, and 302nd fighter squadrons to join the 99th in the 332nd Fighter Group, TAAF was forced to accommodate even more cadets and the support personnel necessary to train and equip them. That announcement helped to solve one problem, by creating openings for the men who had qualified for flight training. (According to the NAACP, by 1942 blacks had to wait an average of eighteen months before they were called to flight cadet training, whereas the average wait for whites was ninety days.) But the addition of the three squadrons also made it necessary for the combat crew training phase to be moved to another base—in this case Selfridge Field, Michigan.[25]

In addition, the base was home to signal corps detachments, a medical corps, quartermaster cadres, and various air service units—all of which TAAF personnel were responsible for organizing, training, and processing. After 1943 the base also trained bomber pilots for the newly conceived, all-black 477th Medium Bombardment Group, which, among other complications, meant that TAAF's aircraft mechanics became responsible for the maintenance of at least half a dozen different types of aircraft. By the end of that year and likely much sooner, TAAF had on top of everything else become a catch-all for the classification and training of blacks in the Air Forces for any conceivable specialty, and base historian Ambler wrote, "Other stations were inclined to send troops to Tuskegee just to get rid of them." "Tuskegee would also have to play the role of furnishing trained personnel for replacements in the tactical outfits," Ambler noted. He described TAAF as "a classification center for all Negro personnel in the Air Forces." On an administrative level alone the Jim Crow air force proved a logistical nightmare.[26]

Brig. Gen. Walter R. Weaver's initial plan for the Tuskegee Flying School envisioned a maintenance crew of eleven white officers and fifteen white noncommissioned officers to be based at TAAF "until a sufficient number of Negro officers were trained for their replacement." The members of TAAF's initial all-white officer corps either volunteered for the assignment or were promised their respective choice of assignment after getting the base up and running, and the base was fortunate to receive the men it did among the initial cadre.[27]

According to official sources, TAAF's original executive officer, Lt. Col. John T. Hazard, and post adjutant, Capt. Clyde H. Bynum, provided the pragmatic approach needed to operate TAAF efficiently. Hazard, a graduate of the ROTC program at Georgetown University, had been commissioned in 1931 and spent nearly his entire prewar military career building, organizing, and supervising Civilian Conservation Corps (CCC) camps before being assigned to Tuskegee—excellent preparation for the duties he faced at TAAF. (On the other hand, another source described him as "an impoverished, not-well-trained former Civilian Conservation Corps officer…given to explosive cursing tantrums of temper.") Hazard and Bynum were in place in their positions by October 1941, joined by a group of young officers who found themselves thrown directly into the deep end of base administration. Lt. Carl Luetcke Jr., for example, reported for duty on August 1, 1941, and found himself appointed simultaneously to the duties of summary court officer, acting post quartermaster, acting post signal officer, acting post utilities officer, acting air corps supply officer, project officer for malaria control, and project officer for the establishment of an auxiliary airfield; at other times over the next year he served as the post weather officer, post communications officer, post operations officer, and post technical inspector.[28]

Because infrastructure was so limited in Macon County, the Army had to build an entirely new system of municipal utilities to serve the airfield. The chosen site was heavily forested, subject to flooding, and required major grading work. That work began in the early summer of 1941 even as the War Department chose the first class of trainees to be trained at Moton Field and TAAF. The development progressed on schedule, but an unusually wet autumn and winter combined with the recently denuded landscape to produce a "bottomless morass" of mud and delayed the project. Then again, the base itself was expected to last no longer than the war itself, so buildings on the base would be built to a Spartan construction code. Builders could make up for lost time by throwing up temporary, unheated wooden buildings.[29]

When an AAC engineer's report indicated in August that the construction project was in danger of lagging, the Air Corps Southeastern Training Command reminded the engineer: "The project at Tuskegee is considered by the War Department as No. 1 priority due to political pressure that was brought to bear upon the White House and War Department to provide pilot training for colored applicants.... For this reason training must be initiated on schedule regardless of cost." Another thorough inspection of the progress of construction at TAAF in September led Commanding Gen. of the Air Forces Henry H. ("Hap") Arnold to the reluctant conclusion that the field would not be ready in time to accommodate the first class of cadets on schedule. "In view of the fact that this is the first class of Negro Aviation Cadets to ever receive flying training in the Military Establishment," he assured the War Department's inspector general—none other than Benjamin O. Davis Sr.—"every phase of their training, administration, and other factors are [sic] being very seriously scrutinized by this office."[30]

In fact, the six men in Class 42-C who passed the primary phase of flight training at Moton Field began basic flight training at TAAF on November 8, 1941, as scheduled, even though the facility was only two-thirds complete. The cadets lived in a hastily constructed tent city, and another cluster of tents served as their Corps of Cadets headquarters, day room, and classroom. When the Japanese attacked Pearl Harbor and brought the United States into the war there were 156 men, only twenty-five of them white, stationed at TAAF. Gen. Weaver's plan to replace whites in lower-level job categories with blacks as the latter gained experience ran into resistance from local whites, however. When black military policemen arrived to provide base security, they replaced civilian employees who then "objected strenuously and in a threatening manner to being replaced by Negro personnel."[31]

The training of support crews continued on schedule. The AAC activated the 99th Pursuit Squadron at Chanute Field in Illinois, on March 22, 1941, as construction at TAAF proceeded. The AAC filled the squadron by assigning quotas to various regions of the country; the Southeast met its quota almost immediately, with enlistees mainly from the Atlanta area. In contrast, the AAC had to advertise heavily in Chicago newspapers to drum up enough enlistees from that region, a problem that the *Chicago Defender* attributed to northern African Americans' refusal to volunteer for segregated units.[32]

The initial cadre of 268 black enlisted men and officers trained at Chanute in specialties such as aircraft maintenance and repair, armoring, communications, weather observation, and administration alongside white trainees under white instructors. Training classes may have been integrated, but living conditions were not. While white trainees lived in brand-new barracks, blacks bunked in World War-I era buildings. The men of the 99th who graduated from the Chanute training programs, 90 percent of whom had graduated from high school and many of whom had attended or graduated from college, hailed from every part of the United States. They approached their work with an amount of pride not unlike the pilot cadets' and similar consciousness of the publicity their service was generating.[33]

Elmer Jones, a graduate of Howard University where he had been a CPT classmate of Yancey Williams and a protégé of Judge Hastie, trained in the engineering and mechanics courses at Chanute and became the 99th's engineering officer and later commander of its service squadron. While he acknowledged the historic nature of the opportunity, he described his own motivations for pursuing the training in individualistic terms. "I think I can speak for most of [my comrades]," he added. "We were doing it for ourselves. I mean, we were proud people, most of us with college degrees. When we were overseas or in the states, we hardly ever talked about, 'Well, we've got to do this. We've got to be better than the average to make it,' that we're doing this to uplift our race. None of that. All of that thought and discussion has come about since we've matured. We wanted an opportunity to do a good job, not to pull up our people. Of course, it's good that we did it as we did, but we were individuals." They transferred to Maxwell Field, where they lived in a tent complex separate from whites on the base, in mid-November 1941 and arrived at Tuskegee later that month. Another 324 enlisted men arrived at TAAF in January 1942.[34]

Training programs ramped up at TAAF in 1942 to accommodate everything from a medical detachment to the all-black 313th Army Air Forces Band. Maj. DeHaven Hinkson supervised six black medical officers, five black nurses, and a twenty-five-bed hospital with an operating room. P. D. Davis, a civilian clerk at the base and formerly the director of the Tuskegee Institute student band, began rehearsing the band, but he was soon relieved by Lt. Frank Drye, another former director of the campus outfit. Drye ran a tight ship and explained his approach in much the same terms that a check pilot on the base might have: "It is my duty to see that you soldier and that you play music and when you fail in either of these it becomes my duty to take disciplinary action," he told his charges. "As I perform my duty with pleasure, I am as happy at assigning you to hard labor in the guardhouse as I am in granting you a three day pass."[35]

The growing base employed an increasing number of civilians, many of them women from the area like Mildred Hemmons, a native of Tuskegee whose father worked at the VA Hospital. Hemmons had been a Tuskegee Institute student, a majorette in the marching band, and the first female graduate of the school's CPT program. After graduation she applied for the Women's Air Service Pilots (WASPs) program. She exceeded the program's entrance requirements but was turned down because, she was informed, there were "no plans to train Negro women."[36]

Intent on finding work in aviation, Hemmons worked as the building contractor's secretary at Moton Field. With construction at Moton completed, she was hired as the first civilian employee of the Quartermaster Corps at TAAF. She later worked in the offices of the commandant of cadets and the signal corps, and recruited other Tuskegee alumnae to work at the base. During the period she kept up a unique courtship with Herbert Eugene Carter, whom she had first known as a Tuskegee Institute football player. Carter, too, was a graduate of the Tuskegee Institute CPT program, and he was accepted as a flight cadet in the class of 42-F.[37]

Cadets had almost no free time, so the couple had to be creative. She recalled, "He would call me up and say, 'Are you going to fly this weekend?' I'd say, 'Yes, I plan to fly Saturday,'" even though she had to scrimp and save to come up with the $5 she would need to rent the CPT program's Piper Cub. "He'd say, 'OK, I'll meet you over Lake Martin at two o'clock.' We could see each other and wave at each other. We didn't really get to see much of each other [otherwise], and that was the way we kept in touch." They married soon after Lt. Carter's graduation in the summer of 1942. Everything—the courtship, the work at TAAF, the association with so many bright minds from all over the country—was, she said, "quite exciting."[38]

As TAAF expanded, the mechanics and radio technicians who had graduated from the original technical training school at Chanute had to train an increasing number of their counterparts. A few were given temporary duty assignments to attend specialized training schools at other bases, where they sometimes took classes in integrated settings, and some received their training at other bases and transferred directly into service groups assisting the 332nd or 477th without ever setting foot on the base in Tuskegee. But the bulk of the new mechanics' instruction took the form of on-the-job training at TAAF.[39]

Leslie Edwards was one of the mechanics who graduated directly from training at another base into service in the 477th. Though he was never stationed at Tuskegee, his story is emblematic of the importance of the instruction that went on there for the trainees themselves. Edwards was a Tennessee native whose family had moved to Cincinnati when he was very young. His father died soon thereafter, leaving Edwards's mother alone to raise three children in an unfamiliar city. The family suffered terribly through the Great Depression; for Edwards "there wasn't any sort of thing like lunch money. Wasn't no such thing. I went to school barefooted." So he dropped out of school and got a job washing dishes in a segregated restaurant. Edwards was working for a meatpacker and had just gotten married when he was drafted into the Army. After induction he was to be sent to cooks' and bakers' school, but an officer noticed something unusual in Edwards's test results and tested him again. Based on his new test results, Edwards was reassigned to the Air Forces and transferred to aircraft mechanics school at Sheppard Field, Texas. Edwards remembered this training—he was in an all-black group living under thoroughly segregated base conditions, but they trained under white instructors alongside all-white classes—as having made all the difference in his life.[40]

"I didn't know a screw from a wrench," Edwards said. He fell behind his classmates, "and now they're telling me if I don't learn all this, I'll be sent over to Europe [in the infantry], and I'm thinking about how I may not see my pregnant wife again. I became so nervous and everything, so upset. I broke out in shingles, my nerves were so bad. But the fellows that I met—from Detroit, New York, Chicago, Los Angeles, Florida, Alabama—the fellows I met, they rallied around me, and they said, 'Edwards, we can learn this. We can get this.' They said, 'You can do it.'"[41]

"We would stay up all night studying," he continued. "It was a good feeling among the fellows; we were going to do this. And I found some of the fellows were exceptionally good at studying. I was amazed at how much they could retain. And as I studied I began to find out that I could retain as much as they could! I felt like this is something that I can handle. When we finally finished up, I was at the top of the class. They had me doing things I never did before. I began to build a certain amount of confidence in Leslie Edwards." He transferred directly into the 617th Bomb Squadron of the

477th at Selfridge Field, Michigan, and worked his way up to flight chief of the squadron.[42]

The flight cadets who graduated from the Moton Field primary phase of training transferred into the basic training course at TAAF; if they made it through that phase they remained at the base for advanced training. In basic and advanced training they flew increasingly powerful aircraft with increasingly complex instrumentation and learned formation flying, long-distance navigation, gunnery, combat tactics, and other increasingly specialized skills. Charles E. McGee described the essence of the training at TAAF. Whereas the primary phase had introduced cadets to developing a "feel" for flying in the open-cockpit Stearmans, in the BT-13s and AT-6s cadets flew at the AAF base, "You have higher speed capability, so your thinking processes are advanced. If you're going to keep ahead of your aircraft, you're going to think about a few more things on different [levels], because things happen a little faster."[43]

Just as Tuskegee Airmen folklore blamed Lt. Magoon for the high washout rate at Moton, it blamed the director of basic training at TAAF, Capt. Gabe ("The Hawk") Hawkins, for the high standards TAFS officers enforced in the more advanced phase. Horace Bohannon summed it up: "Gabe Hawkins was a nigger hater. He didn't like no niggers. [He] was somebody who would chew you up and spit you out. Everybody was afraid to fly with him." Cadet Charles Kerford recalled, "That's what everybody said: 'If you draw Capt. Hawkins, you can forget getting your wings,' because he was a man that was designated to wash us out. I drew Capt. Hawkins, and I got washed. A lot of [cadets] got knocked out with the Hawk, Capt. Hawkins."[44]

A terrific legend grew around the Hawk. There are many different versions of the story, but Sgt. George D. Abercrombie, a clerk who worked under Hawkins, offered this account:

Major Hawkins was a Mississippian. At that time, Alabama was neck and neck with Mississippi in lynching. And Hawkins was a fairly large, rugged Southerner. In fact, he struck fear into most of the people who came in contact with him because he spoke with a lot of authority and he spoke loudly. I mean, he had a directness, and that was a time in the South and especially in the military, where if you're a black soldier and a white major ordered, "Shit," you started farting. If you were caught disobeying an order from an officer, there could be a shooting and all that stuff. I mean, it was a tough time.

Before I came to Tuskegee, it had been rumored to me that Maj. Hawkins had been involved in a plane crash. He had done some maneuver where he crashed. Now, of course, it's all hearsay to me, but I understand that he was just near dead. They had to scrape him up with a shovel. But they took him over to the hospital, which was staffed with black doctors and nurses. That's at Tuskegee. And they put him back together.

I understand that his wife at that time said, "If the only blood you have on this base is black, don't give him a transfusion, let him die." I understand that when he came to, he said the same thing. But they went ahead. They had to do the right thing, and they went ahead, and he recovered. But I understand his wife divorced him.[45]

In another version of the legend, the Hawkinses remained married, and Mrs. Hawkins had a daughter a year after the accident. In this version the black men on base kidded the Hawk that his daughter had a darker complexion than either he or his wife and wondered out loud how that could be.

The legend personalized an impersonal reality: black would-be pilots had a harder time earning their wings than their white counterparts did. The washout rate was higher at TAFS than at other AAF training programs, but the real quota system existed on the front end. By restricting black involvement in its flying forces to the minuscule numbers that could be accommodated by the 99th (and later the 332nd and 477th) and confining their training to a single complex in central Alabama, the AAF determined that it would not offer African Americans equal opportunity or equal treatment.

It would be difficult to overstate the enormity of the challenge TAAF trainers and administrators faced; flight training was the raison d'être for the base, but only a fraction of the men assigned to the base worked in immediate connection to it. Since the rapid expansion of the post-Pearl Harbor Air Forces resulted in raw recruits being inducted and assigned in large numbers directly to TAAF, the post had to create a basic training detachment in 1942. On top of all its other challenges, TAAF had to deal with the failures of the American educational system. Black students were crowded into inferior schools in northern and Midwestern cities, and the South—where the majority of African Americans lived—did not provide black schoolchildren with anything approaching an adequate education. In 1940 the state of Alabama, for example, reported spending nearly six times more per white public school student than black. The nation's black schools were separate enough, but they did not provide an equal, much less meaningful, education for the young men who ended up being drafted into the AAF. Many of those men required remedial education in the technical specializations to which they were assigned at TAAF. "Since the Negro men who manned this station had not been accorded any opportunity en masse to become engaged in the technical phases of aviation," base historian Ambler wrote, "there was no source in civilian life from which these men could be drawn. They had to be trained here."[46]

Oversight of all of these training programs and base operations fell to Col. Frederick von Kimble, who succeeded Ellison as post commander in January 1942. Von Kimble called on his previous experience in the Air Corps's Division of Buildings and Grounds to expedite the remaining construction at the base.[47] He succeeded in this regard, but ultimately proved unequal to the greater task of commanding TAAF and providing leadership to the black air force. Von Kimble did have something of an excuse: War Department policy on race relations and racial segregation was inherently self-contradictory and left TAAF's commanders standing on shaky ground. A 1940 policy maintained that "the service of negroes will be utilized on a fair and equitable basis" throughout the Army, and "The strength of the negro personnel...will be maintained on the general basis of proportion of the negro population of the country." Black officers were to be trained to command all-black units, combatant and noncombatant, in every branch of the service, including the Air Corps. However, it was also War Department policy to segregate African American and white personnel into separate regimental organizations. "This policy has been proven satisfactory over a long period of years and to make changes would produce situations destructive to the morale and detrimental to the preparation for national defense," Adj. Gen. E.S. Adams, the author of the policy, added. "It is the opinion of the War Department that no experiments should be tried with the organizational set-up of these units at this critical time."[48]

Von Kimble interpreted the policy as a prohibition on desegregated facilities of any sort. But the black enlisted men who trained at Chanute Field had done so under effectively integrated conditions with white enlisted men on the Illinois base. They expected to continue the practice after they were transferred to Tuskegee. "A large percentage of us who were from the north and didn't have the same attitude about our rights as people who had been culturally conditioned in the South," said LeRoy Gillead, a New Yorker and veteran of the Chanute training. "Therefore, there was a lot of friction going on at Tuskegee Army at the time, to integrate the PX [post exchange]." In May 1942 two enlisted men staged a sit-in in the "whites only" section of the PX restaurant and left only after ordered to do so by a white officer. There were many other attempts to desegregate base facilities forcibly. Von Kimble insisted to his superiors at the Southeastern Training Command that his practice of segregating facilities on the base was in line with War Department policy. If, however, the commanding officers of bases in the north allowed integration, he could understand why black soldiers might be confused after being transferred to TAAF. "Such inconsistency is difficult to explain," he wrote. "At present there are 1100 enlisted men on this station and some 150 Civil Service employees.... A considerable portion of these men are from the north and inconsistencies in policy to them appear them as sectional prejudices."[49]

Von Kimble went further and attempted sociological analysis. "Should the War Department be pressed to remove the separation of the races at messes and in quarters by legislation or order[,] this cannot expect to affect the established practices of a people," he continued. "Any mixture of the races, particularly in the southern stations, will have not only a tremendously adverse reaction throughout this entire section of the country, but will undoubtedly lead toward an attempt on the part of certain colored individuals or groups to encroach on established customs within local civil communities." Von Kimble concluded, "It is felt that the result would be immediate friction and probably strife," and recommended that the War Department clarify its policies and force all installations to segregate the races in all facilities—in effect, to nationalize the Deep South's approach to race relations.[50]

Maj. Gen. George E. Stratemeyer, commander of the Southeastern Training Command, backed von Kimble aggressively, blaming TAAF's troubles on "Commanding Officers of stations and activities in other sections of the country" and "a very small minority" of radical agitators on the base. But the rank and file of men under von Kimble's command considered his position unjust and openly challenged the strict segregation of base facilities. Von Kimble's policies were, one pilot recalled, "very abrasive as far as we were concerned. We just didn't like the guy." Hundreds would have agreed with an enlisted man who served under von Kimble and remembered him in essentialist terms: "He was a racist."[51]

Von Kimble was not an inspired choice for the command of TAAF, to say the least. Parrish considered his commanding officer's attitude toward the entire effort "rather difficult," "strange," and "ambiguous." As a career military man (von Kimble graduated from West Point in 1918), Parrish thought, von Kimble was determined to do his duty at Tuskegee and please his superiors. But von Kimble, Parrish suggested, must have received mixed messages from those superiors as to what that duty entailed. He "wasn't quite clear in his mind," Parrish said, "as to whether his duty consisted of trying to make this thing a success, and therefore saddle the Air Force with the problem of what to do with the graduates, or whether he could inconspicuously allow it not to succeed, and therefore do everybody a favor." New War Department regulations, for instance, forbade the segregation of base facilities such as restrooms and drinking fountains. But according to Parrish, "Von Kimble was encouraged to feel, I suppose by some officers in the Air Corps, higher ranking plus some political people, that these rules were just made for political reasons"—in other words, to

Stearman PT-17 trainers prepare for take-off at Moton Field, the primary training facility Tuskegee Institute operated under contract with the Army Air Forces. *U.S. Air Force Historical Research Agency.*

What began as a small pool of civilian flight instructors at Moton Field mushroomed in the course of the war as the training program expanded. *U.S. Air Force Historical Research Agency.*

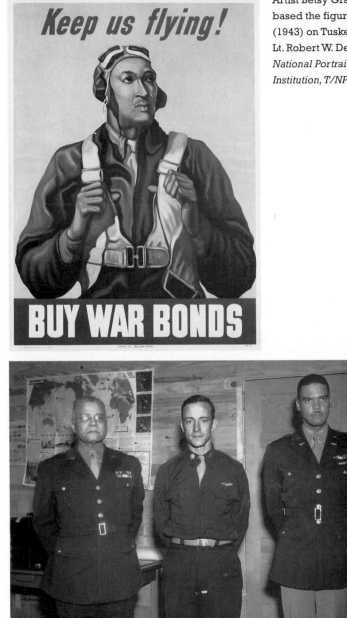

Artist Betsy Graves Reyneau based the figure in "Keep Us Flying!" (1943) on Tuskegee Airman Lt. Robert W. Deiz of Portland, Oregon. *National Portrait Gallery, Smithsonian Institution, T/NPG.89.167.*

Left to right: Brig. Gen. Benjamin O. Davis Sr., Lt. Col. Noel F. Parrish, and Lt. Col. Benjamin O. Davis Jr. Parrish and Davis Jr. were fortuitous choices for the leadership of the Tuskegee military flight program. *U.S. Air Force Historical Research Agency.*

Charles A. ("Chief") Anderson, chief instructor pilot at Moton Field, tutors a cadet. *U.S. Air Force Historical Research Agency*

Enlisted men being trained as mechanics learn the intricacies of a P-40 engine at TAAF. *NAACP Collection, Library of Congress Prints and Photographs Division.*

Nurses from Tuskegee Army Air Field (TAAF) base hospital prepare for a sightseeing flight. *U.S. Air Force Historical Research Agency.*

In the course of the war Tuskegee Army Air Field (TAAF), seen here in an aerial view, became the equivalent of a small, highly functioning, nearly all-black city. *U.S. Air Force Historical Research Agency.*

Members of the first class of graduates from the Tuskegee Army Flying School (TAFS) discuss flying with Robert M. "Mother" Long. Left to right: George "Spanky" Roberts, Benjamin O. Davis Jr., Charles H. DeBow, Long, Mac Ross, and Lemuel R. Custis. *U.S. Air Force Historical Research Agency.*

Pilots of the 332nd attend a mission briefing at Ramitelli, March 1945. They include Jimmie D. Wheeler (seated, with goggles), Emile G. Clifton (seated, with cloth cap), and (standing, left to right) Ronald W. Reeves (cloth cap), Hiram Mann (leather cap), Joseph L. Chineworth (dress cap), Elwood T. Driver (leather cap), Edward Thomas (partial view), and Woodrow W. Crockett (dress cap). *Toni Frissell Collection, Library of Congress Prints and Photographs Division.*

The contingencies of combat led to ad hoc integration in Italy. Captain Morris S. Young removes a particle of flak from the jaw of a white 15th Air Force bomber crewmember. Surgical technician Wellington R. Mills assists. *NAACP Collection, Library of Congress Prints and Photographs Division.*

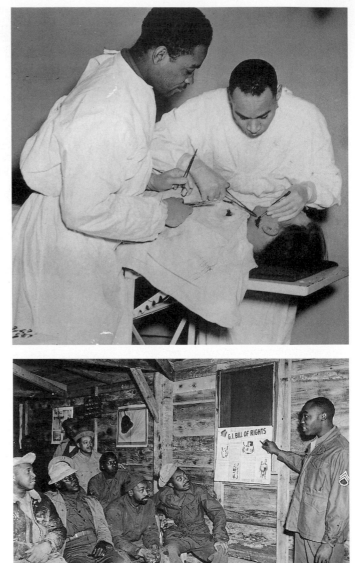

Staff Sgt. Herbert Ellison of Albion, Michigan, a member of a quartermaster trucking company attached to the 332nd, leads a discussion on the G.I. Bill at a post somewhere in Italy. "The men ask questions and we bring out the meaning of the G.I. Bill of Rights and what it holds for them in the way of a better life when they become civilians again," he said. The expectation that wartime service would lead to greater postwar citizenship rights was never far from the minds of many black airmen and soldiers. *NAACP Collection, Library of Congress Prints and Photographs Division.*

Pilots of the 477th fly B-25s in formation. Training African Americans to fly and maintain the world's most powerful and sophisticated killing machines implicitly challenged Jim Crow. *U.S. Air Force Historical Research Agency.*

Captain Anthony N. Chiappe reviews arrested officers of the 477th at Freeman Field in preparation for their removal to Godman Field. *NAACP Collection, Library of Congress Prints and Photographs Division.*

By the end of World War II, experienced black officers had fully assumed leadership of the 477th Composite Group of Tuskegee-trained fighter and bomber pilots. Having proved that they could successfully fly in combat, maintain aircraft, and manage complex operations, there was little justification left for segregating blacks in the Air Force. *NAACP Collection, Library of Congress Prints and Photographs Division.*

mollify the civil rights organizations—"and it would be wise not to enforce them too strictly in the South."[52]

G. L. Washington attributed von Kimble's difficulties to "the manner in which he catered to southern prejudices in fostering and maintaining segregation at the Base. Considering that Colonel von Kimble was an Oregonian one would not expect this. But our own experience in the south did not support such expectation." He observed, "Too often northerners would lean further backwards in the practice of discrimination than the southerners themselves." Parrish lost all faith in von Kimble as a leader when Secretary of War Stimson visited Tuskegee in 1942 to discuss the uses to which the black pilots might be put in the war after graduation. "Von Kimble hadn't flown with any of them," Parrish remembered. "[H]e didn't really know anything about them, but he did not lack opinions" and did "a great deal of generalizing about blacks which I found tedious."[53]

Von Kimble's control of TAAF began to break down in the spring of 1942 amidst racial and military-civilian tensions. In early April, military police from the base clashed with civilian authorities for at least the third time that year. In the first instance, civilian police had arrested an enlisted man from the base on charges of public drunkenness in the town of Tuskegee and then refused to release the prisoner to TAAF authorities. In the second, Tuskegee police had arrested a base sentinel who had been detailed to guard a quartermaster's warehouse in town and had for some reason taken it upon himself to direct traffic in front of the facility. (White drivers objected to being told what to do by an armed black.) In the third incident, which took place on April 1, Tuskegee policemen demanded custody of a soldier whom a TAAF military policeman had placed under arrest for disturbing the peace in the town of Tuskegee. The MP brandished a pistol in the resulting fracas and refused to surrender the soldier. A crowd of approximately fifteen heavily armed white civilians and a larger number of black soldiers and civilians gathered and threatened to escalate the situation into a full-blown race riot. A Macon County deputy sheriff and two members of the Alabama Highway Patrol arrived to control the crowd; they then helped the civilian policemen disarm the MP and beat him badly enough that he required treatment at the local VA hospital. Airmen from TAAF armed themselves, boarded a truck, and started for town, but Parrish intervened and was able to convince them to return to the base.[54]

Benjamin O. Davis Sr.'s report for the War Department's inspector general blamed the incident on the MP's poor judgment, and von Kimble impressed upon all base personnel, and the military police detachment in particular, the importance of cooperation with, even submission to, civil authorities. He instituted a top-to-bottom review of TAAF officers and noncommissioned officers "whose ability, leadership, and personality might be considered as being such as to render them unqualified to perform the duties assigned to them." In case that cryptic sentence left anything to the imagination of his superiors, von Kimble assured them that "a small minority of personnel on duty at the station concerned are radically inclined and are participating in agitation to keep alive race questions and questions of social equality." He continued, "Steps have been taken ... to ferret out these individuals and eliminate them as a disturbing source to the morale of the personnel assigned to that station and as an antagonizing element to the civilians within areas surrounding the reservation."[55]

Black newspapers exaggerated the threat. A screaming headline in the Los Angeles-based *California Eagle* was typical in this regard. "TUSKEGEE RIOTS! MOB ATTACKS NEGRO FLYING FIELD," the paper reported in the wake of the incident. Hyperbole aside, the local atmosphere was unquestionably charged. Local whites responded to rumors that the War Department was considering additional bases for the training of black Americans with outraged letters to Gov. Frank Dixon, petition drives, and an attempt to pass a resolution (known as "The Tuskegee Resolution") in the state legislature demanding that the War Department cease and desist creating Negro camps in the state. The problem was not confined to the Deep South; internal War Department deliberations over the 1942 Troop Basis candidly acknowledged the "difficulty of finding suitable stations" for large black training units anywhere in the country. "Should this reluctance not be overcome and should more Negro units [not] be added, a considerable part of our Army will become a strictly home force contributing little if anything to winning the war," it concluded.[56]

An attempt to expand the Tuskegee program with an auxiliary facility near the community of Fort Davis in Macon County elicited an especially spirited response. After Gov. Dixon succeeded in killing the project through quiet consultation with the War Department, a Tuskegee attorney wrote to "express the thanks of the Mayor and the Council, and the people generally, for your splendid efforts on our behalf." Richard H. Powell Jr. gushed, "We all recognize that in these matters that tend to protect our white citizens from the determined encroachment of our colored population, you have promptly taken the lead, and we know that it is due to your bold, outspoken, and unhesitating stand in matters of this kind that White Supremacy and all that it stands for still controls in Alabama." Such sentiments ignored the reality that at its peak TAAF had a population as large or larger than the town of Tuskegee, and its monthly civilian payroll alone exceeded $100,000—this, in one of the most economically ravaged counties of the most hard-hit region of the country in the Great Depression.[57]

Soon after the near race riot, Parrish was named base commander, replacing von Kimble, who received a promotion and a new command elsewhere.

When he assumed command of TAAF, Parrish later wrote, "There existed no precedent, no set of customs, no established procedures to guide military men in their efforts to build a functioning military organization in the midst of endless theorizing and uninformed discussion concerning racial characteristics and social proprieties."[58] He would surround himself with professional, pragmatic military men and make the best of the situation, but it was Parrish's individual attitude and his approach to the men he commanded that ultimately won him respect. In contrast to von Kimble and others, Parrish "thought of you as a man, just like he was a man," pilot John W. Rogers remembered. "He wasn't like one of these guys that are going to look down on you because you were black. That was the thing." Parrish quietly integrated TAAF's facilities within his first several months in command, backed by a new War Department policy that outlawed segregation in all base recreational facilities.[59]

In September 1942, Lt. Nora Green, a nurse at TAAF, travelled to Montgomery to go shopping before she was to ship overseas herself. Wearing civilian clothes, she bought a bus ticket to return to Tuskegee and boarded the bus. When the driver informed her the bus was for whites only, she refused to leave because, she told him, she was due back on duty at TAAF, and waiting for a later bus would make her late. Montgomery policemen beat and arrested her, then turned her over to TAAF authorities. If the MP incident offered the impression that the world outside TAAF's front gate was enemy territory, Green's experience only solidified it. Blacks stationed at TAAF did not leave the friendly confines of the base and Tuskegee Institute's campus unless they had to. Under Parrish's command, TAAF became a small, self-contained city.[60]

Robert L. Carter, a supply officer with the 96th Air Service Group, remembered his brief time at the base fondly. Carter had grown up in New Jersey and attended Lincoln University, Howard Law, and Columbia Law, and he was reunited at TAAF with several friends from his college days. He enjoyed his time at the station: "When I was on the base, I didn't have any difficulties," he recalled. "I was reunited with people I had known for some time, and we were just having fun because we were all preparing to go off to war, and you didn't know what was going to happen to you. So you're living your life at a very intense time there."[61]

In contrast, he explained, "The negative experiences would come from when you went off-duty." Carter found that when he went to Atlanta or "places like that, cops would try and prey on you. When you were coming back [to TAAF], they realized that you probably had liquor. If they caught you or stopped you, they would try to threaten you with jail, and then if you got out, they would try to shake you down for some money." Carter emphasized that he never had this experience personally. "I do remember being stopped, but fortunately we didn't have any liquor in the car, so they were frustrated," he said. But many others did have the displeasure of dealing with Pat Evans, the sheriff of Macon County, and they recounted similar experiences.[62]

Parrish assembled an upper echelon of white officers who were competent professionals and who, no matter what they personally thought about African Americans or the merits of segregation, proved that they could complete the mission they had been assigned. "I had some people working for me who were basically segregationist in their attitude, but they did their job," he recalled. "They did what was agreed necessary to make a contribution toward winning the war[.]" Speaking of the white officers who served under him at TAAF, Parrish said, "Nobody [was] assigned there who didn't want to serve there." Most volunteered for the assignment because they were originally from the area and wanted to be stationed near family, he recalled. "They were good men; they did a good job and were quite conscientious." Parrish tapped as his director of advanced training Maj. Robert Long, of the first family of Louisiana politics. Known affectionately as "Mother" Long (behind his back, at least) because his flock thought he watched over them like a mother hen, Long won respect from the pilots that placed him in a category with Parrish. Pilot Lee Archer concluded that Parrish and Long "were as fair as they could be under the system. They were crackers and rednecks, but they were fair."[63]

Fair or not, Parrish and Long worked within a system that continued to treat African Americans separately and unequally. Hastie had fought for two years to change the system from the inside, but in early January 1943 he again attempted to resign from his position at the War Department. He offered as his sole reason for the resignation the treatment of African Americans in the AAF. No longer could Hastie advocate effectively for democracy within the armed services, he felt; his "future usefulness" to the war effort, he wrote, "is greater as a private citizen who can express himself freely and publicly." Hastie objected specifically to eleven disparate instances of discrimination in the Air Forces, including the service's creation of a segregated officer candidate school; its refusal to acknowledge the excellent results that had accrued from the initial training program under relatively desegregated conditions at Chanute Field; and its refusal to admit blacks to specialized training programs such as those for weather observers and flight surgeons.[64]

Most importantly, Hastie charged that it had become impossible for him to reconcile the ideals that had once led him to support the war effort so totally with the present situation on the ground at Tuskegee. "The racial impositions upon Negro personnel at Tuskegee have become so severe and demoralizing that, in my judgment, they jeopardize the entire future of the

Negro in combat aviation," he wrote to the secretary of war. "Men cannot be humiliated over a long period of time without a shattering of morale and a destroying of combat efficiency." At the time of Hastie's memorandum, the 99th had been fully staffed, trained, and rated ready for combat for more than three months, but continued to fly the skies of central Alabama with no plans for overseas deployment.[65]

The AAF could offer no substantive answer to Hastie's charges. Stimson had refused Hastie's offers to resign in the past, but had little choice but to accept this time. He did so on January 31, 1943, and Hastie returned to Howard Law. Truman Gibson was named acting civilian aide, and he assumed the role permanently later that year. Gibson was an effective advocate in many ways that his predecessor had not been, his work made easier by the very public criticism Hastie leveled at the War Department. Indeed, Hastie's resignation had exactly the desired effect, spotlighting the effects of white supremacist attitudes in the AAF much more successfully than his work from within the system ever had. In 1946 Robert Patterson, who had been one of the few officials to work collegially with Hastie in the War Department before succeeding Stimson as secretary of war, said that advances in "[d]emocracy in the Army during the war [were] due largely to the effective, brilliant and sincere work done by Mr. Hastie."[66]

Hastie had told Stimson that he wanted to return to being "a private citizen who can express himself freely and publicly," but the secretary of war could not have imagined quite how free and public Hastie's expressions would be once he returned to civilian life. The judge made several published statements concerning the treatment of blacks in the armed forces and later in 1943 published a pamphlet titled *On Clipped Wings: The Story of Jim Crow in the Army Air Corps* under the auspices of the NAACP. He pulled no punches.[67]

He accused the Air Corps of having created the Tuskegee program and the separate, all-black pursuit squadrons only under duress. Three years after Roosevelt's surprise announcement in October 1940, the AAF still had not managed to define a function for the squadrons. The Tuskegee program had proved itself successful beyond doubt in preparing black aviators for service, but the AAF had only recently agreed to expand the program, and the 99th Pursuit Squadron still had not flown in combat.[68]

Hastie pitched his arguments in favor of a fully integrated Air Forces to the emergency at hand, but he was simultaneously speaking to the future. "It is simply impossible to maintain racial segregation of pilots in a combat area," he reasoned. "[T]he only sensible thing to do is to...[provide] interracial associations in training such as [pilots of every ethnicity] are bound to have later on."[69]

Hastie's incendiary pamphlet brought unwanted attention to TAAF. Among the most pressing of Parrish's duties in his first several months as commanding officer of TAAF was managing the press coverage of the base and its programs that resulted. Following soon on the heels of Hastie's resignation, the *Pittsburgh Courier* published a charge by an anonymous reporter who had recently visited TAAF that America's black air force was "not the splendidly functioning unit it ought to be." TAAF's commanders had created a beautiful new base of which all who worked there were justifiably proud, the *Courier* reported. But "officers and enlisted men [were] smoldering with resentment" that led to "dangerously lowered morale." All because "they feel that the Command at the post has tried to placate the hatred of a poor, insignificant little Southern town like Tuskegee, rather than assert the authority of the United States Army and protect the men at any cost."[70]

The sentiment surely existed in quantity, but Sgt. Charles M. Bowden, a Chicago native who had been at TAAF for fourteen months, objected to Hastie's actions and the black press's coverage of the Tuskegee program in general. Bowden wrote in a letter to the editor of the *Chicago Defender*, "I enlisted in the U.S. Army Air Corps...I never expected to conquer the universe. I just wanted to be a plain, ordinary American." Bowden understood that the editors of the *Defender* objected to racial segregation, but challenged them to stop "doing your d—est [sic] to tear down" the TAAF program just because "we of the Tuskegee Army Flying School are not going into town and tearing up everything in sight." He called out Hastie by name. "Your manner, to my estimation, is strictly un-American," Bowden charged. "Who do you think you are? The 'Liberator' of the American Negro? Don't make us laugh. How you, to whom this country has given so much, can desert your post in these critical times, beats me beyond all human understanding."[71]

During his assignment at the Coffey School in Chicago, Parrish had cultivated a personal friendship with Claude A. Barnett, the director of the National Negro Press Association. Barnett now introduced Parrish to the publishers of black newspapers, and Parrish invited several of them to the base to see its operations firsthand. In time he was able to turn the tide of negative press coverage.[72]

Even a cursory look at black newspapers of the period makes it clear that TAAF shouldered the hopes and dreams of literally millions of black Americans. Few weeks went by in the war years in which the major black press outlets did not contain some report of activities at TAAF or the combat exploits of the black Air Forces. The reports generated interesting responses from the public. For instance, a group of underprivileged black boys at the Wissahickon Boys Club of Germantown, Pennsylvania, learned of the pilots in late 1941 and insisted on sending the airmen hand-made Christmas gifts. According to the club's director, the thank-you notes the boys received in return from the men of the 99th impressed the lads beyond words. "If you could have witnessed the delight of the youngsters when those letters arrived!... Thanks again for helping us stress the idea of service to others," Laura M. Coleman wrote to TAAF. "My boys always end the story [hour] now with the prayer, 'God bless the soldiers everywhere.' Now they add, 'Especially the 99th Fighter Squadron.' "[73]

Despite the protests from men like Elmer Jones and Charles Bowden who insisted on being treated as individuals who could rise or fall on their own personal merits, the men and women of TAAF knew they were being watched by the wider black world. Roy Chappell recalled what the Tuskegee program meant for black civilians in personal, poignant terms. "There was one thing that happened to me that I didn't understand completely until maybe ten years or more after it happened. I went home to Monroe, Michigan, the first time I had a furlough. I went home in my uniform and everything. Here's this second lieutenant. And I had an older brother. He had a heart murmur and couldn't get in the service, and he was crazy about me and crazy about this idea that I was a lieutenant in the Army.[74]

"He says, 'Come on, I want to take you downtown. I want to see some of those folks salute you. We've got to go. We've got to go.' I didn't even want to do it. I said, 'Oh, that's just wasting my time.' But he insisted, so I said OK. We got downtown. And we'd run into white soldiers. They would salute and I would salute and everything. If he would see somebody across the street he'd say, 'Cross the street and make them salute.' Every time he would just fall out: 'Oh, that was good!' See another one, salute. Oh, he'd have a good fit.[75]

"What I realized later is that this meant so much to him, he was so proud of his brother, the things that I had accomplished and everything. He was really proud of it. The longer I live, the more I realize what that meant to him. At that time, anywhere we would go, seeing a black officer with wings was really unusual; people were really looking. That was one of the things that was driving all the guys to be successful, because it meant so much to everybody, to an entire race, to be successful. See, we can't be failing. Here we are with this great big chance to do something and fail? No. We had to be successful."[76]

Such mundane factors as providing basic living amenities for the men and women who worked at TAAF made achieving that success more difficult than it needed to be. The base faced a critical housing shortage throughout its short life. Initial plans called for roughly five hundred Air Corps personnel to be stationed at TAAF, but by 1943 nearly twice that many were fighting for living space on the base. Civilian employees were even more crowded, having found few rental options available in the black community of Tuskegee. The Federal Works Agency commenced construction on a thirty-unit "defense housing project" just to the west of Tuskegee Institute in 1942, though the entire project was not completed until 1944. TAAF completed a dormitory-style facility to house 145 civilian employees in 1943 and a one hundred-unit development, Mitchell Village, for civilian workers' families in 1944, but still could not meet demand. Like thousands of other American communities, Tuskegee was a very crowded place in the war years.[77]

Pearl Harbor was the turning point. Every one of the military branches expanded rapidly after the attack, the Army Air Forces most dramatically of all. For TAAF, which had been designed as a small flying school that would also serve as a base squadron, rapid expansion meant that the 99th would be joined by three additional fighter squadrons and a bomber group, all of which would have to be staffed by pilots and service crews trained at the airfield. What was initially planned as a relatively small facility with no more than five hundred men assigned to the base at any one time would have to expand, and in a hurry. By the end of 1942 TAAF was home to nearly 3,500 officers, enlisted men, pilot cadets, and civilian employees—a more than twenty-fold increase in one year's time—and it was still growing.[78]

TAAF expanded according to no discernable logic save that of Jim Crow. Had the base's sole reason for being been the training of combat pilots, it would have developed much differently than it did. Maj. Ambler's official history of the base's evolving organization put it plainly: "For a flying training station the Tuskegee Army Air Field has probably had the strangest aggregation of units imaginable." Not all of the units on the base fell under the post commander's direct supervision. Even worse, the post's administrative difficulties were complicated by what Ambler termed the "tendency" of every other command in the Army Air Forces "to drop their Negro problems in the lap of the Post Commander and then try to forget them."[79]

From an administrative standpoint, the base's two most intractable problems by 1943 were the presence of too many officers and too many washouts from the flight training program. Parrish and his executive staff engaged in a constant juggling act. At times twice as many officers had been assigned to TAAF as there were jobs available. Ambler wrote, "[I]t is impossible to find work for them so they are a constant liability."[80]

The problem of the 286 washouts who remained on the base in September 1943 was an especially prickly one. White cadets who were eliminated from flight training could be shifted into one of several other AAF specialties, but until then, for blacks it was service in the fighter group, the base command, or nothing, an arrangement that the black press portrayed as a grievous injustice. TAAF administrators worried that the washouts, few of whom could be put to productive work, posed an additional morale risk. Ambler wrote, "Vitally interested in all phases of flying...[t]hese men were living on a hope that some day something would be done to get them [back] into the air." Their hopes were realized in September 1943 when the Army Air Forces authorized the creation of an all-black bombardment group. The group's pilots were to be trained at TAAF. But the 477th would also need navigators, bombardiers, communications technicians, and any number of mechanical specialists, and the men who had been eliminated from flight training could be slotted into the new positions in training programs at TAAF and other bases. Of course, while activating the 477th solved one problem, it only added to the predicament of overcrowding on the base.[81]

Original War Department plans had called for TAAF to be staffed by a white commanding officer and white officers and non-commissioned officers at the highest echelons of the specialty training units. "All other duties will be filled by Negroes," the plans stipulated, "and [white] instructors will be relieved at such time as is found the Negroes may replace them." Hastie anguished in 1942—more than a year after the base's establishment— over the fact that not only were the white officers who had originally been considered temporary assignments to the base still there, but others had been transferred in to join them. TAAF had a surfeit of black officers, but the Air Forces demonstrated little urgency in moving them into positions of responsibility. The situation rankled black officers who perceived little opportunity for advancement.[82]

The problem was especially apparent in the Tuskegee-trained bomber group. By 1944 the officers of the 477th bombardment group had made so many complaints about officer advancement through official channels that the First Air Force launched an investigation into the group's poor morale. The problems, the investigation found, stemmed from black officers' belief that "Negro officers are qualified and should be advanced to [command] positions; that the stage of training has arrived when a minimum of supervision is required" by white officers. Col. Robert R. Selway, commander of the 477th, dismissed the complaints and received the full backing of his superior, Gen. Frank O'D. Hunter. The resentments simmered and would boil over the following year.[83]

Base facilities were desegregated soon after Parrish took command of TAAF, but complaints about overcrowding and delays in training black officers for supervisory roles could conceivably have damaged morale at TAAF overall. Instead, spirits generally remained high. The top-flight entertainment that passed through TAAF added to the community's cohesion. Many black performing artists toured the United States to entertain African American troops during the war, sometimes under the auspices of a black auxiliary to the United Service Organizations (USO), and a black soldier in a unit attached to an otherwise all-white base might see one of the acts once a year, if that often. Few other military bases in the country would have been able to offer the large, enthusiastic black audiences TAAF had on hand, so the base was a popular destination for entertainers.

World heavyweight champ Joe Louis, comedian Eddie "Rochester" Anderson, actor and singer Paul Robeson, and Hollywood star Lena Horne made visits. Highlights of the base's morale program in the first two years of its existence included concerts by Earl "Fatha" Hines and the Count Basie and Jimmie Lunceford orchestras. A national radio network broadcast the Louis Armstrong Band's performance from Hangar Two on the base as an episode of the Coca-Cola "Spot Light Band" program. The performers were impressed with what they saw at TAAF, too. Actress and singer Etta Moten, who was best known for her portrayal of Bess in George Gershwin's "Porgy and Bess" on Broadway, performed at the base in March 1942. "I had no idea that the field was so large," she told reporters. "This is the finest group of young men I have ever seen. I am so proud of them and am certain they will uphold the finest traditions of the air corps and the reputation for bravery which the American Negro soldier has always held."[84]

By the summer of 1943 the base also had its own dance orchestra, The Imperial Wings of Rhythm, and a well-appointed service club that served as the orchestra's home. (Shows at the service club must have swung. The Imperial Wings' drummer, Private First Class Arthur Herbert, formerly a member of the Coleman Hawkins Orchestra, was named one of the nation's seven best drummers in Esquire Magazine's 1943 readers poll before he was drafted into the AAF.) When they were not entertaining the troops, the Imperial Wings of Rhythm and Lt. Drye's 313th Army Band toured the South to support war bond drives and showcase the Tuskegee program before all-black audiences.[85]

Yvonne Plummer Terrelongue, a Tuskegee Institute graduate who spent many hours at TAAF in an official capacity as an assistant to local photographer P. K. Polk, also "went there almost every evening" for various social affairs or to shop. The base post exchange, she claimed, had a better selection of groceries and consumer goods for sale than any store in town. She reminisced about TAAF as though the social calendar there were always full. "A lot of people came there to entertain. We had everything," she said. "They were a lot of fun! Gosh, wouldn't you come and dance to Earl Hines?"[86]

TAAF had graduated enough pilots and trained enough specialists that the 99th Pursuit Squadron reached full strength by August 1942. A month later the squadron was placed on full alert and expected to be deployed at any moment. Awaiting overseas assignment, the pilots trained some more. And then some more. "The waiting got tiresome," Davis wrote. "The on-again, off-again deployment situation created confusion and inconvenience." While on alert the officers could not go on furlough, and qualified enlisted men could not enroll in officer candidate school. Both pilots and enlisted men had developed an intense pride in their bustling airbase, and their respective bonds grew even closer. As Charles Dryden, one of the original pilots of the 99th, remembered this period, "To me life at Tuskegee was mighty sweet." He referred to it as "the glory days in the nest of Black eagles."[87]

But six months passed, and morale among the pilots did suffer. "We trained and trained," Dryden's classmate Clarence Jamison recalled. "I had three hundred hours in the P-40. I'd take that fighter plane and do anything with it. We were good. We were flying some *bad* formations and acrobatics, practicing dogfighting, and everything." If anything, he said, "We were over-trained. The white classes were finishing, and they were sending them to the Pacific, to Europe, because they needed the pilots. But, hell, nobody seemed to want us."[88]

"Spratmo," the base grapevine, hummed with reports that the squadron would ship out any day now—or maybe in two months—to the Caribbean or for the air defense of Brazil or Liberia or to the China-Burma-India Theater or,—actually the men had no clue where they were headed. But the constant hurry-up-and-waiting, the uncertainty and fear, weighed on them. Davis worried that it would affect their readiness. Finally, word reached the base that the 99th would ship out via train to New York for deployment on April 1, 1943.[89]

4 Combat on Several Fronts

After flying on alert for roughly five months, the 99th Fighter Squadron and its support personnel finally received orders to leave TAAF in late March 1943—nearly two full years after the first cadet class began its training. Lemuel Custis knew that he and the other pilots were capable of finally putting their instruction to use, but when the orders arrived, he candidly admitted later, he was fearful. "At that time, the squadron's TO [table of organization] had been established, and we were up to strength as far as the TO was concerned. We had the personnel. We all knew that we were going, at some point in time, but we didn't know when. But when the official word came down, it was pretty traumatic." Their training had given them almost everything they would need to be successful overseas: the pilots of the 99th had amassed much more flying time than a typical white fighter pilot would have gained before being sent to combat, and they had achieved remarkable unit cohesion. "I felt a strong sense of being a part of a special group," Charles Dryden reminisced. "I felt an unusually strong bond, a linkage with each and every man of the squadron.... I was extremely proud to be a member of the 99th!" The one thing they lacked was experience. A typical pursuit squadron deployed overseas with at least a few combat veterans mixed in with the rookies, but because no black combat veterans were available and the War Department would not integrate squadrons, the new pilots of the 99th would be on their own.[1]

The squadron's 287 enlisted men and forty-two officers arrived by train at Camp Shanks, New York, on April 4, and disembarked by ship for North Africa on April 15. Col. Davis was ranking officer on the U.S.S. *Mariposa*, which in all likelihood made him the first African American officer in history to be responsible for white troops, of whom there were more than three thousand on board. "When he was introduced as the executive officer in charge of the ship, it looked like some of them could have just dropped," the 99th's adjutant officer, Bernard Proctor, recalled. The *Mariposa* had a relatively short, uneventful crossing to Casablanca, French Morocco, and before the month ended, the 99th's airplanes had arrived and the pilots had flown their first practice missions over North African territory.[2]

They flew in combat conditions for the first time two months later. In the meantime the men of the 99th hosted several curious visitors at their base on the outskirts of the town of Oued N'Ja and were the toast of nearby

Fez, where they socialized with the expatriate African American entertainer Josephine Baker. They trained with an unlikely mentor, Maj. Phillip G. Cochran, the prototype of Flip Corkin, swashbuckling hero of the popular "Terry and the Pirates" comic strip. Having flown against the Luftwaffe in the North African campaign, Cochran taught the airmen about German pilots' tendencies in combat along with several dogfighting maneuvers the pilots would use to great effect in the coming months.[3]

After moving to a new base at Cape Bon, Tunisia, in early June, the 99th flew its first tactical reconnaissance missions in brand-new P-40s. This was months after the Allied forces had pushed German forces under Field Marshall Erwin J. E. Rommel off the continent. "Where we were in North Africa, there was no fighting at that time," said pilot George Bolling of the 99th, "so it was ideal for training." Attached to the 33rd Fighter Group, 12th Air Force, under the command of Col. William ("Spike") Momyer, the squadron was slowly introduced to combat situations. The black pilots received minimal guidance from Momyer's outfit. Lt. Spann Watson, a pilot of the 99th, remembered the first and only set of preflight instructions he received from the 33rd before a combat mission: " 'You boys keep up.' That was our briefing." The enlisted men of the 96th Air Service Squadron, the 99th's maintenance cadre, so distinguished themselves in readying the brand-new P-40s for combat missions that several received Bronze Stars within months of their arrival.[4]

Lts. William A. Campbell, Charles B. Hall, James T. Wiley, and Clarence C. Jamison flew the squadron's first combat sorties alongside white pilots of the 33rd in dive-bombing missions against German installations on the Mediterranean island of Pantelleria as part of the Allies' Operation Corkscrew. After pushing the Axis armies from North Africa, the Allies intended to hopscotch across the Mediterranean and into Italy from the south. Neutralizing the heavy Italian and German fortifications on Pantelleria, midway between Tunisia and Sicily, would be a crucial first step in that effort. On July 2 Hall, who had interrupted his pre-med curriculum at Eastern Illinois Teachers College to join the AAC, became the first African American pilot to shoot down an enemy plane, a Focke-Wulf 190, in a dogfight over Sicily. Upon return to base he consumed the squadron's prize possession: the iced-down bottle of Coca-Cola that fellow pilot Lt. Louis Purnell had saved for weeks in the squadron safe for the occasion of the first enemy kill. The celebration was tempered, however, by the news that two pilots of the 99th, Lts. James L. McCullin of St. Louis, Missouri, and Sherman White of Montgomery, Alabama, did not return from the mission.[5]

Charles Dryden described the adrenaline rush and physical sense of relief he felt upon his "baptism by fire" in those first missions: "Up until that very moment I had harbored a fear deep within myself.... [but] I knew I had conquered my fear of possibly turning yellow and turning tail at the first sight of the enemy." On June 9 he was one of thirteen pilots of the 99th escorting American bombers back from targets on Pantelleria when several Messerschmitt 109s engaged them. At least eight of the pilots of the 99th remained with the bombers, but Dryden led a group of five who turned and attacked in formation, scattering soon thereafter to follow the retreating Germans in hopes of registering their first "kills." They did not shoot down any Germans that day. Breaking off to attack the enemy was an entirely common thing for rookie pilots to do, but the decision would reverberate over the months to come.[6]

In training Charles Dryden had spent countless hours wondering if he would be "a tiger or a pussycat," as he put it, when the time came to face the enemy. He later explained that the life of a fighter pilot was "boring, unless you are under attack by flak along the way or enemy fighters, and in those seconds you can experience terror depending on your circumstances. If you're on his tail, then it's sheer joy. They're very murderous thoughts, but that's the life of a soldier." He continued, "In no way can you think it's fun. War is terrible, war is horrible. There is nothing glamorous about it; it looks like it, but it is not. Especially in hindsight when you think about the fact if you have been involved in killing people, if you have any kind of human sensitivity, you begin to have some second thoughts about it."[7]

Dryden found the need to rationalize his actions. "At the time patriotism takes over. You're saying, 'I'm going to fight for my country, I'm going to defeat those so-and-so's.'" Fighting in the air, as opposed to in the trenches with all of the accompanying sights, sounds, and smells, had its advantages. "Even if I could see him, it was very impersonal because you're trying to shoot down a machine, you're not even thinking that there's a pilot in that machine. You're trying to down him before he downs you."[8]

The 99th saw much heavier action in support of the Allies' invasion of Sicily beginning in July, flying strafing and, with increasing frequency, bomber-escort missions in the 33rd Fighter Group as the Allied Forces aimed toward opening a front on the mainland of Italy. George Bolling was the victim of a friendly-fire accident in the Sicily campaign and ejected over the water; he spent nearly twenty-four hours in a dinghy. "Here I am in the Mediterranean," Bolling said. "In all directions: nothing! You have a lot of time to think, and you think about your mortality, and you think about your past experience, and you think about your friends. And you think about, most of all, God. So from that point of view, it was an eye-opener for me and a worthwhile experience. I learned a lot from it." He hitched a ride on an infantry landing craft that returned from Sicily to Tunisia a few days later.[9]

The 99th moved to a new airstrip on the Sicily beachhead; by August the Allies controlled the island. Momyer now assigned the all-white squadrons under his command to missions over the Italian mainland, leaving the 99th to patrol the Sicilian airspace that had been vacated by German fighters. The white squadrons racked up "kills" that the 99th had no opportunity to gain. "We went for months without seeing enemy aircraft," Spann Watson claimed. "Col. Momyer knew it. He waited until all of his squadrons had gained victories in the invasion of Italy, then criticized us" for lack of aggression. That criticism would nearly stop "the experiment" in its tracks.[10]

The following month Davis was transferred stateside to take command of the newly created 332nd Fighter Group, leaving Capt. George S. "Spanky" Roberts in command of the 99th. Truman Gibson, who had begun to hear reports of dissatisfaction with the 99th's performance from white commanders in theater, arranged for Davis to meet with the Washington press corps on September 10. Davis lauded his men for their performance in combat and the AAF for the excellent training the pilots had received. Davis surely went overboard in his praise of the latter; he told the assembled reporters that no unit had gone into combat with better training or better equipment than the 99th. He would come to regret those words. Above all, however, he emphasized the heavy sense of duty the men under his command shared. "All members of this organization were impressed at all times with the knowledge that the future of the Negro in the Air Corps probably would be dependent largely upon the manner in which they carried out their mission," Davis said at the press conference. "Hence, the importance of the work done by this squadron, the responsibility carried by every man, be he ground crewman or pilot, meant that very little pleasure was to be had by anyone until the experiment was deemed an unqualified success."[11]

The reports of the generals' dissatisfaction with the 99th that Gibson had heard leaked onto the pages of *Time* magazine on September 20. A news item tellingly titled "Experiment Proved?" reported on Davis's press conference and praised his military bearing but contradicted Davis's opinion of his men's fighting prowess. The 99th "has apparently seen little action, compared to many other units, and seems to have done fairly well; that is as far as anyone [in the Air Forces chain of command] would go," *Time* reported. "But unofficial reports from the Mediterranean theater have suggested that the top air command was not altogether satisfied with the 99th's performance."[12]

The news article prompted a response that Davis might have wished his wife could just keep to herself. "Are you justified in saying that the record of the 99th Fighter Squadron is only fair?" she asked in a letter to the editor. "My husband tells me that his judgment...is that the record of the 99th Fighter Squadron is at least worthy of favorable comment." Agatha Scott Davis charged that "by publishing an article based on 'unofficial reports' you have created unfavorable public opinion about an organization to which all Negroes point with pride." The editors responded, "TIME's 'unofficial reports' came from responsible sources which could not be quoted. Those reports—on operational results—raised no question about the Negro's fighting ability. If the 99th's record has been only fair, the blame must at least be shared by the Army Command responsible for the squadron's segregated training and operation. Perhaps too much was expected of such an experiment."[13]

Col. Momyer's report on the 99th—clearly the source of *Time*'s item—reached the War Department's Advisory Committee on Negro Troop Policies, better known as the McCloy Committee after its chairman, Assistant Secretary of War John J. McCloy, in early October. It portrayed the pilots of the 99th as wholly ineffective, even cowardly. "Their formation flying has been very satisfactory until jumped by enemy aircraft, when the squadron seems to disintegrate. Attempts to cover this deficiency so far have been unfruitful," Momyer claimed, though he based his sweeping conclusions on an alarmingly small sample size. He pointed to a single mission, Dryden's flight in which he and others "allowed themselves to become engaged" with German fighters when they should have been escorting American bombers back from Pantelleria, as evidence that the 99th pilots were undisciplined. "It is my opinion that they are not of the fighting caliber of any squadron in the group," he concluded. "They have failed to display the aggressiveness and desire for combat that are necessary to a first class fighting organization."[14]

Momyer's report, which had been channeled through Gens. Edwin J. House and Carl Spaatz in Europe on its way to Gen. Arnold's office in Washington, did not give Davis the chance to rebut the charges. House editorialized, "On many discussions held with officers of all professions, including medical, the consensus of opinion seems to be that the negro type has not the proper reflexes to make a first-class fighter pilot." He recommended reassigning 99th to coastal patrol in northwest Africa. Arnold was only too happy to share Momyer's report and House's recommendations with the McCloy Committee. He proposed that the 99th be removed from combat, that the entire 332nd be assigned to coastal patrol, and that the plans for the 477th be scrapped. The "experiment," in his mind, had been completed, and not successfully.[15]

Gibson arranged for Davis to testify before the McCloy Committee on October 16. He began by contradicting what he had previously said about the unit's training: "The squadron was handicapped in that no one in the squadron had combat experience" and was operating under a shortage of manpower. Davis expressed his dismay at the way Momyer's charges had come to his attention: "The report is a surprise to me—that the squadron disintegrates when jumped was brought to my attention only one time.... The reason for that failure was inexperience." But that criticism no longer held true. The pilots of the 99th were no longer greenhorns. "If there was a lack of experience, it was at first; later we had it," he claimed. "What's so disturbing," he continued, was that "this impression was not given me over there. I carried out my mission—if given a mission to bomb a target, I went ahead and bombed it."[16]

Davis's testimony refocused the black press's attention on the War Department's use of the 99th and galvanized black public opinion behind the squadron. The resulting publicity forced the War Department to acknowledge that Momyer's opinion was not the last word on the subject and that the 99th deserved an objective assessment of its performance. Gen. Marshall commissioned a study on the 99th's effectiveness. It concluded that there was "no significant general difference" between the 99th's performance and that of other fighter squadrons in the Mediterranean Theater of Operations. Meanwhile, Arnold was forced to admit that Momyer had denied the 99th significant opportunities to display the squadron's collective abilities in combat and that it would be unfair to kill the "experiment" based on a single combat mission.[17]

The War Department dictated that there would be no coastal patrol for the 99th. Instead, the squadron transferred to Foggia Air Field on the Italian peninsula near the Adriatic coast, attached to the 79th Fighter Group, in which its pilots more often flew alongside whites in combined actions.[18] In stark contrast to Momyer, group commander Col. Earl E. Bates saw to it that the officers of the 99th were integrated into the work of the group and treated them as equals. Bernard Proctor said, "We administrators met [in an integrated group with counterparts from the 79th] every day, and then the pilots flew together. For the first time, we were not black. We functioned, visited, did everything that the normal group would do."[19]

Walter White had a chance to witness the work of the 99th—and the difference that the squadron's attachment to the 79th made—at close hand when he toured widely through the European Theater of Operations as a war correspondent for the New York Post in 1944. White observed thousands of African American troops in Italy, the vast majority of whom were menial laborers, "unloading ships, repairing airfields, and driving trucks." He had talked with hundreds of disaffected black troops who chafed under discriminatory conditions nearly everywhere he went. (He would repeat the experience the following year when he toured the Pacific Theater.) But morale among the black laborers in

Italy was different, better than that of the troops he had seen elsewhere. "[T]here was a new pride among them because of the 99th Pursuit Squadron," he wrote. "Negroes were being given an opportunity to do something more than menial army chores," and the pilots of the 99th became symbols for other blacks in the service of what blacks could accomplish if offered a fair chance.[20]

"But to me," White reported, "the most remarkable development was the total obliteration of consciousness of difference in skin color among both white and black flyers of the 79th Group." He documented a 1944 incident in which white pilots of the 79th disobeyed an order from Lt. Gen. Jacob L. Devers, commander of the Mediterranean Theater of Operations for the AAF, and held a desegregated dinner party with dancing to celebrate the anniversary of the 79th's entrance into combat. "We have fought together for a year, some of our members have died together, and when we celebrate we are going to do it together no matter what the top brass says," White quoted the white pilots as saying. His observation of the 79th led him to develop a theory explaining why race relations were so much better at the front lines of the war. "I became convinced in Italy of the soundness of the formula which has almost mathematical exactitude," he explained, "that race prejudice flourishes in inverse ratio to proximity to actual fighting. The pettiness of race and creedal differences are sloughed off when men face sudden death."[21]

The 99th moved with Allied forces up the boot of Italy toward Rome. As late as January 1944, when the unit stationed at an airfield in Capodichino, near Naples on the Mediterranean coast, the 99th had still not particularly distinguished itself in combat. Charles B. Hall's remained the squadron's only kill. The late winter season of 1943–44 was an especially rainy one, and the men of the 99th spent more time in the mud than they did in the air. An eruption from nearby Mount Vesuvius further deteriorated flying conditions.

As quickly as it had appeared that Momyer's report would end the "experiment," however, the squadron's fortunes changed. With the other squadrons of the 79th Fighter Group, the 99th flew air cover in the Allies' Operation Shingle, the amphibious invasion of the central Mediterranean coast near Anzio. The assignment gave the pilots more chances to engage German fighters and the opportunity to earn recognition for the unit. The pilots of the 99th shot down twelve German airplanes over two January days. Robert Deiz, who would soon be immortalized on a poster encouraging black Americans to buy war bonds, and Buster Hall got credit for two kills each; Vash Eagleson and Lemuel Custis downed one apiece. They silenced for good the critics who had questioned the squadron's effectiveness. Even Gen. Arnold congratulated the 99th for its "very commendable" performance. But the increased opportunity for glory brought with it a new level of danger. The bulk of these missions involved dive-bombing defensive harbor fortifications. In addition to the Luftwaffe, the 99th had to contend with massive anti-aircraft installations. Lt. Samuel M. Bruce of Seattle died while attempting to crash-land his damaged P-40 on the Nettuno beachhead. He was the third of sixty-six Tuskegee-trained pilots who would die in combat in the Mediterranean-European Theater.[22]

Time gave the 99th due credit after the outburst: "Any outfit would have been proud of the record. These victories stamped the final seal of combat excellence on one of the most controversial outfits in the Army, the all-Negro 99th Fighter Squadron." Maj. Roberts spoke sagely of what the 99th's record in the Anzio campaign had proven: "We have not turned out to be super-duper pilots—but as good as the U.S. Army turns out," he told a magazine reporter. "That's important. Because we had one handicap: people assumed we were not producing because we were Negroes.... But now that we have produced, things have changed." *Time* also quoted a white pilot of the 79th, a Missourian: "They are a first-rate bunch, fighting the same war that we are." Lemuel Custis told a reporter from the *New York Times* a short time later, "When the Ninty-ninth first went over the general impression was that it was an experiment. Now I think the record shows that it was a successful experiment."[23]

Having at least achieved some combat experience and the respect of their peers, if not quite the glory they had aimed for, small groups of pilots from the 99th began rotating back to the states in the spring to provide combat crew training for the newly formed 100th, 301st, and 302nd pursuit squadrons at Selfridge Field, Michigan. (Along with the 99th, the three new squadrons made up the 332nd Fighter Group, commanded by Davis.) After the three new squadrons deployed overseas in January 1944, several of the combat veterans remained at Selfridge to work with the Tuskegee-trained pilots assigned to the 553rd Replacement Squadron who would replace the original pilots as they rotated back to the states. (AAF fighter pilots were supposed to rotate out of combat after fifty missions, but TAFS could not graduate a sufficient number of pilots quickly enough to make that possible for the 99th. Many of them flew more than one hundred missions before returning stateside.) "Our job was to teach these people coming out of flying school at Tuskegee what things you run into in combat: maneuvers and so forth and so on," recalled William A. Campbell, one of the first flyers to return to the states.[24]

Campbell and the others came back to the United States changed men. Lucius Theus, a personnel officer who remained stateside through the war, explained the transformation as he saw it:

What was very noticeable to me was a comfort in their position in life; in other words, knowing that they had succeeded and demonstrated that they could do their jobs well. They could point proudly to their records that clearly demonstrated that they were as good as anyone else, and so I think they exuded, if you will, a more confident attitude toward things.

We did not see the anxiety that you see in a new recruit, a person just coming in, wondering if they were going to make it and so forth. These young men had already...engaged in combat, they knew they were good, they were of course happy to have gotten back alive and all of that. So I think that the word would be they were much more confident in themselves.[25]

But the base commander at Selfridge, Col. William Boyd, insisted on classifying every black pilot on the base, including Campbell and the other combat veterans, as "trainees" or "transient personnel." Boyd was new in command of Selfridge; his predecessor had been abruptly court-martialed, reduced in rank, and removed from command of the base after he got drunk and shot his black chauffeur. The investigation into that scandal also revealed that base officers had arranged for powerful local whites (including Henry Ford's grandson Benson) to be transferred to Selfridge for "cream puff" duty, that noncommissioned officers engaged in widespread bribery and appropriation of government property, and that drunkenness was rampant in the base officer corps.[26]

The men who had trained at TAAF under professional conditions and effective leadership found Selfridge inferior in comparison. The returning pilots' anger over Boyd's classification scheme, a bald rationalization that allowed him to keep the base officers' club segregated, was especially intense. Campbell tired of arguing with Boyd and Lt. Col. Robert R. Selway Jr., the commanding officer of both the replacement squadron and (as of January 1944) the newly formed 477th Medium Bombardment Group, and volunteered to return overseas. He rejoined the 99th, rose quickly to the rank of captain, and had assumed command of the squadron by the time the war ended in Europe.[27]

Selfridge was roughly 25 miles from the racial tinderbox of Detroit. War industries brought more than two hundred thousand new residents to the city, more than half of whom were black, during the 1940s. The new black migrants moved into already crowded neighborhoods such as Paradise Valley and Black Bottom, whose dilapidated housing stock had, one former Detroit resident wrote, "a definite shortage of indoor plumbing." When they sought better living conditions in previously all-white public housing projects and neighborhoods, racial tensions began to boil. "Detroit is Dynamite," *Life* magazine reported in 1942. "It can either blow up Hitler or blow up the U.S." Those disputes erupted into a full-blown race riot in the summer of 1943, which resulted in the deaths of twenty-five blacks, seventeen of whom were killed by police, and nine whites, along with 675 serious injuries and nearly two thousand arrests. The riot cost Detroit an estimated $2 million in property losses and a million hours of absenteeism by war industry workers. Generals in the AAF began worrying about the danger posed by black airmen stationed so close to the city.[28]

At least one Tuskegee Airman, however, was glad to have been stationed at Selfridge. Alexander Jefferson grew up in a racially and ethnically mixed, mostly Polish American, working-class neighborhood of Detroit. After graduating from Chadsey High School in 1938 at the age of fifteen, he enrolled at Clark University in Atlanta, where he excelled academically. Jefferson graduated from Clark with a double major in chemistry and biology and minors in physics and mathematics. In 1942 he narrowly passed the AAF's physical exam—he had to guzzle water and devour bananas to meet the minimum weight requirement of 117 pounds—and was sworn into the Army Reserves. He arrived in Tuskegee in April 1943 as a member of the class of 44-A and graduated the following January. Jefferson's maternal grandfather, who had been born a slave in Georgia, lived to see his grandson in an officer's uniform of the Army Air Forces.[29]

Jefferson was assigned to the 553rd Replacement Squadron and transferred to Selfridge Field for advanced training in the P-39 Airacobra. He and his fellow pilot-officers made frequent visits to Detroit's black entertainment districts in Paradise Valley and Black Bottom. They were glad to have that outlet, mainly because "There were . . . beautiful young women to be found in the Valley . . . who found a group of cocky young fighter pilots, full of vim, vigor, and vitality, to be quite attractive." But Jefferson and his comrades also resented being prohibited from entering Lufbery Hall, the Selfridge officers' club. It was restricted to base personnel, but they were classified as transient personnel, as were all fifty of the men of the 332nd and their trainers, the combat veterans of the 99th, and the newly arrived members of the 477th Medium Bombardment Group. Nevertheless, they had to pay dues of $6 a month for the upkeep of an officers' club they could not enter.[30]

The pilots clearly chafed under the conditions they found at Selfridge. If the northerners among them expected that once they returned to the safe side of the Mason-Dixon line they would find less white supremacism and less segregation, that expectation went unmet. "[M]uch of the good South 'Nigger Discipline' has been carried over into the groups by men (White) who were appointed as supervisors of the fighter training," Milton Henry, a TAFS graduate and now an officer-pilot of the 332nd, complained in a report to the Philadelphia chapter of the NAACP. "For most of us who, like myself, are aggressive individuals capable of living competitive, free lives, this southern aggression theory is infuriating, and is only serving to retain [sic] the progress of the groups, and lessen any desire for any contact with the enemy." Henry made a laundry list of complaints on behalf of the pilots of the 332nd: they were occasionally forced to fly in bad weather or in aircraft they deemed unsafe, even though they routinely witnessed white pilots refusing to fly in such conditions. They were treated as enlisted men, with bed check at 10 p.m. and roll call every morning at the crack of dawn.[31]

Henry reached the breaking point when the AAF court-martialed and convicted Lt. Leroy Bowman for refusing an order to extend a night flight by twenty minutes after he had already flown for five and a half hours and developed back pain. Henry claimed that Bowman was well within his rights under AAF regulations. Court-martialing Bowman and placing him in a cell for such a minor infraction was, Henry charged, "positively unheard of in the history of the Army Air Forces," and asked the NAACP to take up Bowman's defense. He placed the incident in a larger context: "We want, and are trying as best we can, to prevent a rupture in our fighting effectiveness. We know their aim is to make it appear that we weren't worth a damn... [but] [w]e find it hard to fight against Tyranny in the midst of Tyranny." Bowman's case would drag on for more than a year before his sentence was commuted by President Roosevelt; Henry would be drummed out of the Air Forces within the year.[32]

Henry was hardly the only AAF officer to fight discriminatory treatment in Michigan and pay the ultimate price. Robert L. Carter was another. Carter was drafted in 1941, graduated from the Officer Candidate School of the Army's Quartermaster Corps, and received his commission as a second lieutenant in May 1942. In 1943 he asked for and received a reassignment to the 96th Air Service Group because he anticipated that it would soon be transferred overseas in support of the 99th, and he wanted to fight the Nazis. Carter joined the 96th at TAAF and soon moved with the unit to Michigan. In Carter's first eighteen months as an officer, he received one efficiency rating of "Superior," two of "Very Superior," and one of "Excellent." His duties in this period were various; in addition to his service as a supply officer for the 96th, he was a platoon commander, administrative inspector, and trial judge advocate. However, the group's treatment at Selfridge Field and an auxiliary field, Oscoda, complicated his plans for overseas service. Carter's insistence on equal treatment for blacks in the AAF earned him a reputation as a troublemaker. Rather than going overseas as planned with the 332nd, he was instead transferred into a dead-end position under Major Arthur P. Hayes at Alpena Air Base in Michigan.[33]

Hayes deemed Carter's service from October 1943 to January 1944 so unacceptable that he recommended the AAF decommission and dismiss the second lieutenant. The AAF court-martialed Carter on the basis of Hayes's bizarre allegations against him. (These included: "Lt. Carter complains of segregation and prejudice against the colored race.... It is reported that Lt. Carter has told enlisted men to 'do as little to get by as you can, and no more.'...The undersigned by chance caught a remark by another officer to the effect that after the war Lt. Carter planned to be 'An ambulance chaser.'") Carter's civilian defense attorney—none other than William H. Hastie—challenged the allegations and returned some wild ones of his own: "Major Hayes has represented his race as 'white' or as 'colored' as has served his convenience.... [This] reveal[s] traits of character to be considered in an issue of credibility between Major Hayes and another officer."[34]

The court-martial convicted Carter and discharged him from the service, but the Air Forces' loss was the nation's gain. The experience "made a militant of me and instilled in me a fierce determination to fight against racism with all my intellectual and physical strength," Carter remembered. Following his exit from the service, Carter went to work as an assistant counsel to Thurgood Marshall at the NAACP's Legal Defense Fund (LDF). He worked as a lead attorney on the LDF's landmark cases of the following two decades, including *Sweatt v. Painter* and *Brown v. Board of Education*. When Marshall left the LDF, Carter succeeded him as general counsel, a position he held until 1968. Carter won a remarkable twenty-one of the twenty-two cases he argued before the U.S. Supreme Court as an attorney for the LDF. In 1972 he followed Marshall to the federal bench, accepting an appointment to the U.S. District Court for the Southern District of New York.[35]

The unrest at Selfridge continued. Spurred on by active Detroit chapters of the NAACP and the Urban League, and by reporters from the local black newspaper, the *Michigan Chronicle*, the black officers at Selfridge tried to enter Lufbery Hall several days in a row; each time they were turned away physically. When it became apparent that they would not stop trying to use the club, Col. Boyd closed it and called for backup. On Thursday, May 4, Jefferson and several other trainees had their aerial gunnery practice interrupted by a radio announcement: "All officers report to the post theater, as you are, on the double!" The commander of the First Air Force, Maj. Gen. Frank O'D. ("Monk") Hunter had flown in to read the black officers of Selfridge Field the riot act. The men were restricted to base. Within forty-eight hours, the 332nd had been transferred, and the men were on a train headed for they knew not where. Charles Dryden, who had returned from Italy to Selfridge as a trainer, actually wondered, "Are we going to be interned the way the Japanese-Americans...had been only recently[?]"[36]

The troop train arrived the next day at what Dryden called "Godforsaken Walterboro Army Air Base" on the coastal plain of South Carolina. "When our train backed onto the base, we were greeted by white soldiers in full battle dress," Jefferson recalled. "There they stood, one every 30 feet along both sides of the train, with rifles and bayonets at the ready." Dryden and Lt. Spann Watson, native northerners who had swallowed their pride and allowed themselves to be Jim Crowed in Alabama because they had their eyes on larger prizes, who had risked their lives in the skies over North Africa and Italy then refused to abide by segregation as combat training instructors in Michigan, cracked at Walterboro.[37]

Segregation of base facilities was no better or worse, no more or less rigidly enforced, at Walterboro than it had been at Selfridge. What differed were the whites who could use the all-white facilities in South Carolina that were denied the combat veterans. Watson and Dryden were first perplexed, and then outraged, to see whites in uniforms with "PW" stenciled on the backs entering the whites-only area of the post exchange cafeteria. It slowly dawned on the instructors that the men were German prisoners of war housed on the base. "WE WERE INSULTED AND HUMILIATED IN OUR OWN NATIVE LAND!" Dryden later wrote.[38]

Dryden got himself in trouble over the course of a weekend after spending his first week at Walterboro stewing over the German POWs he saw using base facilities he could not. On a Saturday morning in June 1944 he demonstrated for his pupils in the 553rd the landing maneuver that Horace Bohannon so enjoyed showing off in Atlanta. It was strictly forbidden at Walterboro. Early the next morning he led a flight of four on a low-level navigation mission that ended with the aircraft "buzzing" the town's business district. Dryden's superiors charged him with violating the 96th Article of War—"conduct of a nature to bring discredit upon the military service." He was able to talk his way out of punishment for the buzzing incident, but the previous day's "grass-cutting" display had endangered troops and facilities at the air base. The guilty verdict in Dryden's first trial carried a sentence of dismissal from the service, but he got the sentence reduced on appeal. He would have to remain on base for three months, pay a hefty fine, and forego any promotions for a year.[39]

Watson got himself into an even more dangerous predicament. He had the local Ford dealership repair his personal car in January 1945 and somehow got into a dispute with the owner of the dealership. According to Watson, the dealer found Watson's attitude overly "uppity," so the dealer slapped him. Watson responded by punching the man. "He got up, and I floored him again," Watson recalled. "I beat the hell out of him." It was Watson's bad luck that the man he had beaten turned out to be the town's mayor. An angry mob assembled, MPs arrived, and Watson made it back to the relative safety of the base. The base commander gave him a choice: He could ship out for Italy with the next group of replacement pilots or he could transfer to the 477th, but he could not stay at Walterboro. Watson joined the 477th and transferred out the next day.[40]

Several enlisted men of the 96th Air Service Group had similar experiences while stationed stateside. Edmund L. Wilkinson, a native New Yorker, dropped his studies at the City College of New York in 1942 to enroll in a training program for aircraft mechanics. He trained and worked in programs in New York and New Jersey where he was one of a small handful of African Americans. Wilkinson was drafted in 1943 and assigned to Rome (N.Y.) Air Depot as an army private. Despite having already gained expertise in maintaining aircraft hydraulics, Wilkinson was assigned to a labor battalion that dug ditches and cleared forest areas around the base. When the opportunity to volunteer for the 96th ASG arose, Wilkinson took advantage of it and transferred to Oscoda. He was assigned to base accounting—"and I hate accounting," he said. Being so close to the members of the 332nd combat crew flying airplanes and the other members of the 96th ASG who got to work on them was agonizing. But after a month Wilkinson was able to transfer again, into the 367th Air Service Squadron of the 96th. "Ah boy," he said, "I was home then. They couldn't hurt me no more." The 332nd was preparing to ship out for Italy and transferred to Camp Patrick Henry in Virginia, the port of embarkation, shortly after Wilkinson joined the maintenance squadron in December 1943.[41]

Wilkinson recalled an incident at Camp Patrick Henry that Davis glossed over in his memoirs, in which the enlisted men of the 96th and several officers of the 332nd nearly rioted when they refused to be segregated at the base movie theater, and authorities used violence to disperse them. "[T]he general feeling," he said, "was that if that was the way we were going to be treated going overseas, we'd stay here and fight the war." Wilkinson recalled that the enlisted men stayed up late one night discussing how they might obtain ammunition for the empty rifles they had been issued, but an officer made an impassioned plea: "Don't do this. Whatever it is we're going to do when we get overseas, it will vindicate the black people. It will make this incident seem stupid."[42]

"I guess at about 1:30 in the morning we heard a bullhorn, and we looked outside, and here was the base provost martial with a bullhorn on a 6-by-6 truck with a .50 caliber machine gun on it, mounted on a swivel rack," Wilkinson remembered. "And he's telling us that we are restricted to quarters and anybody that leaves the quarters is subject to get shot. And that was the end of our insurrection." Their ship, the S.S. *Josiah Bartlett*, embarked the next day. The incident did not "come as a culture shock," Wilkinson said. People had told him he would be treated that way in the South. But that knowledge "didn't take away the pain; it didn't take away the hurt or the anger. It just made you—I wouldn't even say it made you resolved to do better or do something about it. All it did was make you want to get away from that situation. Frankly, we were glad to get overseas because we figured it couldn't be any worse over there than where we were."[43]

Wilkinson was aware of Double-V ideology that combined patriotism with civil rights consciousness, but because of incidents like the one at Camp Patrick Henry, he said, "That didn't operate for us. Whatever we did, we did out of our own inner pride of self [and out of] being happy that we did have black pilots and we wanted their planes to be absolutely perfect. We did it out of that kind of a thing. Not patriotism, if you would call it that. We were not patriotic because they took that away from us. How could you be patriotic to a country that did that to you?"[44]

The 100th, 301st, and 302nd fighter squadrons and their accompanying service squadrons arrived at full strength in Italy in February 1944, making the 332nd Fighter Group operational. The group moved to Ramitelli Airfield on the Adriatic coast and joined the 15th Air Force late in May. Flying brand-new P-51 Mustangs with distinctive bright red tail markings from Ramitelli's pierced steel-planked runways, the group flew bomber escorts for the 15th Air Force, the missions for which the pilots of the 332nd would later achieve some measure of fame, for the first time in July 1944.

Gen. Nathan Twining, commander of the 15th Air Force, oversaw a strategy that used U.S. bombers based in Italy to pound away at German industrial targets, and he believed that the attrition rate was too high in his bomber groups as they flew deep into Axis-held territory. He impressed upon Davis the importance of providing fighter escort, as opposed to "happy hunting"—seeking out individual German fighters to rack up "kills." (It was a typical maneuver for an individual German fighter to draw escorts away from the bomber stream so that others could ambush the bombers.) Woodrow Crockett, a pilot of the 100th Fighter Squadron, explained the calculus:

> A fighter, German or U.S., only cost $50,000 [and] one man. A B-24 or B-25—it costs $225,000, with ten, eleven people in it. Late in the war one outfit one day went out and shot down nine enemy Focke-Wulf 109's: $50,000 times nine and only nine people. [However, at the same time] they lost seven B-17s with eleven fully combat-ready people in each airplane. [That's] no kind of tradeoff, and [there is] no way you could ever win anything with that kind of ratio.[45]

Davis, in turn, demanded that his pilots provide the effective shepherding. Several pilots recalled him advising, "Don't come back if you lose a bomber."

In February 1944 the 99th separated from the 79th and joined the three other all-black squadrons of the 332nd; not everyone in the squadron was happy to be leaving an effectively integrated group to be segregated again. By the end of the year the pilots of the 332nd had impressed their counterparts in all-white bomber crews. "Unofficially you are known by an untold number of bomber crews as the Red Tails who can be depended upon and whose appearance means certain protection from enemy fighters," Col. Davis informed the pilots of the 332nd that December. "The bomber crews have told others about your accomplishments, and your good reputation has preceded you into many parts where you may think you are unknown." He continued, "The Commanding General of our Fighter Command has stated that we are doing a good job and that he will so inform the Air Force Commander. Thus, the official report of our operations is a creditable one." When not providing bomber escort, the pilots of the 332nd typically struck at rail traffic and infrastructure throughout Central Europe; they also provided air cover for invasions of southern France and Greece.[46]

Alex Jefferson's group of replacement pilots arrived just in time for the 332nd's transition to the brand-new red-tailed P-51s. Jefferson remembered some of his bomber escort missions in great detail, but by the time he published his memoir in 2005 he had forgotten most of the particulars of his first eighteen missions. In contrast, his nineteenth, his first strafing mission, was more than memorable enough. A German antiaircraft battery shot Jefferson and at least two other pilots of the 332nd down while they were attempting to take out radar stations at Toulon, on the southern coast of France. The other pilots on the mission had seen Jefferson's aircraft go down but they did not see him exit; in Detroit his parents received a telegram that he had been killed in action. But Jefferson escaped his burning aircraft and parachuted to dry land—"right in the middle of the 20-mm gun crew that had shot me down." He spent the next nine months in German POW camps.[47]

The German intelligence officer who debriefed Jefferson at a central interrogation center surprised him by producing a thick file on the 332nd Fighter Group. According to Jefferson, the officer picked Jefferson's face out of a group photograph of his graduating class at TAAF; told him how much Jefferson's father earned as a laborer at the Detroit Lubricator Co. and how much he paid in property taxes for the family's home; and even remarked on Jefferson's college grades. He was shocked to learn that the Germans had a copy of the ten-hour inspection report for his P-51 *Margo*, which had been completed the morning of the day he was shot down over France. "The Germans had to have had somebody at Ramitelli Air Base or higher up the line who was giving them information," he ruefully assumed.[48]

Jefferson persevered through nine months in POW camps and kept notes and a sketch pad that served him well when he later reconstructed the ordeal. Two experiences stood out in his memory. The first occurred on his first day at Stalag Luft III, a camp holding five thousand American and British air officers who had been shot down over German-occupied territory and where the inmates were allowed to choose who would live in their barracks. Jefferson was picked out of a lineup by a "dyed-in-the-wool-cracker with the deepest southern drawl imaginable" with these words: "Ah think I'll take this boy." Jefferson soon learned why: His new roommates hid escape materials in the barracks, and they wanted to make sure that they were not bringing a German spy into their midst. "At home," Jefferson mused, "black soldiers caught hell from SOBs just like the guy who had selected me. Now, five thousand miles from home, they can trust a black man because they are scared to death of a strange white face. Ain't that a bitch!"[49]

The second event brought Jefferson closer to the majority of the officers with whom he was confined, men who "had been prisoners for more than two years and had no idea that blacks were now pilots and officers in the Army Air Corps." One day a crewmember of a B-17 that had recently been shot down arrived in camp and embraced Jefferson. "You're a Red Tail!" the man enthused. "If the Red Tails had been with us [on our last mission], we'd have made it back home! You guys saved our asses so many times!" Following the encounter, Jefferson, wrote, he and the eleven other members of the 332nd in the camp were treated more or less as equals.[50]

Accounts from members of other bomber crews corroborate the B-17 crewman's claim. Larry Fleischer, a New York Jew who was drafted at the age of eighteen, trained as a navigator-bombardier and joined an all-white, ten-man crew in the 777th Bomb Squadron based just south of Ramitelli, recalled his experiences flying under the protection of the 332nd. Compared with other all-white squadrons who provided bomber escort, the pilots of the 332nd "stayed up close," he said. "They didn't get way out. A lot of times, those [other] guys were so far out that if some aircraft came out of the clouds, they wouldn't have been able to get over there quick enough. [But] they escorted us."[51]

Fleischer and his crewmates discussed what made the Red Tails different. "I mean, you can't tell what the color of the pilot is when he's got his helmet on and everything, but we never knew that they were black. We just knew that they were there," he remembered. "We couldn't figure out why are these guys so damn good, and all the [other] guys just come out there, they leave early, before we're not completely out of enemy territory. And here are these guys—I mean, when we would see them we'd say, 'Man, we've got it made today,' because they were right there, all the time.

They were our lifesavers." The co-pilot of Fleischer's crew, George G. Barnett, concurred: "They just gave us comfort, where the other escorts didn't. You know, we were glad to have the other escorts, but we would have preferred to have the Red Tails escorting us. But goodness, there were a dozen fighter groups [operating out of the area]. We couldn't get Red Tails all the time. They went with other groups some of the other times."[52]

Fleischer's crew learned of one significant factor, the color of their skin, that made the Red Tails different when the crew was forced to make an emergency landing following a bombing run on industrial targets on January 20, 1945. "The mission was to Linz, Austria," Fleischer recounted. "Linz sits at the [northern] base of the Alps. In other words, from there on, going south, it's all Alps," he said. "We got hit by antiaircraft flak going over the target; they hit us in the bomb bays. We couldn't close the bomb bay doors. Two of the four engines were hit." Because of the damage to the bomb bays, it fell to Fleischer to release the bomber's payload manually. The plane was flying at roughly 150 miles per hour, 25,000 feet over the Alps, so the temperature of the air coming through the bays was approximately 60 below o. Fleischer had to make several attempts at jettisoning the 100-pound bombs, and in the course of his efforts he lost a boot; the resulting case of frostbite continued to bother him at the time of his 2001 interview.[53]

The crippled B-24 made it back over the Alps and crossed over Yugoslavia and the Adriatic, but could not summon the power to make it all the back way to the crew's base. Pilot Murl D. Brown spotted an unknown airbase just off the Italian coast and successfully landed the damaged plane. Fleischer said, "Before the plane hit down, we really were expecting it to be [an abandoned] German field because [otherwise] why wouldn't it be on one of our maps? I mean, it was so secret they didn't even have it on our map, and we were supposed to have the latest maps." To the crew's unending surprise, "here were all these Red Tail P-51's" parked off the runway. Brown had landed at Ramitelli.[54]

"So when we land there at Ramitelli and see those Red Tails—man! And these are all black guys! It was complete shock," Fleischer recalled. He was stunned, "Because in my experiences up to that time, as far as black people, the only black people I ever saw in the military was when I was at Ellington Field [Texas]. They were in the kitchen. They were cooks, and they served the food, and that's the only black guys I ever encountered in the military. And here they were." The existence of black pilots in the Army Air Forces was, he said, "more secret than the atom bomb! I mean, nobody knew about it." Francis X. Connolly, a gunner in the crew, was equally surprised: "All these trucks and jeeps came up with black men in them, in

American uniforms. All these black men spoke English. We didn't know exactly where we were."[55]

Fleischer entered the Ramitelli base hospital to have his foot treated, and the crew's remaining enlisted men moved into six-man tents with members of the Ramitelli ground crew. The officers—Brown, Barnett, and navigator Stan Kay—were shown to officers' quarters and offered beds. According to Barnett, Brown asked, "Who sleeps here?" Their escort from the 332nd answered, "One of the pilots who's on R&R." Brown (again, according to Barnett) replied, "I'm not sleeping in any bed a nigger's slept in."[56]

Fleischer continued, "I didn't find out until years later that Murl D. Brown went out and slept in the airplane that night, which I can tell you was pretty cold. And the next night he decided it wasn't that bad, and he actually did sleep in that bed." Unlike Brown, Barnett loved the accommodations, in contrast to those at his regular base. There, he said, "We didn't even have heat in the tent we lived in in the wintertime. We just slept in our clothes and slept in as many blankets as we could get on us." The men at Ramitelli had built their own heaters and made life more bearable in other ways. "They had an old Italian barn that they converted to a theater," Barnett remembered. "And about every night of the week you'd go over there, and anybody who could do anything got up on stage and performed. They had a small orchestra, comedians." He mused, "They knew how to live better than we did. Their food was a notch better than ours. I think they must have traded with the local Italians for eggs and beef and things like that. They had things that we never had that I wished we had." Even Brown came around. The crew spent nine days at Ramitelli, and as they loaded up in the back of a troop-carrier truck to return to their base, Barnett remembered that Brown turned to him and said, "You know, George, they're not so bad after all, are they?"[57]

Of course, not all stories of forced intimacy between white and black Airmen had such happy endings. Inclement weather had forced a different bomber crew to spend the 1944 Christmas season at Ramitelli. The Tuskegee Airmen did not remember that visit pleasantly. Louis Purnell was the base censor at Ramitelli, and when he read one of the crew member's letters home he found the words, "Dear . . . The most sentimental time of the year is approaching. It makes my heart bleed to know that I'll not be with you at Christmas. May God speed the end of this war. . . . [I]t's bad enough I'm not on my own base. I'm stranded at a nigger base, eating nigger food and sleeping in a nigger bed."[58]

But in general, emergency landings did have the unintended effect of breaking down segregation. Edmund Wilkinson's service squadron joined up with the 332nd at Capodichino. Rather than moving to Ramitelli when the group moved there, however, he was assigned to a detachment at an emergency field at Falconara, roughly 200 miles up the Adriatic coast. "[O]ur role was to make a place for these planes to land and then do whatever we needed to do to treat the crew if they were injured or the plane was busted or whatever the heck happened. If it was fixable we'd fix it. If it crashed and burned, well, we'd just use the parts for part supply or whatever." The group serviced planes from the 332nd and all-white fighter squadrons of the 15th Air Force, but also crippled bombers that could not make it back to their bases, along with the occasional British or Canadian airplane.[59]

"Now, we were dumped cold into planes—B-17s, B-24s, B-25s, A-26s— dumped cold into that and expected to fix them," Wilkinson said. "And we did fix them! It was a very rewarding experience to be able to translate out of your head. Of course, we had the tech manuals—you could always get the tech manual; if there was something confusing, you could go look it up. But you had that basic skill. All the guys, the propeller specialists, the engine specialists, sheet metal man, whatever it was they learned, they learned well." A black medical detachment patched up any injuries the pilots and crewmen might have sustained, and the quartermaster corps fed and housed them until the mechanics could get their aircraft flying again. "And so that turned out to be a very interesting thing," Wilkinson said, "because there you have integration under war conditions."[60] Walter White's mathematical formula—"race prejudice flourishes in inverse ratio to proximity to actual fighting"—proved accurate again.

Segregation broke down in Europe in many ways. "The life of enlisted personnel of the ground crew in the U.S. Army Air Corps is very drab at times," a unit history recorded, but the rare trip to one of the Italian hotels or resort areas that had been requisitioned for rest and relaxation camps could go a long way toward relieving the tedium. This was so in part because "[t]he esprit de corps that existed among the negro and white troops" in the camps "was admirable." Another sort of esprit de corps seems to have been apparent in the camps as well: the group's flight surgeon, Dr. Vance Marchbanks, dispensed thousands of condoms between the 332nd's arrival in Italy and VE Day, but venereal diseases remained a challenge to the group's effectiveness.[61] Officers could wangle leave for an R&R camp near Naples. Joe Louis, the heavyweight champion of the world, visited the camp, and the men found other ways to pass the time. Enlisted men traveled to Rome and points beyond. William Surcey and a group of resourceful airplane mechanics and welders even made a boat out of spare parts in their downtime. The *Miss Adriatic* floated on excess fuel tanks and had an air compressor for a power plant.[62]

The men needed such outlets, because their work was grueling. Charles E. McGee, a replacement pilot of the 302nd Squadron who joined the 332nd in Italy in January 1944, flew more than fifty bomber-escort missions (out of the 136 total missions he flew in the war) in a little more than eighteen months. He described an escort mission from Ramitelli to the Ploesti oil fields in present-day Romania that fed the German industrial machine, an immensely valuable target at this point of the war, from the perspective of a fighter pilot. "Your day starts pretty early," he said. "The wake-up call for the pilots would be, say, 5:30 in the morning. You'd have a half hour to get up, throw some water on your face, get coffee, go get food and so on, so that you could report to operations, say, by 6:15."[63]

A short intelligence briefing provided information on the composition of ground forces in the area. "You'd get your operations briefing," McGee said. "By 6:30 you're going to personal equipment and putting on your gear that you're going to need for your mission. And by 6:45 you're at the flight line with all your information." A conversation followed with the airplane's crew chief. "And of course he probably got awakened at 4 to go get the pre-flight done and begin to get the aircraft ready and be sure the armament and all of that's done." He continued, "You're strapped in the aircraft at five minutes of seven, and get the signal, and your flight starts up and taxis out so that by 7:10 the takeoff rolls start."

Under normal operations pilots took off in pairs and circled the field once. As a given squadron's entire flight of eighteen aircraft (two of whom were spares) took off, "The lead would make a great big circle. By the time he made a circle around the field, heading out in the direction of the bombers, everybody is pulling in." He continued, "As you're climbing out you're in fairly loose formation, but everybody is keeping an eye out as you approach the rendezvous point. We'd climb out across the Adriatic, but our rendezvous point with the bombers might be along a river just into Yugo-slavia or the Yugoslav-Romanian border." McGee explained, "You'd begin to look for your bomber stream, and, of course, you're at the rendezvous point to be with them, based on the intelligence you've been given and what they might expect from the enemy."

If all four squadrons participated in a given mission, "We'd have sixty aircraft in the air. But you might have one squadron on one side of the bomber stream, and, of course, they're strung out for miles in their flights, because there could be more than one bomb group going." One squadron might have responsibility for defending Luftwaffe attacks from the side; another might have top cover. "If you ever heard the term 'swivel neck,'" McGee said, "that's a fighter pilot."

McGee was never relaxed on the missions, he claimed, but "I didn't find any fright in it because the training pretty well set you up for what you wanted to do. We had good briefing leadership and great respect for Ben

Davis. These were folks that we respected. And we were ready. We had been trained to do the job. Let's have at it. Let's do it."

McGee recalled B. O. Davis's directions regarding bomber protection. "Davis said, 'If you go happy hunting and haven't been dispatched, you're going to be in trouble if you come back before me. Our job is to protect the bombers.' 'Happy hunting' is if you get a report that there's enemy aircraft in the air and you go leave your bombers, trying to find the enemy. You don't know where they are. That's just what the Germans wanted in some cases, because they could have somebody just sitting there, waiting for you to leave and go on. They used decoys."

By that point in the war the Luftwaffe had been all but crippled, but "Every once in awhile you did have a dogfight. Combat happens pretty rapidly, because once you start after somebody and see him, you're trying to maneuver. You're also looking. You hope your wing man is keeping your tail clear. And suddenly you're diving or climbing." McGee described one instance in detail:

In this one particular case I chose to dive down, and of course I'm following him, trying to get a bead on him, and the next thing I know, we're down right over his airfield. In fact, that's my last memory as I got a shot into him. He's turning. The airfield had already been bombed. There were a number of fires. A hangar was on fire. And as I'm coming in and got a shot on him, he went off in a right turn into the ground, and I'm gone, and only a couple of minutes had passed from the time when the whole thing started. Maybe two and a half. I didn't put a stopwatch on it. But, again, you're on the move. Again, you don't know whether somebody's on your tail. So you climb immediately back out, and you're jinking around to avoid any ground fire if there is any, and climb back out to altitude and join back up if they haven't gone too far, or head for home. In my case I ended up heading for home. After I got up to altitude and the bomber stream, everybody had moved on too far for me to be able to climb back up and catch them. Head for home.

"The average mission was four and a half hours," he said. "It's a pretty small working area to spend that much time there. But you learned to shift around. In fact, I used a British parachute because their seat packs were much more comfortable than ours were. I've spent six and a half hours in a P-51 cockpit." A few of the 332nd's missions took them deep into German-held territory. "Some of the missions were very tiring. When you come back, you've sweated a bit. I mean, it's a working mission. When you come [home], it might be 1, 1:30, something like that." The post-flight routine amounted to preflight in reverse. "When you land, you go fill out your form on the aircraft, tell the crew chief if anything was wrong, then you go to get rid of your personal equipment, hang it back up, and go to intelligence. That's where you get the debriefing, the critique of the mission, and they go through the whole mission, from your takeoff all the way through—if you had anything to report, any problems, they'd critique it all the way through. Do a mission report on that. Get through the intelligence briefing, get your shot of liquor, and you're free."

Roscoe Brown, a pilot who earned his wings at Tuskegee in March 1944, was assigned to the 100th Pursuit Squadron. He joined the group as a replacement pilot at Ramitelli and flew his first combat missions in August 1944. The son of a dentist who was responsible for overseeing the U.S. Public Health Service's programs for black Americans during the Roosevelt administration, Brown had attended the same Washington, D.C., public schools that educated such members of the Talented Tenth as Judge Hastie and Dr. Charles Drew. He entered the Army Air Forces the day after he graduated at the head of his class from Springfield College in Massachusetts. Brown had been exposed to segregation in Washington, he recalled, but never internalized its messages. "That's what they taught you at Dunbar High School: that you had to be better to be equal, and that you can be good and you've got a long history and heritage of being good. Every day in my school was Black History Day." Speaking of his fellow pilots who had grown up in similar environments, he said, "We were a pretty cocky group of people—confident bordering on cocky—but you almost had to be."[64]

When Brown joined the 332nd at Ramitelli, the Allied air forces were pounding away at the German interior. Following the successful invasion of the Italian peninsula, Allied troops had invaded France and were pushing toward Germany from the west; the Soviets had turned the tide on the eastern front and begun their own offensive. The 15th Air Force, based in Italy, was streaming up from the south to bomb industrial targets within Germany and in occupied areas in an effort to destroy the German empire's war economy and hasten its surrender. By mid-1944 the German Luftwaffe was a shell of its powerful former self, but it still provided effective defense. The bombing runs remained dangerous for Brown and his fellow escort pilots. "The way we saw it, our job was to protect the bombers, not to become heroes," he said. "We knew that if we let the bombers get shot down, even if we shot down a lot of fighters, we would probably lose our opportunity to fly. The race factor was there all the time."[65]

Brown proved to be a gifted airman. On March 24, 1945, he and other pilots of the 332nd participated in the longest mission in the history of the 15th Air Force, rendezvousing with B-17 bomber groups based in Italy and escorting them the 1,600 miles to Berlin. After the bombers had unloaded their payload on their intended target, the Daimler-Benz tank factory, Brown turned around to escort them home when he noticed unidentifiable "streaks" overhead. They turned out to be Messerschmitt 262s, the first jet aircraft deployed in combat. Brown's P-51 could not climb fast enough to engage the jets on their own terms, so he dove. When a Me-262 followed, Brown was able to engage it from underneath, fire, and destroy it. He was one of the first American pilots to shoot down a jet.[66]

What most Tuskegee Airmen remembered about the mission was not Brown's prowess in the air, however, but the derring-do of the maintenance crews that made it possible. The 332nd learned of the "max effort" mission at 10:30 the evening before it was to take place, less than nine hours before takeoff. The P-51s' combined inboard fuel tanks and standard 75-gallon auxiliary tanks limited their flying range to far less than 1,600 miles and would not have allowed the 332nd to fly the mission. So several members of the 96th Air Service Group found and stopped a train hauling 110-gallon auxiliary tanks, brandished their weapons, and "requisitioned" the larger tanks. The flight crews worked overnight to deploy the tanks, making the 332nd operational for the mission, and the so-called "Great Train Robbery" was memorialized in Tuskegee Airmen lore.[67]

The 332nd flew its last combat mission on April 26, 1945, when six pilots of the 100th and 301st fighter squadrons shot down four German airplanes. The Germans surrendered two weeks later. The pilots of the 99th and 332nd had flown more than 15,000 individual sorties in 1,500 missions in their two years in combat, including the 311 bomber escort missions that did so much to hasten the German surrender. They destroyed or damaged 136 German planes in the air and another 237 on the ground, along with nearly a thousand rail cars and transport vehicles and, most incredibly, a German destroyer. Thirty-two Tuskegee-trained pilots were shot down and captured as prisoners of war; sixty-six were killed in action.[68]

One of the latter was Lt. Walter D. Westmoreland of Atlanta. "He was a Georgia boy, the youngest of four children," Walter White wrote of his nephew and namesake in a moving remembrance. "He, like me, could have passed for a white man." Westmoreland, who had earned a master's degree in economics from Atlanta University before joining the AAF in 1942, "hated war, he loathed killing," White wrote. "But he believed that Hitler and Mussolini represented the kind of hate he had seen exhibited in Georgia by the Ku Klux Klan and the degenerate political demagogues. He believed that the war would bring all of that hate to an end." Westmoreland had been shot down in the Anzio invasion, bailing out and breaking his leg in two places. He refused an opportunity to return home, recuperated in a field hospital, and resumed flying. Westmoreland was shot down again over Hungary in a bomber-escort mission in October 1944; his comrades last saw his airplane striking a tree and bursting into flames.[69]

The War Department recognized how successfully the Tuskegee Airmen had protected the bombers; one press release credited the fighter group with having flown more than two hundred escort missions without ever having lost a bomber under its care to enemy fighters. The "Never lost a bomber" claim would develop a life of its own. Later, historians questioned the assertion, but the Airmen had demonstrated objectively that they performed every bit as well on average as all-white groups. Based on that performance, the Tuskegee Airmen did not expect to return home to a United States that had changed dramatically, but they did expect that their service would be honored. They knew that they had not killed Jim Crow, but many took it as a given that they would receive a greater measure of respect within the flawed system. After all, they had earned it by risking their lives for their country. Many, like Charles Hall, hoped that at the very least they would be able to pursue their dreams of careers in the flying business. "Some of us are interested in military aviation and others in commercial, but we all want as broad a span of opportunity as we can get," he said. Lemuel Custis concurred and suggested that the returning black veterans would not just ask politely for what they believed they had earned. "When they come home they expect to get some of the things they've been hearing about and fighting for," he told a reporter in June 1944. "I believe they will be both aggressive and progressive about it all."[70]

Alex Jefferson certainly did not remember his experience as a POW fondly, but he did recall that the German officers he encountered were infinitely more respectful toward him than average whites in the Army Air Forces were. Patton's army liberated Stalag Luft VIIA, to which Jefferson had been moved when the Russians approached Stalag Luft III from the east, in April 1945, and he made his way home. When his troop ship, the U.S.S. *Lejeune*, arrived in New York Harbor, Jefferson was filled with intense patriotism and "indescribable jubilation." Then he disembarked. "Whites to the right, Negroes to the left," the private at the bottom of the gangplank instructed. "Back to the so-called good old days," Jefferson thought to himself. "Back to the United States."[71]

5 The Trials of the 477th

"[C]onditions at this base are deplorable for colored soldiers...The whole camp here is rotten with prejudice and discrimination," Pvt. John S. Lyons wrote from Army Air Base Alamagordo (N.M.) to the NAACP. "I would appreciate it very much if you would kindly look into a big problem that confronts the negro soldiers here in Sioux Falls, South Dakota," Pvt. William Bryant petitioned from an AAF Technical Training School. "We are not being treated as human beings here." Black servicemen at Carlsbad Army Air Field in New Mexico lodged a formal complaint with the War Department because the base theater, post exchange, and buses had been divided into whites-only and colored-only sections. The massive social disruptions of the war led to similar conflicts at bases throughout the United States, proving that the problem of unequal treatment on the basis of race was not confined to the South.[1]

Through the course of the war the NAACP continued the campaign it had begun before 1941, loudly advocating for equal treatment for blacks in every branch of the military. When individual blacks believed they had been mistreated and sought redress, they were as likely to appeal to what was by then the nation's unquestioned premier civil rights organization as they were to the War Department or First Lady Eleanor Roosevelt—and their appeals to those two institutions arrived by the bagful. The NAACP claimed that thousands of new dues-paying members joined during the war years, which gave the association a larger budget for investigations into discriminatory treatment and for publicity. The NAACP fielded what would seem to be a disproportionate number of complaints from officers and enlisted men of the AAF.

Forcing the AAF to train black Americans as fighter pilots was a significant victory in the civil rights coalition's campaign for equal opportunity, but it was an incomplete one. The formation of the 99th Pursuit Squadron opened the door for three dozen aspiring African American pilots and hundreds of technical specialists; the creation of the 332nd tripled those opportunities. But there were nearly 13 million blacks in the United States at the time; making available one hundred slots for fighter pilots (all of whom had to be shorter than 5 feet 10 inches tall and weigh less than 170 pounds) could not take full advantage of the contributions blacks wanted to make in the air war. If African Americans were to realize their aspirations and achieve a condition even approaching equality in the flying forces, they would have to be trained in all the areas whites were, although in reduced numbers. Within the context of the segregated AAF, that necessitated the creation of all-black bomber crews, and the coalition that had forced the War Department to create the 99th continued its efforts to force the department to deploy blacks in multi-engine bombers.

In 1942 Roy Wilkins, assistant secretary of the NAACP and editor of *The Crisis*, asked the War Department whether it planned to train blacks for bomber crews. The response he received late that year was dispiriting: "War Department policy precludes the training of Negroes as navigators, bombardiers, et cetera, until such time as the feasibility of organizing medium and heavy bombardment squadrons of all negro personnel is proved." Acting Adjutant Gen. H. B. Lewis candidly admitted that the department was waiting to see whether the Tuskegee-trained fighter pilot could "prove his worth as a combat aviator" before it would commit to devoting the training resources for a bombardment unit. (At the same time, of course, the generals in the AAF were denying the pilots of the 99th the opportunity to prove their collective worth as combat aviators.) The War Department intended to stall the development of such a program for as long as was politically possible and the AAF for longer than that.[2]

Leaders of the War Department had signed off on plans for the development of an all-Negro combined fighter-bomber group by May 1943, but civilian aide Truman Gibson reported that the AAF was doing nothing to train ground crew personnel and was still insisting that the fighter pilots had to prove themselves before it would organize such a group. Gibson argued that the creation of a normal bombardment group, as opposed to the fighter-bomber hybrid, was much more feasible in an organizational sense and more likely to be effective in combat and thereby prove the "experiment" a success.[3]

The AAF finally bowed to the civil rights coalition's pressure from without, and Hastie's and Gibson's from within, in 1943 and announced the creation of the all-black 477th Medium Bombardment Group; the group was activated in January 1944. Typical—that is, all-white—bomber groups were manned, trained, and sent off to combat in a matter of three to four months in the wartime AAF, but commanding officer Col. Robert R. Selway Jr. had to build the 477th from scratch. Because TAFS was the only training school in the country producing black pilots, the 477th would have to compete with the 332nd for the limited number of pilots graduating each month, and the AAF had never yet trained a black navigator or bombardier. Training programs for those specialties would either have to be built from the ground up at the already overcrowded TAAF or appended to previously all-white programs throughout the states. The AAF decided on the latter course, which initiated other, more serious problems.[4]

The effort was doomed from the start. The AAF just could not get the numbers to work: the branch would now pay the price for strictly limiting the numbers of black pilot cadets it had admitted to training since 1940 and for refusing to train African Americans in other technical specialties. TAAF could not train pilots and specialists at a fast enough rate to resupply the 332nd and build the 477th at the same time. The plan to staff the black group's leadership with experienced fighter pilots after they returned from combat overseas, which would require them to be retrained to fly the group's multi-engine B-25 bombers, delayed the group's formation further. Something had to give.[5]

The AAF first chose to lower aptitude requirements for the 477th's pilots, bombardiers, and navigators. White applicants required a score of at least seven on a nine-point scale on an aptitude test to enter such training programs; after 1944 the AAF felt the need to accept blacks with scores as low as four on the same scale just to get warm bodies into the 477th's openings. Training for these specialists was, moreover, chaotic; they trained in small groups at bases throughout the country, which ensured that they would never develop the esprit de corps that characterized the 99th. Elements of the 477th moved more than thirty times in the twenty months between the group's inception and the end of the war. Nine months after the group's activation—more than twice the time it took to ready white groups for combat—only twenty-three of the group's authorized 128 navigators and navigator-bombardiers and half of its authorized 176 pilots had joined the black bomber group.[6]

The group finally assembled enough trained crew members to begin combat crew training just short of the first anniversary of its activation. The 477th achieved a remarkably proficient safety record in that year of routine flying: 17,875 flying hours with only two minor accidents, which won the group two commendations from the commander of the First Air Force. But the slow pace of training gave the men of the 477th even more time to dwell on the treatment they received from their white superior officers. They were entitled to better as officers and gentlemen, they believed, and as the months wore on they became increasingly determined to receive the respectful treatment they had earned. Most galling of all was commanding officers' practice of defining the officers of the 477th as "trainees," who were therefore denied entrance to officers' clubs at a series of stateside bases that had been restricted to supervisory personnel, all of whom were white. "For many of us, and mostly those from the north, this was just something they were going to fight," said Lt. LeRoy F. Gillead, a navigator-bombardier of the 477th from New York. "That was something I was going to fight.... I had a right to go to the officers' club."[7]

The 99th had been in combat for six months by this point, and the remaining squadrons of the 332nd had just arrived in Europe. They had not produced nearly the number of combat-tested officers the 477th would need to form the group into a proficient fighting force under the original plan; so Selway staffed the 477th with white leadership, with the pledge that as more black officers gained experience they would be rotated in. He never fulfilled that promise. Rather, Selway devised what blacks derisively called a "promotion mill" that ensured that black officers never commanded whites, and whites without combat experience moved into supervisory positions over black combat veterans.[8]

The 477th had foundational morale problems dating back to its very activation, in January 1944 at Selfridge Field, Michigan, where replacement pilots for the 332nd were also training. One member of the 477th, a career Air Force officer, later charged that throughout its history the bomber group "was subverted by the very persons responsible for its success." The 477th would not be considered combat-ready until more than a year and half after its activation. The numbers game surely hampered the development of the 477th, but the experience of the 332nd would seem to prove that with effective leadership the bomber group could have been trained into an effective fighting unit despite that obstacle. Instead, the group was crippled by morale problems that flowed from resentment on the part of black junior officers toward white senior officers' insistence on rigid racial segregation, and the black officers' equally firm determination to fight the injustice.[9]

At Selfridge the officers of the 332nd and 477th petitioned the base commander, Col. William Boyd, for equal access to the lone officers' club on base. Lt. Milton Henry, the pilot who had already gotten in trouble for defying Jim Crow on a Montgomery bus and complained about conditions at Selfridge, went so far as to physically enter the officers' club and demand his rightful privileges. Boyd denied the petition and Henry's demands, and his superior officer, Maj. Gen. Frank O'D. Hunter, backed him to the hilt. Hunter, a Georgian, had been a World War I flying ace, and he vastly preferred the lily-white Army Air Corps of his early career to the increasingly heterogeneous force he commanded in World War II. If anything, he proved even more determined than Boyd to segregate the officers under his command when he traveled to Selfridge Field to address the men of the 477th. "The country is not ready to accept white officers and colored officers at the same social level," he said. "I base that opinion on the history of this country for the past 125 years."[10]

Hunter was not shy in expressing his theories and opinions on American race relations, of which he had many. "I recognize no racial difficulty at Selfridge Field," he told the men. "We are in the army to win a war and not to settle the race issue.... This thing here [the attempt to desegregate the club] is caused only by downtown [Detroit] agitators, some from among you. I will weed out all of the agitators in this command and lop them off." Boyd's actions clearly violated Army Regulation 210–10, issued in 1940, which prohibited the racial segregation of base recreational facilities, but Hunter went even further, arranging for the creation of a nominally separate-but-equal officers' club for blacks at Selfridge. However, the AAF transferred the group to Godman Field, Kentucky, before the club could be completed.[11]

Hunter's support for Boyd's segregation policy was total, but the secretary of war reprimanded the base commander harshly. In Gen. Benjamin O. Davis Sr.'s report to the War Department on Boyd's conduct, he informed the colonel, "Investigation by the Office of the Inspector General has disclosed that racial discrimination against colored officers was due to your conduct in denying to colored officers the right to use the Officers Club. Such action is in violation of Army regulations and explicit War Department instructions on this subject." Davis recommended that Boyd and another officer who had performed poorly in the crisis be court-martialed and removed from their respective commands, though the AAF declined to act on those recommendations. (Instead, it court-martialed Lt. Henry and discharged him from the service.) The AAF's investigations into the incident concluded that black newspaper reporters, racial agitators, and "communisitic elements" in nearby Detroit, not Boyd and Hunter, were ultimately responsible for the problems. The service's first official response to the Davis report concluded: "[W]hite and colored officers jointly using a club and drinking there together or jointly attending dances would create an intolerable situation and one which is fraught with the possibility of the greatest danger."[12]

Those sentiments were unacceptable to civilian leaders in the War Department because the civilians were susceptible to public pressure. (The incident at Selfridge Field had appeared on the radar screen of the War Department in the first place after the ladies of a Chicago civic club wrote Eleanor Roosevelt to ask her to look into reports from the base they had read in a black Detroit newspaper.) Boyd and Hunter's actions at Selfridge forced the War Department's hands and resulted in service-wide reforms ensuring that "the designation of recreational facilities for the use of a particular race or color group would not be permitted." The Selfridge Field crisis made the War Department much less likely to tolerate further incidents from the AAF and proved a watershed event in the history of blacks in the service.[13]

In the wake of the confrontation AAF Commanding General Henry H. ("Hap") Arnold left little room for his generals' personal interpretations of the policies governing the treatment of African Americans in the service. He let it be known that he was under intense pressure from civilian leaders in the War Department to resolve the situation. "Recent racial difficulties within the Army Air Forces, particularly at Selfridge Field, have brought to light the fact that some War Department agencies feel that the Army Air Forces are not complying and do not desire to comply with War Department policy as affects handling of Negro troops," he announced in a memorandum for the chiefs of all Air Forces headquarters offices. "I personally was not conscious of this fact," he continued—which might not have been a lie, but only if he had been able to ignore Hastie entirely over the previous two years—"however, in the event that there is a feeling in the Army Air Forces anywhere which is in opposition to War Department policy it must be immediately stamped out." The matter should have ended there, but it did not. Gen. Hunter was a stubborn man.[14]

The generals of the AAF now believed that they needed to find new places for the 332nd and 477th to train; Selfridge Field and nearby Detroit had become racial tinderboxes. The Air Forces recommended transferring the black groups to the Caribbean island of Antigua, where "good flying weather would prevail and [more importantly,] where it would be too far away for newspaper reporters to interfere with personnel and training activities and all outgoing mail would be censored."[15]

But the War Department could not allow the political firestorm this would have caused. Instead, when the fighter pilots moved from Selfridge to Walterboro, the 477th transferred to Godman Field, a small AAF facility adjacent to the army's Fort Knox on the outskirts of Louisville with inadequate housing and minimal training and operational facilities. Its short, deteriorating runways could not safely accommodate the B-25J, the aircraft the 477th was supposed to be training to fly in combat and the heaviest in the AAF's inventory. The officers of the 477th could therefore be forgiven for thinking that they were being transferred to Kentucky because of the incidents at the Selfridge officers' club and not because they could be better trained for combat at Godman. Godman was simply inadequate for the purposes of a medium bombardment group in training—almost laughably so. Unlike Selfridge, it had no air-to-ground gunnery range. As compared with the group's previous home base, it had one-quarter the hangar space, one-seventh the total acreage, and one-fifth the gasoline storage capacity.[16]

The 477th's commanding officer, Robert Selway, was made commanding officer of Godman as well. He immediately made clear why the 477th had been transferred to such an inferior facility when he turned over the base officers' club entirely to blacks; white officers on base could use Fort Knox's facility, but blacks could not. This was not good enough for the men who had already forced the issue of equal treatment at Selfridge. If the clubs at Fort Knox were available to white officers stationed at Godman, they contended in full voice, they should be available to every officer stationed at Godman. Selway rebuffed these arguments.[17]

The unequal treatment of black officers in the 477th extended to other areas of the base. When a white private at Godman refused to salute Capt. Clarence G. Southall because, he explained, "he was from the South and did not salute Negroes," Southall attempted to bring the man up on charges in a court martial. The private was transferred from the base, and Southall's superior officers threatened to charge him with inciting a race riot.[18]

Members of the 477th in training at other stations throughout the country faced similar obstacles. In September 1944 a group of twenty-two black officers stationed at Midland Army Air Base, Texas, for bombardier training lodged a formal complaint with the War Department over the base commander's segregation of recreational and mess facilities. "This group finds the treatment accorded them, and the deprivation of limited recreational facilities to make it extremely and unwarrantedly difficult to maintain morale," they wrote in a scathing statement of their grievances. "The continuance of such a policy in force is hardly in accord with the struggle to which our nation has committed itself. We feel that it makes a travesty of 'the four freedoms,' finding, as we do, that to be a Chinese American, a Canadian student, a member of the Free French, to be anything, is better than being an American Negro seeking decent treatment in America."[19]

The men had used the base officers' club without incident for approximately two weeks before the base commander decided that a race riot was imminent—perhaps because the club was planning a dance at which white women would be present—and redefined the club as off-limits to the black officers. They could not be denied service entirely, so now they were the only officers in the Air Forces with access to room service: "We could call up, and they would deliver us a hamburger and a milk shake and all that," bombardier-navigator Roy Chappell remembered with a chuckle. "Gimme a scotch and soda!" James C. Warren of the 477th impishly recalled telling the officers' club employees over the phone. " 'I'll have a martini!' And here comes this dude." "But at the same time," Chappell said, "we started writing everybody and calling everybody that we knew that had something to do with this."[20]

A confidential War Department investigation pinned the blame for the Midland protests on Lt. Coleman A. Young, whom the investigation deemed an "agitator ... who has been under investigation at Midland Army

Air Field since 16 August 1944 for engaging in Communistic activities prior to his induction into the Armed Forces." (Warren recalled Young as the author of the complaint that drew the War Department's attention.) Young, the anonymous investigator reported, "has been the organizer of a colored 'equality movement' at the station. He has called on the Commanding Officer on three occasions entering complaints of not having the liberties and concessions that were afforded white personnel." Young, it was alleged, had told a colored Women's Army Corps officer that "he had called all colored officers together at meetings on several occasions for the good of the colored race," which branded him a racial agitator. He had also "engaged in an altercation with a white cashier and a white sergeant as to where he would sit in the Post Cafeteria. Upon his departure, he remarked that 'he would have to start some action, if his race was ever to be accorded equality.'"[21]

The AAF investigation into the problems at Midland revealed that the source of the problem was base commander Col. Charles Dowman's insistence on defining all black officers as trainees and all white officers as instructors even if they were detailed there to receive instruction. Dowman had allowed black officers to use the base officers' club until that September, "at which time the Commanding Officer determined that an emergency had arisen which might result in riot and bloodshed, and placed a temporary restriction on the use of the officers' club by student officers (colored)." He claimed to have kept all other base recreational facilities open for the use of black officers, though the black officers disputed this.[22]

The investigation backed Dowman, who in any case had reopened the club to the black officers soon after the supposed emergency passed, apparently at the insistence of white officers on the base. James Warren believed that white instructors who had flown overseas alongside the 332nd convinced Dowman the black officers were worthy of inclusion. In fact, he believed that black officers enjoyed an unusually close relationship with their white counterparts at Midland, in part because blacks held a relatively equal level of power within the base's specific environment. Pilots on the base could log flying time in B-25s on the weekends to visit friends and families, but AAF regulations stipulated that if the destination was more than 500 miles away the pilot had to fly with a rated navigator. The men of the 477th were the only rated navigators on the base, so they could pick and choose their weekend destinations. "I'd go home and visit my family [in Chicago] overnight, then come back," said Warren, who emphasized that he and other navigators of the 477th had close contact and strong working relationships with their white fellow officers on those long journeys.[23]

By May 1944 dissatisfaction among the officers of the 477th at Godman over issues of equal treatment and, perhaps even more significantly, command structure and promotion, had reached a critical stage. A confidential investigation for the AAF's Air Inspector found "general resentment" on the part of the men of the 477th at having been "transferred below the Mason-Dixon line where the law is not in their favor." The group's chaplain reported dangerously tense conditions: the officers resented being blocked by whites in the upper ranks of the group; the enlisted men considered their superiors incompetent. "Colonel Selway has forfeited the respect of his officers," the chaplain reported. He regretted the existence of a " 'lack of unity' stemming from the disparity between the white and Negro officers of the Group." Rather than investigate the chaplain's charges, however, the inspector shot the messenger. "Chaplain Clanton impressed me as lacking in sincerity and as harboring an active dislike for Colonel Selway which borders on disloyalty." All of the warning signs of a dysfunctional unit were plainly there for the AAF to see and act upon, but the leaders of the service chose to ignore them. "The Negro personnel at Godman Field are well provided for and have no just cause for complaint," Col. John E. Harris's investigation concluded. "Colonel Selway enjoys the confidence of his staff and is reputed to be alert to his responsibilities. There is nothing in the immediate situation to cause alarm; however, the activities of the chaplain will bear watching."[24]

A later investigation by the NAACP disputed that assertion, finding that the black officers, to say nothing of enlisted men, chafed under Selway's leadership structure. More than a year after the group's activation, each of its four squadrons was still structured so that white officers held every single position requiring command responsibilities. "Not only do they question the competence of many of the white officers holding key positions in the squadrons," Walter White reported to Secretary of War Stimson, "but they indicate that most of the so-called supervisory personnel do not have much more flying experience than they themselves have." The 477th's flying officers had by their count an average of seven hundred hours experience in the air, yet not one of them had been entrusted with a command position. They also claimed that whites classified as "instructors" at Freeman had an average of only two hundred flying hours.[25]

The black officers grumbled that their outfit had become a promotion mill for "second-rate" whites. They cited the case of twenty-two-year-old Robert F. Mattern, who was transferred to the 477th just days after being promoted from the rank of lieutenant to captain. After a month in a squadron command position, he was promoted to the rank of major and transferred out; another young white officer replaced him. The men of the 477th saw this happen again and again; they estimated that squadron command positions turned over once every four months. As soon as whites had gained experience as squadron commanders in the 477th, they transferred out to commands in white units, and other whites moved in to replace them. The NAACP's report on the 477th's troubles concluded, "[S]ince the simplest way of obtaining a promotion is by being assigned a higher function, Negro Squadron Officers are never able to secure such promotions because the Squadron Command is limited to white personnel."[26]

The War Department took no action on the NAACP complaint, but in March 1945 the AAF did transfer the 477th from Godman Field to a better facility, Freeman Field on the outskirts of Seymour, Indiana. Freeman had longer runways, a firing range, and other amenities that made it far superior to Godman for the purposes of the group. Black officers and enlisted men would work in close proximity with white personnel on the base, and the officers would live alongside whites in a public housing project immediately adjacent to the airfield.

The town of Seymour was no Shangri La for African Americans, however; the populace was less than 1 percent black, and local businesses began displaying "Colored will not be served" signs for the first time as soon as the black airmen arrived. ("Great field! Great facilities! But the town was lousy," remembered one Airman.) Seymour was little different from hundreds of towns throughout the United States in this regard. By 1945 the War Department's files bulged with correspondence from white people throughout the country who objected to having blacks stationed in their respective communities. When the Rapid City, S.D., city commission discussed the possibility of black troops being stationed at the local air base in December 1942, City Manager J. H. Lake wrote U.S. Rep. Francis Case to complain, "Colored troops in Rapid City would present a problem that I cannot, at this time, see how we could handle." Case forwarded the concerns to the War Department. Representatives of the Albuquerque, N.M., Chamber of Commerce petitioned the War Department not to transfer a black unit to Albuquerque Air Base, as did the city fathers of Bangor, Maine, and dozens of other communities.[27]

The arrival of the 477th would strain Freeman Field's facilities, increasing the number of officers on base, for instance, from fewer than three hundred to more than seven hundred. Selway arranged for the reclassification of Club No. 1, the noncommissioned officers' club, into a second officers' club at Freeman in anticipation of the group's arrival. He classified all the black officers of the Combat Crew Training Squadron, or Overseas Training Unit, as trainees, even though some of the "trainees" had been in the service for nearly four years by this point and at least four had already served in combat with the 332nd in Europe. Four others had completed training as pilots, bombardiers, and navigators, possibly making them the only triple-rated officers in the Air Forces. Several of the pilots in the group had logged more than nine hundred hours of flight time, and the group's surgeon, Dr. James Ramsey, had reached the rank of major in the Army Air Forces Medical Corps. At the same time, Selway classified all white officers among the base personnel and the white officers of the Overseas Training Unit as instructors. When the men of the 477th learned that Club No. 1 had been designated for the use of trainees and the much better appointed Officers' Club No. 2 for "supervisory and instructor personnel," they understood the basis of the decision. They quickly dubbed Club No. 1 "Uncle Tom's Cabin" and refused to patronize it.[28]

In public statements, Selway attributed his decision to the belief that fraternization between instructors and trainees would have an ill effect on the group's training. In truth, the effort was a transparent attempt to circumvent both the letter and the law of War Department Memorandum No. 97 and Army Regulation 210–10, which prohibited segregation of base facilities by race, and which Selway mistakenly interpreted as having no application to "Club facilities on training stations."[29]

In early April the bulk of the 477th and the personnel of the group's associated 118th Base Unit, whose officers held special orders designating them as base personnel, as opposed to trainees, made the move from Godman to Freeman. Selway received a tip from a black officer of the 477th that his comrades were planning something for Officers' Club No. 2 on the evening of April 5. ("Some traitor—that's all I can call him—called ahead," James C. Warren recalled disgustedly.) Selway stationed Lt. J.D. Rogers, the field's assistant provost marshal, and Maj. A. N. White, base mess and billeting officer, at the club. Rogers was prepared to physically block any blacks' entrance to the club. When thirty-six black officers entered in small groups and refused White's direct order to leave, White placed them under arrest in quarters and closed the club. Selway was apparently convinced that these thirty-six were the only "agitators" on the base, so the club opened normally the following night. Then another thirty-five black officers entered in small groups. Major White ordered the men to leave, arrested them when they refused, and, under Selway's orders, closed the club indefinitely, and held three of the arrested officers in confinement.[30]

Following the arrests, 110 men of the 477th signed an appeal to the Army's inspector general asking for an investigation of what they believed were violations of Army and War Department regulations at Freeman Field. "The continuance of this policy can hardly be reconciled with the world wide struggle for freedom for which we are asked, and are willing, to lay down our lives," they wrote. In an effort to clarify base facility policies, Selway issued Base Regulation 85–2, which spoke to the assignment of housing, mess, and recreational facilities for officers on the base. The regulation reinforced Selway's previous policy separating facilities for supervisors and trainees, and stated that it was fully in line with the standards of the Army Air Forces.[31]

When Leslie S. Perry of the Washington, D.C., branch of the NAACP arrived in late April to investigate the incident, he was able to meet informally with several black officers of the 477th and had an official audience with Selway. Selway freely admitted that he had instituted curfews and other policies that tended to separate blacks from whites on the base. He considered these reasonable applications of the lessons he had learned while at Selfridge during the 1943 Detroit race riot. Before the colonel instituted the reforms, he claimed, "white and colored personnel spent most of their time standing about in groups glaring at one another." But with the new policies in place flying time had increased, and the accident rate had decreased dramatically. Selway also maintained that it was standard operating procedure in the AAF to separate instructors and trainees in officers' clubs, but he was unable to name another base where such a policy was in use.[32]

Having put the policy in writing, Selway then elevated the confrontation by providing each officer assigned to the base with a copy of Base Regulation 85–2 along with a form that read, "I have read and understand the above order" and included a line for the officer's signature. He had to have known that many of the black officers would refuse to comply. Selway must have welcomed the confrontation as a way of weeding out perceived "agitators" from the 477th. He may not have expected the extent of the black officers' resistance, but he precipitated a full-blown challenge to his command.

Several participants insisted later that the revolt had not been planned in advance—in part, one suspects, because they knew that if there had been evidence of conspiracy at the time they could have faced additional prosecution under the 66th Article of War. "Everybody really was on their own. There was no leadership telling you what to do or what to say," LeRoy Gillead later insisted. Nonetheless, the events at the officers' club were clearly organized beforehand; the participants certainly behaved in a disciplined fashion at the time of the protests that indicated prior planning. When the order came to sign the acknowledgement of Selway's policy, they were not quite as unified. "There was no collaboration in terms of what you should do," Gillead said. "[It was] left up to you whether you would agree to sign or not sign. You didn't know what anyone else would do."[33]

Not surprisingly, an officer with extensive organizing experience found himself at the center of the protest effort. Coleman Young, a bombardier who had also graduated from Infantry Officers Training School at Fort Benning, had worked as a United Auto Workers organizer in Detroit before the war and learned the tactics of mass action. He had also led the 1944 protest at Midland Army Air Field that resulted in the desegregation of that base's officers' club. Young was "the most vocal person" among the officers who challenged Selway, according to Gillead; in meetings with fellow officers of the 477th, he discussed possible tactics for the challenge and what their legal ramifications would be. For his part, however, Selway found it impossible throughout the ordeal even to imagine that the officers of the 477th could have conceived and acted on the plan themselves. As Boyd and Hunter did in the conflict at Selfridge, he blamed the mutiny on "outside agitators." Selway singled out for blame Lowell M. Trice, a journalist for the *Indianapolis Recorder*, a black newspaper. Also an official in the nearby Indianapolis branch of the NAACP, Trice had visited the base on April 5 and other occasions.[34]

Selway convened a board of six officers to conduct a punitive ritual. One by one, every other officer on the base would be led into a room and ordered to sign the form attesting that he had read and would abide by Base Regulation 85–2. (He went through the pretense of treating every officer at Freeman Field equally for once, ordering whites to sign the form, too. All 292 did.) Selway designed the procedure in a way that made organized resistance difficult, quarantining the officers who had gone through the process from those who had not and thus had no idea what the others had decided to do. The board proceeded by rank with highest-ranking officers going first, and leaving the second lieutenants and flight officers who were presumably more likely to protest for last. Though direct communication among the officers was limited by the quarantine, a strength-in-numbers strategy suggested itself. The officers had read the document and had an idea what to expect Selway would order them to do behind closed doors. They reasoned that if one man refused to sign, he would be court-martialed, but gambled that Selway would not risk the public relations problems that would result if he sent dozens of them to jail.[35]

They appeared individually before the board and were ordered to read the policy and to sign the statement attesting to their understanding of the policy. Those who hesitated to sign were given the chance to amend the form or to add personal statements attesting to their disagreement with the policy below their signature. Many took advantage of that loophole, but 101 others still refused to sign. To these Selway read the 64th Article of War, which forbids the willful disobeying of a lawful direct order from a superior in wartime and can be enforced with penalties up to and including death. He then placed the 101 under arrest and arranged for their transfer back to Godman Field, with the rest of the 477th soon to follow. It bears mentioning that if only 101 of 422 refused to sign, more than three-fourths of the black officers who had been segregated into the separate and unequal "Uncle Tom's

Cabin" found a way to rationalize the treatment and signed the regulation. "Some people, for whatever reasons, signed," LeRoy Gillead said. "I resented that originally, but [now] I can understand why." They wanted careers in the postwar Air Force.[36]

The decision whether to sign was a wrenching one for each officer, and the 101 who refused had almost as many reasons for doing so. For Gillead, the decision hinged on what kind of example he wanted to demonstrate as a parent. "My wife and first son were living in the housing compound there," he remembered. "I recall quite definitely when I was given a direct order to sign the regulation or suffer the punishment of death if I disobeyed my immediate commanding officer. I was trembling in fear, but I had the feeling that my son would at least know his father was not afraid to stand up for what he believed in. That was a turning point in my entire life."[37]

Lt. Quentin P. Smith, a pilot and an imposing man with a booming voice, recalled the theater of the signing ceremony. "Are you familiar with the 64th Article of War?" a major asked him. "The 64th says failure to obey a direct order of a commanding officer is punishable up to and including death. And the major stands up and says, 'I order you to sign.' My transcript said, 'He shook his head.' They sucked the air out of me." Ordered to answer the command verbally, Smith remembered, "I said [in a high-pitched, squeaky voice]: 'No.'" Smith returned to the barracks under arrest. All he could think about was how much more money he was making in the AAF than he had as a schoolteacher in Gary, Indiana. Had he ruined his chances to make a career of the service?[38]

Lt. LeRoy Battle, a bombardier-navigator, had a simpler explanation for his refusal to sign: "I was just young enough not to give a damn!" The vast majority of the officers were in their early twenties, yet they were forced to make a decision that would resonate throughout their military careers, and in some cases beyond. Flight Officer Haydel White had grown up with segregation in New Orleans, but had never accepted or internalized its lessons. The overseas cap he was issued with his officer's wings at TAAF was the first one he ever wore, he said, because a black man who wore a hat in Louisiana was expected to remove it when talking to a white. "It showed, to me, submission, and I wasn't about to kowtow or be submissive to anybody, so then I didn't wear a hat." For the same reason he refused to bow to Selway's regulations, because that would constitute "re-segregating myself." White refused to sign. He recounted proudly, "I wasn't influenced by anybody. I was influenced by myself."[39]

Hiram Little was a son of central Georgia who had worked his way into Morehouse College, the elite all-black school for men in Atlanta. While at

Morehouse he had responded to an Air Corps officer's recruiting pitch, he said, "Not because I loved flying, not because I was extra-patriotic, but because I didn't want to be drafted" into the army. He trained at Chanute Field as an armorer and transferred to TAAF in 1942. He "loved every minute of" his time at TAAF, he said. "I got a chance to meet people from all over the U.S.A., and meeting these guys was something I probably would have never had a chance to do." But after the 477th was created, Little decided he "wanted to try the flying end of the Air Force" and was able to become reclassified for bombardier-navigator training. He completed training programs at TAAF, Eglin Field in Florida, and Midland Army Air Base in Texas, earned a commission as a flight officer, and transferred to Godman Field in December 1944 to join the unit.[40]

Little transferred with the rest of the 477th to Freeman Field in 1945 and immediately found himself caught up in the officers' club controversy. He was among the 101 who refused to sign and in retrospect made his decision seem like the most natural one he had ever made in his life, hardly even a decision at all. But Little was not a rebel: he had never been arrested before, he had been a good student, and he had never challenged authority figures: "I got along with all of them because I did what they told me to do. I was used to it. Taking orders just never bothered me, never bothered me at all." His decision to challenge the camp policy came down to the fact that the instructor/trainee designation "was a lie everybody saw through," and Little could not abide it. "So we all decided at the mess hall and where we gathered that we're going to force this issue."[41]

Little could not have cared less about socializing with white officers. He had enjoyed being at Godman on the outskirts of Louisville because the city was "just full of beautiful [African American] women, all kind of bars, all kind of restaurants. You can do anything you want in Louisville." The Kentucky city was less than an hour from Freeman by bus. Given those nearby attractions, he asked, "Why would I want to worry about going up here in this officers' club with these white people? I ain't particularly enamored of them, particularly fond of them. They're just somebody that are on the earth as far as I'm concerned." Little objected to the policy not because he wanted to patronize the club, but because he perceived that Selway and Hunter "decided they were going to put these black people in their place."[42]

In fact, Little never did set foot in the Freeman officers' club. But when he was called into Selway's signing ceremony, "before I even went in there, I knew I wasn't going to sign that order. I didn't talk to anybody about it, but I knew I wasn't going to sign that order that I was going to bow down willingly to segregation, because I'd been doing that all my life, and I was sick of it." He had only one worry: "I hope my mama doesn't read the paper. It's going to get in the paper, and they'll print the names of all these black people who were up here mutinying—and that's what they said: 'mutiny'—she's going to see my name, and she's going to be disturbed."[43]

Little decided that defying the order was worth the risk. "I've got to do it sooner or later," he reasoned. "I might end up in jail, I might end up out yonder in federal prison. I'll still get out with a dishonorable discharge, but I'll never get a government job. I'll probably end up working at somebody's grocery store or drugstore somewhere. I don't know what will happen, but I have to go through with it." In fact, before he defied the order and refused to sign, Little had planned on making a career of the Air Force. But he feared that the incident would follow him anywhere he went in the service. "Every time I come up for promotion," he thought, "somebody's going to open my file, and this is what they're going to say: 'This nigger is a troublemaker.'" Little left the service after the war, but he need not have worried about finding government employment. He worked for the postal service for the next thirty-three years.[44]

On the night he sent the 101 to Godman, Selway received another telephone tip from a member of the 477th. He had re-opened Club No. 2. His informant told him that "the Negro officers of the base had resolved to make an issue" of his segregationist policies and to cause a commotion that could not help but attract national attention. "[T]he proposed action was backed by approximately 100% of the Negro officer personnel," the informant told Selway, and it threatened to mushroom into something much larger than the previous protests. It would include, he said,

1. Cancellation of the Negro training program.
2. Grounding all aircraft at the base.
3. Precipitation of a mass incident which would result in a mass arrest and a mass trial.

Selway closed the club.[45]

He held three remaining officers of the 477th, lieutenants Roger C. "Bill" Terry, Marsden A. Thomson, and Shirley R. Clinton, at Freeman for a few more days and prepared their courts-martial based on Lt. Rogers's testimony that the three had "jostled" him as they entered Club No. 2 on April 5. Terry did not dispute that he could be classified as a "trainee" on the base, but Thomson and Clinton had special orders classifying them as base personnel. Both Thomson and Clinton had been in the service for more than three years and had completed the training for their respective MOS (Military Occupation Specialty); Thomson had held the position of executive officer of the 618th Squadron for several months and had served as billeting and club officer at Godman. He was no more a trainee than Rogers or Selway.[46]

Terry was held in solitary confinement as he awaited trial. "If I wanted to go to the bathroom, I'd have to ask the guard," Terry recalled. "He would have to get the officer of the day, and he would go with me down to the bathroom, and then I'd use the bathroom because they only had one bathroom in these barracks," he said. "And then I ate alone. I had three books. I had *Pilgrim's Progress, The Rise and Fall of the Roman Empire,* and a Bible. I read the thing from one end to the other. I threw my knife at the door. I painted a circle and put a target up there. Just anything to keep from going crazy.[47]

"You become anxious after a few weeks," Terry said. "I was looking for some help because I was in custody for eighty days or so. I came to the conclusion that they weren't playing with me, that they wanted their pound of flesh." He was held incommunicado. "My mother, Edith Terry, had been trying to get in touch with me, as had my brother, and various friends [of the 477th], like A. Philip Randolph. The guys from the Committee Against Jim Crow in Military Service were trying to get in touch with me, but they couldn't."[48]

The 101 whom Selway had arrested for refusing to sign had a frightening initial experience when they returned to Godman. "We were very apprehensive. It was a hell of a feeling," one of the arrestees, Mitchell Higginbotham, said. "We didn't get it really impressed upon us until our arrival at Godman Field, when we were met by these huge vehicles, like buses with bars on the windows, and armed troops with bayonets and so forth, and transported back to the barracks. They had equipped the whole area with huge floodlights. So then it dawned on us that we were in prison, and this was a serious situation." Worse, said Wardell Polk, "Just across the tracks [from Godman] was Fort Knox, and they had German and Italian POWs there. They jeered at us and whatnot until the administration declared the area off limits to them."[49] "We could not in our wildest imagination believe that a group of United States Army Air Force officers were being treated in this manner," wrote one of the 101, but "I have never seen morale so high in a group of men who were under such great stress."[50]

The facilities at Godman made it impossible for a multi-engine unit to put in the training hours necessary to achieve combat readiness. By all appearances, the AAF acceded to Selway's request to transfer the entire group simply because Selway had 104 officers under arrest (the 101 who refused to sign, plus the three who remained under arrest for the "jostling" incident) and felt he needed the large cadre of white MPs stationed at Fort Knox available in case of race riot. The transfer signaled beyond doubt that the service had given up on training the 477th for combat readiness. James Warren, one of the 101, later charged, "Hunter was far more dedicated to seeing his racist policies enforced than he was concerned with the training of the bomb group to fight the enemy." Fitz-roy ("Buck") Newsum, a pilot in the 477th, put it another way: Hunter and Selway prioritized their "personal desires" over the nation's needs. "[They said,] 'It doesn't make any difference that guys are fighting and dying overseas. No way. Our personal desires come first.'" Warren also uncovered later what he called "the smoking gun," the transcript of a telephone conversation between Col. Malcolm N. Stewart, acting chief of training, First Air Force, and Gen. William W. Welsh, chief of staff of the Air Force for Training. In discussing the 477th's move to Godman, Gen. Welsh admitted, "If we can stave it off in some way for a period of time ... maybe we can eliminate the program gradually and accomplish our end."[51]

Lt. William T. Coleman Jr., an administrative officer in the group (though not one of the 101) who had interrupted his studies at Harvard Law School to join the AAF, thought he knew the reason for the transfer, and it had nothing to do with preparing the group for combat. "The Air Forces struck back," he wrote to the NAACP. The "sole purpose" for the transfer, he reported, was

> the avoidance of letting us frequent the white officers club and to punish us, by sending us away from Freeman with its housing project and north-ern location, for our fight to get equality. The manner of the move (short notice, secret destination, etc.), indicates that it was made without the approval of the War Dept [sic] or if they did approve it they were rushing it so public opinion could not form against it. Everything at Godman is at a standstill. ... The Group, definitely, has not had the training necessary for overseas service as an effective combat unit.

There was no question that morale was so terrible in the 477th and the training so far behind schedule that it could not be deployed in the Pacific by the summer of 1945 as had been planned.[52]

Selway's stubborn mismanagement of the situation necessitated attention from the highest levels of the chain of command. Army Chief of Staff Gen. George C. Marshall ordered the 101 released from arrest on April 23, though Hunter did arrange for letters of reprimand to remain in their personnel files and insisted that the three remaining arrested offi-cers be court-martialed. At the War Department's insistence, Gen. Arnold reassigned Benjamin O. Davis Jr. to command of the 477th and Godman Field, and decreed that the group would have all-black officers by its new readiness date of August 1. Gen. Hunter boycotted the ceremony at God-man in which Selway transferred command to Col. Davis.[53]

Davis became the first black commanding officer of a stateside U.S. military base just in time to preside over the first all-black court-martial board in history. Whether the courts-martial of Clinton, Terry, and Thompson should even take place had been the subject of intense debate within and between the Air Forces and War Department for weeks. Hunter was adamant that the breaches in discipline could not be tolerated and must be punished harshly. On the other hand, Col. R.E. Kunkel, chief of the Military Justice Division of the Army Air Forces, concluded, "[L]ong-range public interest does not appear to warrant a trial by courts-martial on charges growing out of the incident described."[54] Hunter would have preferred to court-martial all 104 but settled for trials of the three. Clinton and Thompson would be tried together in one trial, Terry by himself in another.

On July 2, 1945, Selway and his junior officers testified in the first trial that Clinton and Thompson had entered the officers' club against orders and in the process laid hands on Officer of the Day Lt. J. D. Rogers. Selway was a hostile witness and came very close to committing perjury, but the prosecution was unable to present sufficiently compelling evidence to convict the pair. After a short deliberation the board returned a verdict of not guilty.[55] Terry faced a slightly more serious charge, "offering violence against Lt. Rogers." "I didn't hit him," Terry said later. "Well, anyway, they said that I couldn't get around him without touching him. But I didn't touch him."[56]

As expected, the courts-martial drew intense media scrutiny, particularly from the black press, and Selway and Hunter's superiors at the War Department could ill afford to let those two manage the proceedings on their own terms. The AAF saw to it that the courts-martial would be perceived as fair by blacks. Six black officers of the 477th sat in judgment at the courts-martial (defense motions removed Davis from the proceedings). Yet Terry claimed that he was given little time to plan or participate in his own defense. "I felt it was quite confusing. However, they sent the man that later became my counsel, Theodore Berry. He was a fraternity brother, and he was with the NAACP Legal Defense Fund [sic]. I met him the day that I was tried. I don't feel that that was adequate. However, he did an excellent job." Berry was in fact an exceptionally able attorney with a strong interest in the fate of blacks in the military. He had worked for nine months in 1942 as a morale officer for the Office of War Information, where he was responsible for encouraging African Americans to put up with segregation on behalf of the larger war effort. However, Berry determined, "They wanted to play games with words without making fundamental changes." He resigned the position and returned to his job as a Hamilton County, Ohio, prosecutor and also served as president of the Cincinnati branch of the NAACP. He took on the trio's defense at Thurgood Marshall's request.[57]

Edith Terry, Walter White, and others succeeded in forcing the "mutiny" into the political arena. The NAACP encouraged local chapter members to bombard their elected representatives with requests for information on what had happened at Freeman Field, and at least eighteen U.S. congressmen lodged formal requests with the War Department. The inquiries were, of course, designed not to elicit information, but to impress upon the department the intense interest African Americans had in the case.[58]

When Clinton and Thomson were acquitted of all charges following their trials on July 2, Terry let his guard down. "It was quite disquieting when you think about it. If the case had any importance at all, I should have had more time to prepare. But, of course, I didn't feel I had anything to prepare for because the other guys had been acquitted." Terry would soon understand that he was wrong to underestimate the seriousness of his situation: "Little did I know that they had to get somebody. It was me.[59]

"They started the court, and the guy asked for death on all of the counts, and that shocked me. In fact, the guys say I turned pale every time they asked for death, and they thought they were trying the wrong guy. It was quite disquieting. They went through it. My attorney was quite eloquent, and [William Robert] 'Bob' Ming was the court officer, and he was helpful. They found me guilty and fined me $150 and confined me to the base for three months. They found me guilty of jostling. That means I couldn't get by the officer in the doorway of the club; that I hit him. I didn't hit him, but that's neither here nor there. Then they set me free."[60]

The mixed judgment—acquittal on the charge of disobeying an officer but guilty of jostling and a $150 fine—had to be reviewed and approved by Davis and Hunter. Terry continued, "It went forward, and Frank O'Driscoll Hunter was quite bitter about it. He said the whole damn case was a farce, that I should have been convicted of disobeying a direct order, and all that kind of stuff, but he reluctantly signed it. As far as I'm concerned, he just was a die-hard racist."[61] In signing off on the trial verdict Hunter concluded: "The sentence, although grossly inadequate, is approved, and will be duly exercised."[62]

But Terry deemed the experience worthwhile, all things considered. "It happened to be the one incident that broke the camel's back" of Jim Crow segregation in the armed forces, he said, and then spoke of the collective judgment of the Tuskegee Airmen.

> We think that it broke the camel's back because they had to recognize the fact that 104 officers were arrested, and that they all defied this order, and the order was said to be illegal. We feel, and I think I speak for most of the guys, that it was our advantage that we gave to the Negro people, that there would be no discrimination in the Army Air Force from that time on. Up until that time, they treated us like children. As long as we were flying airplanes and minding our own business and helping them, it was OK, but if we wanted to manifest our own destiny, that was verboten.

And one thing I will say: The guys stood by me. I expected to be left alone, but they stood by me. All of them. A lot of them didn't go to town while I was confined to the base. They also took up a collection and paid the $150. That was nice of them.[63]

When Gen. Arnold named Davis as Selway's replacement, he also supplanted every other white officer in the 477th with a qualified black. Morale improved immediately. The AAF disbanded two of the group's four squadrons in order to concentrate its strengths, and it reassigned two pursuit squadrons from the 332nd, remaking the force into the 477th Composite Group. By May the new group was on track for a planned September deployment to the Pacific Theater. But not even Davis could wave a magic wand and make all of the 477th's problems disappear. He requested housing quarters at Fort Knox for the top cadre of his officers, just as Selway had done. Selway's request had been honored without incident, but Davis's request caused concern. Fort Knox's commanding officer called Hunter's First Air Force Headquarters to deny the request. "I don't know whether you are familiar with Fort Knox or not," he said, "but... we have four General Officers living here... [and] by God, they just don't want a bunch of coons moving in next door to them." Davis would remember it as the worst insult in a career full of them.[64]

Resolution of the Freeman Field "mutiny" now became a matter of policy. The AAF asked the War Department to bring Army Regulation 210–10, which flatly prohibited racial segregation in base recreation facilities, in line with War Department Pamphlet 20–6, which allowed much more leeway for base commanders to establish segregated practices. The Secretary of War's Committee on Special Troop Policies (known as the McCloy Committee after its chairman), the body responsible for setting policy affecting blacks in the armed services, offered its report in May, and the news was bad for the Frank Hunters throughout the military. In sharp contrast to the old-guard AAF generals' wishes, the committee—which included, in addition to its chairman, Assistant Secretary of War John J. McCloy, AAF Brig. Gen. Idwal Edwards, Gen. Benjamin O. Davis Sr., and Truman Gibson—recommended that Army Regulation 210–10 should remain the law of the land, and all other regulations and pamphlets should be brought into compliance with it.

The War Department's clear and decisive response to the Freeman Field affair should have settled the question of racial segregation at individual base facilities, but it did not. The AAF continued to resist the inevitable momentum of desegregation for months. Gen. Barney M. Giles's response was representative of the push-back: "It is believed that the greatest over-all harmony between the white and Negro races will be maintained within the Army," he argued, "if the Army follows as closely as practicable the usages and social customs which prevail in this country with respect to recreational facilities."[65]

Another AAF response concluded, "As a practical matter regulation of this problem must be handled in coordination with accepted social custom. For the War Department to attempt the solution by regulation of a complicated social problem which has perplexed this country for a number of years is bound to produce diversion that may go so far as to affect the full effectiveness of our war effort."[66]

But McCloy had none of it. In an important statement of civilian control of the armed forces, his decision stood. The Freeman 104 forced the War Department to define racial segregation as a discriminatory act by definition, and they placed the institution squarely on the side of integration. The movement toward full integration of the armed forces might be gradual and halting from that point forward, but there would be no going back.

The conclusion of the 477th's troubles coincided with the conclusion of combat in World War II. Benjamin O. Davis Jr. remained in command of the composite group at the end of the war, and he oversaw its move to Lockbourne Air Base, Ohio, soon thereafter. Concurrently, the War Department ordered military induction centers throughout the country to stop enlisting blacks for the AAF. The following year the War Department lifted the ban and rechristened the 477th as the understaffed 332nd Fighter Wing, reactivating the 100th and 301st squadrons and eliminating the bomber squadrons. Bomber pilots could not transfer into other, all-white groups, so they transitioned into fighter squadrons if they were able. Navigator-bombardiers remained on flight status at Lockbourne by crewing C-47 transports, but they performed no essential duties.[67]

For some of the men stationed there, Lockbourne under the command of the man they called "B.O. the C.O." was the best of all possible worlds in a segregated Air Force. Charles Dryden remembered it as "Camelot": "[A]ll activities were conducted with precision and pride.... everywhere on the base there was evidence of striving for perfection," he wrote. Lockbourne was " 'our' base, run, from top to bottom and all in between, by 'us.' ... And, what's more, we had fun doing so."[68] Many of the men of the 332nd and 477th who had worked so hard to create a space for African Americans in the AAF considered Lockbourne their just reward: the world they made for themselves there came closer to making the "equal" in "separate-but-equal" a reality than even TAAF had. But the forces they had unleashed also ensured that separate-but-equal's days were numbered.

6 Integrating the Air Force

When a young musician named Willie Ruff enlisted at Lockbourne Army Airfield to play French horn in the 766th Army Air Forces Band, he learned "what a special place it was and [heard about] the high quality of its officers, doctors, nurses, engineers, and pilots." His mentor told him, "Some of the most accomplished people in all of America are right here on this base." The 766th's leader, Chief Warrant Officer John Brice, dreamed of competing against the all-white Army Air Forces Band and demanded nothing short of perfection from his charges. The band included the drummer Elvin Jones (later a member of the John Coltrane Quartet) and the pianist Ivory ("Dwike") Mitchell Jr., with whom Ruff would later tour the world in the Mitchell-Ruff Duo; in their down time, several members of the band studied with musicians in the Columbus Philharmonic. Ruff remembered the education he earned at Lockbourne as having been every bit as valuable as the one he subsequently gained at Yale.[1]

That all of the base's operations aspired to such levels of excellence was a source of tremendous pride for the men stationed there. But, Dryden acknowledged, "With that situation you have one full colonel and four lieutenant colonels and maybe twenty or thirty majors and the rest are captains, lieutenants, and so forth." Only one person at a time could gain command experience, and "not until he retires or dies will anybody else get a chance to do that. So we were in a prison, so to speak. Apart from promotions, training opportunities, all sorts of perks that go with the freedom to move about through the Air Force: assignment to the War College, the Pentagon, and all those sorts of things escape you." To make matters worse, the postwar 477th Composite Group and its successor, the 332nd Fighter Wing, faced constant practical problems, the results of personnel mismatches that had dogged the all-black flying groups from their inception. By early 1948 the situation had not improved; thirty-five of forty-eight officer positions in the 332nd were unfilled because Jim Crow prevented black officers from achieving particular specialties. By almost any definition, the 332nd had to be considered an ineffective fighting force. The service would have to admit blacks piecemeal to specialist training schools to which they had until then been denied, staff the wing's tactical units with white officers (a decision that would be guaranteed to bring down condemnation from the civil rights coalition), or desegregate once and for all.[2]

African Americans served the Army credibly during the war in segregated infantry, tanker, and quartermaster units in addition to the aviation group upon which their community had pinned so many hopes. But their wartime service produced few immediate breakthroughs; they found it especially difficult to break into the officer ranks. Two years after the war ended there was only one black officer for every seventy enlisted black men in the Army—this at a time when the ratio for whites was one to seven. The numbers were even more inequitable in the Navy, Marines, and Coast Guard. But in the war years black Americans had forced national debates on the fundamental immorality of segregating the men and women who were willing to sacrifice their lives in the world battle against fascism. As those debates proceeded through the courts of public opinion, the armed forces considered the issue on their own terms.[3]

Blacks had an ally in Noel Parrish, who by 1945 wanted desperately to rid the service of a policy that he knew hampered the institution's abilities to function and fight as effectively as it needed to. He deplored what he called the "terribly expensive[,] disturbing aspects of trying to operate an Air Force within an Air Force with a separate personnel system, a separate training system, a separate everything." Parrish calculated that segregation "made it cost several times what it would have cost to have integrated systems." Tuskegee-trained pilots would have had to be worth "three or four white pilots, at least," he estimated, to justify the expense of the entire training facility on a per-pilot basis. Parrish's experience at TAAF would inform the rest of his career in the Air Force.[4]

When he was selected to attend the Air Command and Staff School as a member of its inaugural class in 1946, Parrish was sufficiently concerned about the issue that he devoted his thesis research to racial discrimination's deleterious effects on training, readiness, and morale in the AAF. He concluded his thesis, "The Segregation of Negroes in the Army Air Forces," with this observation: "<u>In the administration of segregated units there is no routine</u>. There can be no <u>consistent</u> segregation policy because segregation is itself inconsistent and contradictory [emphasis in original]." According to Parrish, racial segregation in the armed forces had to end not because it was immoral but because it was wasteful and impossible to implement logically and consistently. That it was unjust attracted a constituency that fought Jim Crow in the arena of public relations, but it was Parrish's argument regarding productivity and economy that ultimately won the day at the Pentagon.[5]

Parrish's thesis project grew from an ironic fear: The Tuskegee program had been so widely expected to fail that he worried its success could "be used as a further excuse for continuing [segregation] policies which we had overcome with only the greatest difficulty." Parrish received no training in researching and writing a thesis, so he used what he considered the best academic study he could find on the subject of race relations in the United States, Gunnar Myrdal's *An American Dilemma,* as a template. Parrish filled the thesis with anecdotes from his own experience and data from academic and military studies. In contrast to military reports on the performance of black troops in the First World War, it was thoroughly researched and firmly grounded both in academic theory and in practical lived experience.[6]

Parrish focused on the operational problems segregation presented for military commanders, but he also allowed himself the freedom to consider a wide range of topics, including the implications of racial segregation for American religious groups and the folklore that whites had constructed about blacks. He began with a very modern understanding of the concept of "race": that the very concept was socially constructed, not biologically determined. Parrish marveled at one phenomenon in particular. For every stereotype whites had devised about African Americans over the years, he found, they had also devised another equally deeply held, though absolutely contradictory, stereotype. "Negroes are gay—Negroes are melancholy; Negroes are devilish—Negroes are deeply religious; Negroes who succeed do so because of white 'blood'—Negroes of mixed 'blood' are worthless; Negroes are loyal—Negroes are undependable." "These beliefs appear trivial, many of them ridiculous," Parrish concluded, but they also informed policies and actions on the part of the AAF. That, he argued, would have to change.[7]

When the United States entered the Cold War contest against Soviet totalitarianism, racial discrimination began to appear even more an embarrassment to the nation as it engaged in a new geopolitical struggle. Parrish related a telling anecdote from his Tuskegee experience, including a debate that was replayed throughout the world after the war ended:

Mr. Abol Amini, member of the parliament of Iran, and Mr. Majid Movaqar, publisher of the daily newspaper Mehre Iran [*sic*], visited Tuskegee Air Field with a party of Iranians under the guidance of the State Department in 1945. Mr. Moqavar was pro-American and pro-British, Mr. Amini was pro-Russian. The former tried to argue that the effective and expensive Negro training program was an example of democracy in action. His pro-Russian companion asked embarrassing questions: "Why were negro pilots and officers kept apart for the rest of the Air Forces? Were they not also citizens of a democracy? Could the reason be that their complexions were dark?"

There were other visitors from time to time, from Africa, from India. They asked the same questions in various forms.... Most Americans in authority seem to forget that foreign visitors have read our Constitution."[8]

Jim Crow segregation was not only an embarrassment to U.S. interests in this context, but it also actively aided the Soviet Union's propaganda efforts in the Cold War contest to lure non-aligned nations such as Iran, India, and the newly independent nations of Africa into the Soviet orbit.

In fact, the military services did desegregate within a remarkably short period of time after the war's end. But the Pentagon did not do so because racial segregation was morally wrong or for Cold War rhetorical reasons, nor because the Tuskegee Airmen and other all-black fighting units had proved so capable in combat. As compelling as these arguments for desegregation were, the changes came for reasons of operational self-interest on the part of the military. Parrish wrote, "As any administrator knows, standardization of personnel procedures is as important to an organization as standardization of parts is to a factory. Segregation prevents standardized personnel procedures." This practical consideration ultimately doomed Jim Crow in the Air Force. In 1939 the Army Air Corps's chief of personnel responded to black advocacy by complaining, "The War Department is not an agency which can solve national questions relating to the social or economic position of the various racial groups composing our nation." Yet this is precisely what occurred in the service between 1940 and 1949. What had been one of the institutions in American life most indifferent to the aspirations of blacks before the war and a rigidly segregated institution during the war became one of the very first institutions to desegregate after the war.[9]

Tracing that development requires a return to the bureaucratic warfare waged by William Hastie, Truman Gibson, and others, because after the war came the committee work. During the war white Americans directed so much violence toward black soldiers, and blacks responded with so much direct action against segregation, that Secretary Stimson appointed a special committee to look into incidents as they occurred and to make recommendations to avoid similar incidents in the future. The McCloy Committee was a natural enough creation. It would have been the logical mechanism through which Hastie could voice his concerns within the War Department and work toward solutions. But Hastie was not informed of the committee's creation and did not learn of its existence until more than a month after the committee held its first meeting in the Munitions Building. The slight, which was all too typical of his experience there, hastened the judge's resignation from the War Department.[10]

The committee's purpose was to consider "social questions... personnel problems and training, and use of Negro troops." Even McCloy admitted that he was not quite sure what that meant, but his most visible committee member, Gen. Benjamin O. Davis Sr., had a clearer understanding. The advisory committee's overriding goal, he wrote, should be "the breaking down of the so-called 'Jim Crow' practices within the War Department and on the military [bases], and the securing of the cooperation of the communities near [bases] to that end.... [M]ilitary necessity requires a closer unity and comradeship among all races." In March 1943, nearly three months after he assumed the position of civilian aide following Hastie's resignation, Truman Gibson joined the committee and became its most active member.[11]

Gibson was in a precarious position. The NAACP's Roy Wilkins publicly criticized him and other civilians in the War Department in 1943 for "pussy foot[ing,]...cater[ing] to civilian prejudices." But Gibson soldiered on. "Being the African American advocate in the War Department required nimble instincts," he later observed. "One moment you were on the defense, struggling to overcome some antediluvian directive or to push back against Jim Crow tradition." Or protecting your flank from desegregationist activists, he might have added. "The next moment found you on the offense, pushing the envelope to modify army policy to overcome the military's ingrained tendency to opt for segregation on every occasion."[12]

Gibson's greatest test had come in 1943, when he arranged for Benjamin O. Davis Jr.'s testimony before the McCloy Committee to defend the pilots of the 99th. He continued the fight through the end of the war, visiting black troops at training bases throughout the United States and in war zones, reporting his findings to the advisory committee, and pushing war planners to use black units in combat. Though Gibson followed the progress of the 99th and 332nd closely, he did not consider the service of those units to have been the decisive action of the war as far as the argument for desegregation went. Instead, he believed, it was the wartime experience of the all-black 92nd Infantry Division in northern Italy that ultimately provided the best argument for desegregating the Army. Gibson also believed that combat in meeting rooms at the newly built Pentagon, not combat on the battlefield and in the skies, would finally determine what blacks did and did not gain from the war. "The battles producing what little progress that had finally been achieved in World War II would have to be fought again" after the war ended, he later wrote.[13]

In 1945 the McCloy Committee paid particular attention to the skirmish at Freeman Field. Gibson recognized that the AAF had created for itself "a ludicrous position. They couldn't have defended it." As a result of the committee's investigation, the War Department rebuked the commanding officer of the 477th, Col. Robert Selway, and insisted that the Army enforce policies prohibiting the segregation of base facilities. The clearest outcome of the "mutiny," then, was the War Department's restatement of a policy that placed the military firmly on the side of desegregation.[14]

"Participation of Negro Troops in the Post-War Military Establishment," a landmark 1945 study and the first major research endeavor after the war's end to take up the question that had concerned the officers of the War College in 1925, grew out of the work of the McCloy Committee. It aimed to consolidate the committee's investigations of how blacks were performing in the field, with an eye toward creating policies on how black troops should be employed in the postwar military and utilized in the next war. In the course of its deliberations, the committee examined extant research and heard expert testimony from high-ranking, experienced officers in each of the services. One of the strongest proponents of complete desegregation turned out to be the war hero Col. James H. Doolittle, who acknowledged that blacks were forcing desegregation on private industry and before long would force it on the military as well. "You are merely postponing the inevitable, and you might as well take it gracefully," he testified.[15]

The AAF's contributions to the study reflected the prejudicial attitudes of its wartime leaders—in one notable case, quite literally. Each division of the force was responsible for completing its own research into the performance of African Americans in the war, which it then forwarded to the Pentagon for review and compilation into the final document. The First Air Force commissioned its research, Gen. Hunter wrote in a cover letter to Gen. Arnold, from "those who have actually had the most intimate connection with the training of Negro air organizations." Its unidentified author was none other than Robert Selway, who focused the review on the wartime performance of the 477th.[16]

Selway criticized the group for having taken so long to achieve combat readiness, the result (he argued) of blacks' general inability to meet the AAF's high standards. This was of course a wildly unfair charge, given the force's refusal before 1943 to train the black navigators and bombardiers the 477th needed. Instead, Selway concluded that the delay in achievement of combat readiness was due to black Americans' general lack of initiative and inability to perform without strict supervision by whites. He further charged that blacks had no "desire to go to combat" and offered as proof for the indictment a May 1945 survey of the 477th that found that more than 90 percent of the 477th's enlisted men and approximately 80 percent of its officers wished "to be relieved from the Army without delay." In the midst of the Freeman Field "mutiny," a direct result of Selway's incompetent leadership, these results should have surprised no one. When he forwarded the report to the War Department under Arnold's signature, Lt. Col. Louis Nippert of Gen. Arnold's staff watered down or ignored Selway's analyses, but the AAF recommended that segregation continue nonetheless.[17]

Col. Parrish offered an eloquent dissenting opinion. He praised the work of black mechanics and administrative personnel, in addition to pilots, at TAAF, and wrote:

> It is a discouraging fact that Officers of the Army Air Forces whose scientific achievements are unsurpassed, and whose scientific skill is unquestioned in mechanical matters and in many personnel matters, should generally approach the problem of races and minorities with the most unscientific, dogmatic, and arbitrary attitudes....
>
> Whether we like or dislike Negroes and whether they like or dislike us, under the Constitution of the United States, which we are all sworn to uphold, they are citizens of the United States having the same rights and privileges of other citizens and entitled to the same applications and protection of the laws.

He had a single, simple recommendation for the employment of Negro troops moving forward: The only consideration should be the "employment and treatment of Negroes as individuals which the war requires and which military efficiency demands." That was a minority opinion in 1945, but the Air Force would come around to Parrish's shockingly modern approach to race relations in a short period of time.[18]

The McCloy Committee disbanded at the end of the war, having brought attention to the mistreatment of black troops and laid the groundwork for desegregation, but the need for consideration of "the Negro question" continued at the Pentagon. In 1945 a new committee, known as the Gillem Board after its chairman, Gen. Alvan C. Gillem Jr., began holding hearings on the Army's racial policies and planned to make recommendations on how the radically restructured postwar force could best utilize blacks' service. The board heard expert testimony from a familiar cast of characters. William Hastie argued for immediate desegregation, but in something of a twist he acknowledged that the Army was closer to desegregating than other national institutions.

Benjamin O. Davis Sr. offered withering criticism of any policy that subordinated military effectiveness to questions of who should or should not sit next to whom in a mess hall. He wondered how "foreign people such as the French, Russians and Brazilians" would interpret such policies in a Cold War context. His son recommended gradual integration with more attention paid to the quality of leadership at the unit level. If the leaders were competent, he argued, integration of troops could occur without incident. In his testimony Parrish made no secret of his disgust with segregation on grounds of morality and military efficiency, but suggested that the military could avoid the problem altogether by ignoring the concept of racial integration and insisting instead on "assignment by qualification"—in other words, true color-blindness. The rest, he said, would take care of itself.[19]

Apart from Parrish, every white officer with experience commanding black troops in combat testified that even the limited and gradual desegregation of troops was inadvisable. In April 1946 the Gillem Board seemed to privilege the testimony of non-combat commanders like Parrish and civilian advocates such as Walter White and William Hastie, and it recommended the integration of forces—but only gradually and only during duty hours. Parrish considered the recommendations too timid. "[T]he breaking up of the big segregated units into smaller segregated units," he wrote, "does not seem a significant step."[20]

The National Security Act of 1947 merged the Department of War and Department of the Navy into the National Military Establishment, which would shortly thereafter be renamed the Department of Defense. The act also created an independent U.S. Air Force. The timing was significant: the reorganization of the Army Air Forces into the newly autonomous Air Force meant that new civilian leadership came on board just as new military leaders emerged to replace Gen. Arnold following the successful conclusion of wartime operations. Advocates of desegregation recognized a window of opportunity. At this point the Air Force was little closer to practical integration than it had been before the war, but the policies developed by the McCloy and Gillem committees had laid the groundwork necessary for a radical restructuring of the force.

The major civilian figure in the movement toward desegregation was the first secretary of the Air Force, W. Stuart Symington, a Missouri businessman and longtime Truman supporter who had transformed Emerson Electric Co. into a major defense contractor and integrated its professional workforce during the war. Symington had military allies in Gen. Carl A. Spaatz, the first chief of staff of the Air Force; and Lt. Gen. Idwal Edwards, Air Force deputy chief of staff for personnel, who had also been a member of the McCloy Committee. Edwards did not consider the 332nd Fighter Wing, much less the 477th, to have been an effective fighting unit, but he did not blame blacks for the groups' shortcomings. Edwards was most responsible for the desegregation policies the service would embrace in short order. He and Symington would come to be considered the new service's staunchest advocates of desegregation—on grounds of military efficiency, Cold War ideology, and morality, in that order. They came to understand segregation as unworkable because no military unit was stronger than its weakest members, and segregation illogically bunched together the strong and the weak.[21]

Inter-service rivalry surely played a role in the Air Force leaders' decision to move ahead with integration plans. This was an opportunity for the Air Force to prove it was more forward-looking than the Army and Navy, more professional and less bound by tradition. Besides, as Parrish wrote in his thesis, "The advantages, to the Air Forces, of getting ahead of pressure in its personnel and assignment policies would be well worth the effort. At least the seizing of the initiative in this field would be a new experience." By 1947 Symington, Spaatz, and Edwards had convinced themselves that the Air Force would have to desegregate and were on the edge of creating policy to accomplish it, but they waited for a signal from the commander-in-chief before proceeding further.[22]

They did not have to wait long. President Harry S. Truman created the President's Committee on Civil Rights (PCCR) in December 1946 with his Executive Order 9808, and the PCCR began studying the problem of racial discrimination in the United States in 1947. Truman, a Missourian with ideas about race that were typical of whites in the border South of his time, had nonetheless developed a decent civil rights record as a U.S. senator and had proved sympathetic to efforts to desegregate air training before the war. After ascending to the presidency, by all reports, Truman was moved to action by news from the South of black veterans being brutalized by white authorities. According to one account, in the city of Birmingham, Alabama, alone, Police Commissioner T. Eugene ("Bull") Connor's force killed as many as five black war veterans in the first two months of 1946.[23]

There were similar incidents reported in Louisiana, Texas, Georgia, Florida, and Tennessee, but the most notorious case was that of Isaac Woodard, an Army veteran who returned from fifteen months' service in the South Pacific to be honorably discharged at Camp Gordon, Georgia, in February 1946. Woodard immediately boarded a Greyhound bus bound for North Carolina, where he planned to meet his wife and then make a visit home to New York. But Woodard, still in uniform, had words with the white bus driver over a perceived racial transgression soon after the bus crossed into South Carolina. The two argued in the town of Aiken, and the driver radioed ahead to the police of Batesburg. When the bus arrived in Batesburg, Police Chief Lynwood L. Shull and a deputy removed Woodard from the bus, arrested him, and beat him savagely while in their custody. When Woodard finally received medical care the next day, doctors determined that the chief and deputy had damaged Woodard's eyes with their nightsticks so severely that he would never see again. Confronted with the news of this and other outrages, Truman reportedly exclaimed, "My God! I had no idea it was as terrible as that! We have to do something." He wrote an acquaintance, "When [local authorities] can take a Negro sergeant off a bus, beat him and put out one of his eyes, and nothing is done about it by State Authorities, then something is radically wrong with the system."[24]

Creating the PCCR was Truman's response. It was one of his most brilliant political moves, arguably his master stroke. The PCCR would educate the white public about what Truman and others saw as the need to extend constitutional protections to African American citizens and align his political interests with those of civil rights advocates, but in a way that minimized the damage done to his reputation among white southern Democrats. It set in motion a chain of events that resulted in the immediate desegregation of the U.S. military—a decade before the U.S. Supreme Court's *Brown* decision began to desegregate the nation's schools "with all deliberate speed." The PCCR's influential committee report set the agenda for the civil rights movement into the mid-1960s, but it would be another twenty years before direct action campaigns finally forced Congress to outlaw Jim Crow segregation in public accommodations and guarantee their voting rights.[25]

Facing a tough 1948 re-election campaign, Truman walked a political tightrope in giving the PCCR its mandate. He had real reason to fear alienating white Southerners; as it happened, in 1948 the previously solidly Democratic South did abandon Truman for the States Rights, or "Dixiecrat," party and its standard bearer, Gov. J. Strom Thurmond of South Carolina. Truman also worried about losing support from his left to the New Dealer Henry A. Wallace, who became the candidate of the Progressive Party in the midst of Truman's tough campaign against Republican Thomas A. Dewey, the popular governor of New York. At the same time, as they had in 1944, black voters were signaling that they needed new, concrete reasons to turn out in numbers for the Democrats.[26]

PCCR Director Robert K. Carr, a professor of government at Dartmouth, led a small staff that held public hearings with testimony from forty witnesses, corresponded with more than two hundred private organizations and individuals, and solicited data from twenty-five federal agencies over a span of several months in 1947. In the public hearings government witnesses tended to make the case for a greater effort on the part of the national government to educate the white public about blacks' lives and the contributions they could make to American society if given a fair chance. Civil rights advocates such as Walter White argued the need for greater federal intervention on behalf of blacks' citizenship rights. The members of the PCCR were evidently swayed by the latter.[27]

Events moved astonishingly fast throughout 1947. In the midst of the PCCR's deliberations, Truman became the first American president to address the annual meeting of the NAACP. Speaking from the steps of the Lincoln Memorial before an audience estimated at ten thousand and a national radio audience of millions on June 29, Truman said that the time had come for the United States "to put our own house in order." The federal government, he pledged, would become the "friendly vigilant defender of the rights and equalities of all Americans." At least one Tuskegee Airman was in the audience. A former pilot cadet and intelligence officer for the 332nd, twenty-seven-year-old Percy Sutton, took a break from his graduate studies (he was enrolled simultaneously in programs at Columbia University and Brooklyn Law School) to attend the NAACP's thirty-eighth annual conference in the segregated capital. "All around me," he recalled, "blacks in the audience were reacting with uh huhs and God bless yous as President Truman repeated his words pledging civil rights equality for all Americans." Walter White compared the speech to the Gettysburg Address.[28]

The NAACP kept up the pressure on the administration, however. Just days before the PCCR released its report, the organization submitted a petition of grievances on behalf of black Americans to the United Nations Commission on Human Rights. Authored by W.E.B. DuBois, the petition announced: "This protest is a frank and earnest appeal to all the world for elemental justice against the treatment which the United States has visited upon us for three centuries.... It is to induce the nations of the world to persuade this nation to be just to its own people, that we... now present to you this document." The United States successfully blunted the Soviet Union's proposal that the commission take up an investigation into the petition's charges, but the entire episode damaged the nation's international reputation in the early days of the Cold War. U.S. Attorney General Tom Clark admitted to being "humiliated" not just by the international incident but by the truths the petition contained. In any case, the petition's timing ensured that the PCCR's report would receive maximum publicity and would result in concrete, practical action from the Truman administration, which was anxious to avoid such public displays of black disaffection.[29]

The PCCR's report, titled *To Secure These Rights* and released in October 1947, hewed closely to sociologist Gunnar Myrdal's thesis in the landmark book that had so influenced Parrish, *An American Dilemma*, published in 1944. Myrdal conceived of America's race-relations problem as having resulted from a gap between national ideals of equal opportunity and the realities of racial discrimination. He prescribed a blend of popular education programs and federal intervention that the PCCR would follow closely in its own recommendations, although the PCCR's report went further in suggesting specific, concrete ways in which various apparatuses of the federal government might protect individuals from racial discrimination. *To Secure These Rights* was elegantly and persuasively written. It achieved Truman's goals for the PCCR, attracting millions of readers and drawing attention to the problem of racial discrimination in a way that not even the NAACP's decades' worth of advocacy had.[30]

To Secure These Rights never once mentioned the Tuskegee Airmen, but its most substantive recommendation flowed from their experience. The committee report traced the development of basic constitutional rights as various ethnic and racial minority groups had exercised them over time in the United States, but it paid special attention to the experience of African Americans, and it portrayed World War II as a turning point. The report objected in especially strenuous language to discriminatory treatment toward black war veterans, concluded that discrimination within the military was unacceptable, and recommended vigorous action on the part of the federal government to remedy the wrong. "[A]ny discrimination which, while imposing an obligation, prevents members of minority groups from rendering full military service in defense of their country is for them a peculiarly humiliating badge of inferiority," the committee wrote. "The nation also suffers a loss of manpower and is unable to marshal maximum strength at a moment when such strength is most needed."[31]

The PCCR found most compelling the evidence that segregation of the armed forces provided rhetorical ammunition to the nation's enemies on the one hand and caused costly inefficiencies on the other. "The injustice of calling men to fight for freedom while subjecting them to humiliating discrimination within the fighting forces is at once apparent," the PCCR asserted in one of its most strongly worded conclusions. "Furthermore, by preventing entire groups from making their maximum contribution to the national defense, we weaken our defense to that extent and impose heavier burdens on the remainder of the population." *To Secure These Rights* recommended that Congress immediately use powers that the Constitution had clearly granted to the legislative branch "to end immediately all discrimination and segregation based on race, color, creed, or national origin, in the organization and activities of all branches of the Armed Services." In addition, the committee recommended a concerted effort to recruit, assign, and train troops without regard to race, and to prevent the segregation of military men traveling in uniform within the United States. (This last point should have been moot; the U.S. Supreme Court had already ruled in the 1947 *Morgan v. Commonwealth of Virginia* decision that racial segregation of passengers in interstate travel was unconstitutional. But in a pattern that would repeat itself several times over through the next two decades, federal lassitude left it up to African American activists to see to it that the decision was implemented.)[32]

Somewhere in the White House a closet is full to overflowing with reports from presidential commissions that presidents have chosen to ignore. *To Secure These Rights* would not be one of those reports. The committee supported its recommendations with readings of the Constitution that sanctioned Congressional action on desegregation. But Truman and the commissioners themselves knew full well that Southern Democrats with seniority in the House and Senate would not allow such legislation to proceed, so the recommendations gave Truman the political cover he needed to act decisively if he chose to do so. Truman's prospects for re-election in 1948 made the action more likely: his advisers estimated that black voters could provide the balance of power in New York, New Jersey, Pennsylvania, Ohio, Michigan, and Illinois, and they encouraged Truman to make "a fresh commitment to the Negro cause." He delivered an unprecedented special message to Congress in February 1948 calling for the enactment of several of the PCCR's recommendations. These included the creation of a permanent Commission on Civil Rights and a Civil Rights Division in the Department of Justice, stronger federal civil rights and voting rights statutes, protection against lynching, and other reforms. The message concluded with a bombshell: Truman informed the Congress that he was directing the Secretary of Defense to eliminate "the remaining instances of discrimination in the armed services...as rapidly as possible."[33]

That order was dramatic, but three months later the Department of Defense was still unable to put forth a comprehensive desegregation plan. A. Philip Randolph again threatened to lead a march of tens of thousands of black Americans through the streets of Washington and pledged that he would personally counsel blacks to avoid conscription into the Jim Crow military by any means necessary. The Air Force and Navy submitted plans to desegregate, but the Army dragged its feet through the spring. Truman finally broke the logjam in July with the release of Executive Order 9981, which announced:

> It is hereby declared to be the policy of the President that there shall be equality of treatment and opportunity for all persons in the armed services without regard to race, color, or religion or national origin. This policy shall be put into effect as rapidly as possible, having due regard to the time required to effectuate any necessary changes without impairing efficiency or morale.

Army Chief of Staff Gen. Omar Bradley bucked the order, using language that already sounded antique. Bradley pronounced, "The Army is not out to make any social reforms. The Army will put men of different races in different companies. It will change that policy when the Nation as a whole changes it." Truman reiterated, however, that though the order called for gradual desegregation of the armed forces, the armed forces *would* desegregate. He forced Bradley to issue a public apology.[34]

Truman's request for stronger civil rights legislation was dead on arrival on Capitol Hill, but his actions had at least one desired effect. Blacks and white liberals lined up in large enough numbers behind the president in the November election to assure his re-election. Two of every three black votes in the election went to Truman, and they were decisive in California, Ohio, and Illinois. Had Dewey carried any two of those states, he would have won the election.

Even aside from electoral politics, it would be hard to exaggerate the impact of Executive Order 9981, for exactly the reasons Bradley voiced. By desegregating the armed forces Truman did push the executive branch of the federal government ahead of public opinion. By changing Army policy he did change national policy. And once Truman had placed the agents of federal power on the side of desegregation and forced them to offer black Americans fully equal opportunities, how could there possibly be any going back? Dorothy Height, longtime chairwoman of the National Council of Negro Women, considered the "integration of the armed services...the most significant institutional advance for the civil rights of black Americans since President Lincoln issued the Emancipation Proclamation."[35]

The Air Force finalized its decision to desegregate in the period between the creation of the PCCR and the issuance of Executive Order 9981. It was the swiftest of the armed forces to carry out its plans; the Air Force made substantial progress toward real integration within ten months of Truman's order, whereas it took the Army and Navy another two years to begin even token efforts at integration. Gen. Edwards justified his actions matter-of-factly: "The Commander-in-Chief said that this should be done and so we did it." Symington recalled that Truman had demanded of the Air Force, "I want concrete results—that's what I'm after—not publicity on it. I want the job done."[36]

A major hurdle remained, however. Parrish reported in 1947 that he had "yet to encounter the white Army officer who has found time ever to examine Myrdal's classic summary, or any dependable source of fundamental information" on the subject of race relations or the lives of African Americans. Nonetheless, he had "spent hundreds of hours listening to presentations of limited knowledge and experience that passed for wisdom [on the subject]" over drinks in officers' clubs. The order came down from the Pentagon that black Americans in the Air Force would be treated fairly, as individuals, but it would take years to change this crucial aspect of institutional culture among the overwhelmingly white officer corps.[37]

The Air Force planned to initiate integration by dispersing the officer corps at Lockbourne; so, as it did in every other American institution, the work of desegregating the Air Force fell hardest on blacks. By 1948 three-fourths of all the black officers in the Air Force and every single one of the active pilots in the Tactical Air Command were stationed at Lockbourne. Many of the officers liked it that way, and not all of them went along willingly with the Air Force's plan. Charles Dryden, the pilot who described life in the all-black Air Force at Lockbourne as "Camelot," led an effort among junior officers on the base in early 1949 to challenge the Air Force's plans.[38]

Those plans had not yet been released to the public. Dryden and his fellow challengers had not actually seen the plans' details, so they were left to imagine the worst. It is understandable that they would do so. Having served under Col. Selway and Gen. Hunter during the war, they could be forgiven for assuming that their superiors in the Air Force did not have their best interests at heart. The group lodged a complaint with the NAACP, which sent their former comrade Robert L. Carter to Lockbourne to investigate their concerns. Carter learned that the group's "general sentiment seems to be in favor of integration.... Generally the men feel that if integration occurs, it will be the best thing for all concerned." At the same time, "There are doubts, of course, of being given ample opportunity to advance and prove their proficiency if they are removed from Lockbourne Air Base.... [T]hey present the general cry of professional persons in a segregated unit who believe their careers are safest under a segregated set up."[39]

Dryden's group assumed that under the Air Force's plans the majority of the officers who held command responsibilities at Lockbourne would be transferred out to dead-end assignments commanding black labor battalions at other bases, and that others would be transferred into light-duty positions that prevented them from commanding whites. As an alternative first step they suggested that the Air Force should leave the 332nd in place at an expanded Lockbourne. The Air Force could integrate the base by keeping the existing leadership structure intact and transferring whites in to serve in junior roles. The Air Force had heretofore resisted any arrangements under which whites had to follow the orders of black officers; this scenario offered a chance for the Air Force to prove that it was serious about offering black officers real opportunities in the new service.[40]

For once, however, Dryden and his group underestimated the leadership of the Air Force. On paper, the service's integration plans did offer a fair shot to black officers and enlisted men to rise as high as their talents could take them, and the service's leadership seemed determined to make the plans a reality. If the Air Force leadership could convince the service's middle managers that white officers who did not offer fully equal opportunity to blacks would not advance their careers—if they could change the institutional culture Parrish found so tedious—the plans could work. The NAACP elected to take the service at its word and declined to pursue Dryden's grievance. The 332nd would be disbanded and the Tuskegee Airmen who remained in the service dispersed to other units.

Of the 192 officers of the 332nd at Lockbourne in 1949, 158 were reassigned in their already established occupational specialties to previously all-white units. Twenty-four were assigned for additional training before transferring to other units, and ten were separated from the service as part of a reduction in force. Leaving the 332nd and spreading out to the four winds was a bittersweet experience for the officers of the all-black unit. Pilot Lewis Lynch was of two minds about the breakup. He recalled, "In the segregated Air Force you knew everybody. You didn't have anything to prove in terms of could you fly or couldn't you fly. The people around you knew. You had been marked, for good or for bad. You had a reputation." He was quick to mention a down side to the arrangement, however: "The bad part about the segregated Air Force was that if you're on somebody's shit list, you're on their list forever because you didn't have any chance to convince him otherwise." He continued, "But the worst thing was there was no place to go. The rank structure was fixed. We had a colonel, who was the wing commander, Col. Davis. There was no place for those guys who were aspiring to go further. The squadron commanders were fixed. The flight commanders weren't going anyplace, so you were stuck. You're not going to move."[41]

After the desegregation decision came down, "I was glad," Dryden later claimed, "that we could be assigned to other units and be promoted according to—to quote Dr. King—the 'content of our character and not the color of our skin.'" But Dryden and the other men of the 332nd, many of whom had been together now for seven years, gave up a lot to desegregate the service. "We had gotten to the point where in the air, we knew just how to fly with each other. You knew what the other guy was going to do and what you could depend on him to do, and we had had seven years experience with our own mechanics and instrument people and parachute riggers and all the rest. We had total confidence in all segments of the operation." Now the pilots would be transferring into units where each was the only black or maybe one of a pair. Members of the group that "had become like family" would now be disconnected and redistributed to bases literally around the globe.[42]

Harry T. Stewart, a combat pilot who left the Air Force just before the 332nd disbanded, was candid in his assessment of integration's cost. "I'm not too sure how well I would have fared in a so-called integrated Air Force, because I had the support while I was in Tuskegee," Ramitelli, and Lockbourne, he said. "I was in a group, and we gave each other support. When they integrated, a lot of people went out on their own, and they no longer had that kind of support there. It must have been a struggle and a lonely existence for a lot of them."[43]

What Stewart called the 332nd's "last hurrah" came in May 1949, just before the diaspora commenced. The Air Force held its inaugural ten-day "William Tell" gunnery meet at Nellis Air Force Base in Nevada. Stewart,

Alva N. Temple, and James H. Harvey represented the 332nd (along with an alternate, Halbert L. Alexander) and competed in dive-bombing, skip-bombing, strafing, and aerial target shooting competitions against pilots from all-white fighter groups. When the final scores were tallied, Alva Temple had placed second overall and the 332nd won the team competition. "They didn't expect us to win, naturally, but we did win. Won by a large margin," Harvey remembered. "They thought they were better than us, and we were just as—well, I say we were better. That's all I ever say: We're better. Not just as good; we're better. And we proved we were better."[44]

For whatever reason, however, the Air Force found it difficult to acknowledge the 332nd's victory. "The Air Force Association puts out an almanac once a year," Harvey noted. "One of the items in the almanac is the winners of the gunnery meets, from 1949 through the present day. For 1949, each year the almanac was published, it would say, 'Unknown.'" In 1993, Col. William Campbell, the president of Tuskegee Airmen Inc. (TAI), an alumni group, "got all the data together, presented it to the Air Force, and as of April of 1995 the almanac shows the 332nd as the winners of the 1949 weapons meet. Now, forty-some years, that's a long time. They knew who won. They just didn't want to recognize us."[45]

Harvey cherished the victory in part because it had truly been a team effort. The 332nd flew outdated P-47s against the other teams' P-51 Mustangs and F-82s. "We took four aircraft, [but] we flew the same three aircraft for two weeks," he said. "That's how good our maintenance [crew] was. They were excellent." Alva Temple explained that each group's entire operations team was tested, "in that if an airplane didn't make that mission for any reason, if the guns weren't operating properly, that counted against you" in the competition. "If the engines weren't right and you had to come in [for repairs], that was counted against you. In other words, it was an overall test of the capability of a unit." Harry Stewart recalled, "We only flew in the competition for, at the very most, an hour and a half a day. The rest of the time these planes were being kept in fine tune by the crew chiefs and the maintenance people with our group, and they worked all through the night and part of the day in keeping those planes in tip-top shape. And we were so proud because we never had a malfunction all the time we were out there, and we think this contributed so much to our victories there. We owe our victories to those enlisted men." When the men of the maintenance cadre went out to celebrate the victory, they were denied entry to a Las Vegas casino that served whites only.[46]

The group's final breakup came two months later. Harvey and Lt. Edward P. Drummond of the 332nd were assigned to the 35th Fighter Wing at Misawa Air Base in Japan. "We met with the wing commander when we got there," Harvey remembered, and then described the kind of experience that the men of the 332nd had at bases all over the world. "We had a little chit-chat, and then the commander"—who had apparently never spent much time around black Americans—"said, 'What do you want us to call you?' It's a military outfit! 'What do you want us to call you?!' I said, 'Well, I'm a first lieutenant. Eddie Drummond is a second lieutenant. How about 'Lt. Harvey' and 'Lt. Drummond?' He said, 'OK.' He realized he had screwed up."[47]

Conditions throughout the Air Force certainly did not change overnight, but the service made tremendous strides by the time Truman reinstituted the draft for the Korean War in 1950. Percy Sutton volunteered to return to service in 1950. He considered the Korean War-era Air Force "dramatically different" from the one he had served in World War II. Sutton was named chief legal officer at the newly integrated Andrews Air Force Base in Maryland, a position that required real leadership as it placed him in a command position over black and white officers and servicemen; a black dental officer and a black medical officer joined him at Andrews.[48]

Some men who remained in the Air Force reported that conditions changed gradually enough after the war that Truman's executive order made little substantive difference in their day-to-day lives when it came down. William Gray, a bombardier-navigator of the 477th who had mustered out after the war but then re-enlisted in 1947 as a communications specialist, remembered that blacks and whites worked alongside one another in so many capacities at Randolph Field in Texas that his squadron's softball and bowling teams integrated after the presidential order came down, but beyond that little else changed. Gray earned low-level responsibilities that put him in charge of whites for the first time after Truman's order, but he recalled that he "[n]ever had any problem with attitudes. Those that didn't like me before still didn't like me, and those that liked me before still liked me."[49] Lucius Theus, a personnel administrator who served directly under Davis at Lockbourne, was already so used to having to achieve perfection in everything he did that when he transferred into a previously all-white unit "the transition was not really difficult at all." His new commander could hardly expect more of him than Davis had, Theus thought.[50]

Others found that little changed with Truman's order, but for different reasons. Theopolis W. ("Ted") Johnson, a pilot with the 477th, was recalled to service for the Korean War. "What I found," he said, "is that people paid more lip service to the instructions from the White House and to the instructions from Air Force headquarters than they did to actually trying to make it go. I got the feeling that I was always on trial, that I was always on center stage." Johnson continued,

It was rough, because I was one of two black officers in a fighter wing, which had a complement of maybe three thousand individuals and maybe 150 officers altogether. I remember I considered myself always being tested to see what I could do or to see what I would do in response to a certain situation. So from my view, I was given the dirtiest jobs. I was given the jobs that nobody else would tackle.

It was a constant test to see if I would break. For me, it was a constant test to prove to them that I would not. I don't know if they enjoyed it, but I enjoyed it. I had a ball, proving that I could do what I said I could do. I enjoyed that.

Socially—there were times when, at the club, at a function, they would make comments. Sometimes I ignored them. Sometimes I didn't. Frequently there was the "n" word and the "m-f" word and the "m-f-n" word and so forth and so on. It depends upon how I felt at the time. Most of the time I simply ignored it. But occasionally I would rear up and say [gritting teeth and speaking very deliberately], "Please don't use that term where I can hear it." But that seemed to make things worse.[51]

James Warren, one of the 101 men arrested at Freeman, left the Air Forces in 1945, graduated from the University of Illinois and worked for an architectural firm in Chicago. He was recalled to service for the Korean War and assigned to Mather Field in California. His trip from Chicago to the West Coast provided unwelcome memories of the last war. Hotels in New Mexico refused to serve him, and he and his wife "damn near froze [sleeping] in the car." The couple attempted to enter a Las Vegas casino, but "a guy with the biggest gun I'd ever seen" intercepted them and warned, "No, your people have a place over on the west side."[52]

When Warren was transferred to Langley Air Force Base in southeastern Virginia for combat crew training, he tried to use the base swimming pool but was informed, "The colonel wishes you wouldn't use the pool." Warren wearily asked to see the base commander, who told him, "Well, you know, we're not quite set up down here for integration." "It's not a matter whether you're set up or not," Warren, a lieutenant, said he informed his superior officer. "And by the way, I have more experience in this than you do. I was arrested in World War II protesting just the type of thing that you're trying to do. Does that give you an indication of what's going to happen?" Warren received his pool privileges. "I wasn't a very enthusiastic swimmer" until then, he remembered, but he became one, and he brought guests from nearby Hampton Institute to the pool every chance he got. He went on to fly fifty combat missions as a navigator in Korea and earned the Distinguished Flying Cross.[53]

Warren elected to make a career of the Air Force. He faced few instances of discrimination in the post-integration service that were as blatant as those he had endured under Selway's command. But there were cases that made him suspicious: the promotion paperwork that always seemed to get lost or misfiled; the many superior officers who made sure he remembered that he was the only black officer under their respective commands; the constant questioning of his qualifications. In the late 1960s, when he transferred to Travis Air Force Base in California and put down earnest money on a house, the seller's commanding officer tried to force him to back out of the sale because the neighbors—fellow officers at Travis—did not want a black in their midst. But Warren remained in the service long enough to witness the Air Force's slow evolution into something like a meritocracy.[54]

The private sector was slow to catch up to the Air Force. The coalition of black newspapers, historically black colleges, and civil rights organizations that pushed for anti-segregation and anti-discrimination reforms in the AAC before the war did so in part because its members expected aviation would be a red-hot field after the war. The assumption was correct. Unfortunately, however, the momentum of wartime change did not carry over into peacetime, and blacks were not permitted to fill the new jobs created in the industry's postwar expansion. Black Americans were largely denied the chance to make careers for themselves in aviation.

Not for lack of trying. As he had before the war, Walter White of the NAACP initiated a broad letter-writing campaign intended to win airline jobs for blacks who had been trained at Tuskegee. "During the past two years I have had the opportunity of visiting battlefronts in both the European and Pacific Theatres of War as a war correspondent," he wrote to the presidents of the major airline companies late in 1945. "One of the questions most frequently and anxiously asked me by Negro fliers and members of ground crews was whether an opportunity to use their training and experience would be given them by commercial airlines after the war. It will be a source of great encouragement to these men to know that such opportunities will be afforded." Pilots and service crew members of the 332nd and 477th assured White that they wanted to put their training to use as civilians. "Through various sources I have heard that the NAACP is fighting to place Negro pilots on Commercial Airlines," Lloyd S. Hathcock wrote White, hoping the organization could help him secure a job. "I have been overseas with the 332nd Fighter Group as a pilot, and I am very interested in commercial flying."[55]

The response from Linus C. Glotzbach, president of Northwest Airlines, was representative of the airlines' reaction to White's efforts: "It is our policy to employ our personnel without regard to race, creed or color.... We are working on an extensive training program for all our personnel, but it is not designed to give any special consideration to any particular group."[56] But Northwest would not hire a Tuskegee-trained pilot after the war. Neither did Delta, American, United, Trans World, or any of the other major passenger carriers. Charles "Buster" Hall, winner of the Distinguished Flying Cross and the first black American to shoot down an enemy plane in combat, applied for jobs with all of them after the war, but the only work he could find was managing a restaurant. In fact, of all the pilots affiliated with the Tuskegee program, only James O. Plinton Jr., a Moton Field flight instructor, found employment with a major airline in the immediate postwar years, and he worked not as a pilot but an administrator, beginning with Trans World Airlines in 1957 and rising finally to the position of vice president for marketing of Eastern Airlines. The Red Tails who piloted so many white bomber crew members to safety never had the chance to put those skills to work in the civilian world.[57]

Tuskegee Airmen officers who made a career of the Air Force tended to fare better. Benjamin O. Davis Jr. became the Air Force's first black general officer in 1954. He held several high-profile commands at bases throughout the world through the Cold War and Korean and Vietnam conflicts, and ultimately retired with a third star. Davis had a second career as the city of Cleveland's director of public safety and then as an assistant secretary in the Carter-era U.S. Department of Transportation (following in the footsteps of William T. Coleman, an officer in the 477th and Gerald Ford's secretary of transportation), where he was responsible for anti-terrorist efforts and civil aviation security. President Bill Clinton awarded Davis a fourth star, making him the nation's second black full general, in 1998.

Charles Dryden excelled in the new Air Force, although he always worried that his display of frustration at Walterboro would come back to haunt him. It never did. "Every time there was a reduction in force, I just knew, 'Well, I'm gone; they're going to get me,'" he said. "But I survived them all and finally retired a lieutenant colonel, which people are amazed at and so am I." Charles McGee, the pilot who described his missions escorting bombers over the Romanian oil fields, remained an active combat pilot in the Air Force through the Korean and Vietnam wars, racking up more than six thousand flight hours. He "got along fine on base" through a series of stateside and overseas commands, he said, but found after-hours base facilities slower to desegregate and found housing his family a constant struggle into the 1960s. He retired in 1972 as the commanding officer of Richards-Gebaur Air Base outside Kansas City.[58]

Daniel ("Chappie") James Jr., one of the most gifted graduates of the Tuskegee Institute CPT program, who had first instructed pilots at Moton Field and then talked his way into the TAFS program, graduated into the 477th and rose steadily through the ranks after the war. A large man at 6 feet 4 inches tall and well more than 200 pounds ("I don't climb into an airplane, I strap it on," he was supposedly fond of saying), James was literally a poor fit for the 332nd. Had the Air Force not been forced to create the 477th and generate openings for pilots of James's stature, it would have been denied the service of a man who became of its most effective Cold War-era leaders. The bomber group allowed James to remain in the service until the introduction of the postwar jet fighter aircraft that were large enough to accommodate his size; he was one of the most decorated fighter pilots of the Korean and Vietnam wars.[59]

James became a general officer and after a series of successful stateside and overseas commands became the first African American awarded a fourth star. He ascended to the command of North American Air Defense (NORAD), making him responsible for all strategic aerospace defense forces for the United States and Canada. A gifted public speaker, James delivered countless addresses extolling the virtues of the United States and calling on all Americans—black Americans especially—to be more vocally and proudly patriotic. In the ears of black critics of the Vietnam War, James's preaching sounded all too much like blind apologias for the American mistake in Southeast Asia. James's controversial and sometimes bombastic public pronouncements may have deflected attention from his gifts as an administrator, but they also provided cover for other blacks in the military. With Chappie James manning the public relations hustings, other blacks did not have to give as much voice to their own patriotism.[60]

The Air Force facility that made those careers possible fared less well. Training bases like TAAF closed by the dozens throughout the country as the Army Air Forces demobilized at war's end. TAAF remained open into 1946, training diminishing numbers of aviation cadets and providing a temporary home base for black officers who wanted to make a career of the service. Sheer numbers—the same problem that had bedeviled TAAF administrators from the outset—made it increasingly difficult to operate the base. Returning combat veterans found flying time difficult to come by at the base, and they chafed in their make-work assignments. "I was the assistant-assistant-assistant base message center officer, which is just a job, just someplace to go when you're not flying," recalled Lewis Lynch, one of the returned veterans of the 332nd. "I was just there, wasting time."[61]

Frederick D. Patterson sought to save TAAF by lobbying the Air Force to keep the base open as a training school and headquarters for all-black tactical units. But an outcry from the black community, particularly in the form of *Pittsburgh Courier* editorials and NAACP press releases, was so loud and withering that it forced Patterson to withdraw a formal appeal he made to Gen. Marshall to spare the base. The *Norfolk Journal and Guide*, among other black newspapers, repeated Hastie's earlier accusation, accusing Patterson of placing Tuskegee Institute's interests above those of black

Americans. Black elites still regarded TAAF not as a showpiece of black achievement but an embarrassing Jim Crow relic.[62]

Local whites shed few tears at TAAF's disappearing act. The base historian reported at the end of the war that local "white people are willing... that the station remain in its present location provided it is always under command of a white officer and [has] white officers in positions of control." A few local white merchants, he wrote, "realize that the field is a great source of revenue, but even these would prefer that the colored personnel send their money to town and not come with it." The Army Air Forces formally deactivated TAAF in April 1946. Thereafter black cadets quietly entered flight training at Randolph Air Force Base in San Antonio.[63]

Along with dozens of fellow officers, Lewis Lynch transferred from TAAF to Lockbourne, in his hometown of Columbus. He was flying at Lockbourne when the Air Force desegregated. When the 332nd disbanded, he spent several years at Williams Air Force Base in Arizona as an instructor, imparting the knowledge he had first gleaned years before from Lewis Jackson at Moton Field to flight cadets from NATO nations. "When they integrated the Air Force," Lynch said, "I found that we had to prove all over again that we could fly. I was surprised when I got to Williams how few people knew that there were black pilots in the Air Force. Hardly anyone knew anything. The 332nd itself was the best-kept secret in the Air Force. Nobody knew that we existed except those few bombers that we had escorted." When he was forcibly retired from flying in 1964 because of recurring migraines, Lynch went straight to work for the Air Force as a civilian contracting officer. By then the service's colorblind ethic had begun to take hold, making his civilian career possible.[64]

It is difficult to make broad generalizations about the postwar careers of the Tuskegee Airmen and impossible to list all of their later accomplishments, but by and large they made disproportionately large contributions in civilian life. A few of them continued their trajectory as civil rights crusaders. Robert L. Carter, the legal officer who was drummed out of the Air Forces, and William T. Coleman joined the NAACP's Legal Defense and Education Fund and helped litigate the landmark *Brown v. Board of Education,* among many other cases. Percy Sutton risked his life as a Freedom Rider in 1961 and as an attorney went on to represent scores of civil rights activists who found themselves in southern jails. Sutton was an active leader in the Manhattan NAACP for several years and served as the borough's elected president from 1965 to 1977. Along the way he made millions in the broadcasting industry. Coleman Young, the labor organizer who had also been at the center of the 477th's protests, became mayor of Detroit and one of the most powerful black elected officials in the United States in the 1970s.[65]

Roscoe Brown returned home and entered graduate school at New York University almost immediately, using GI Bill benefits to earn a PhD in education. He remained active in the NAACP and had a long and distinguished career as an administrator at the City University of New York (CUNY). Many other Tuskegee Airmen, including John B. Turner, the longtime dean of the School of Social Work at Case Western Reserve University, excelled in academe. Turner retired as Kenan Professor of social work at the University of North Carolina at Chapel Hill, where the school of social work's building is now named for him. A few, like the black ace Lee Archer, made millions in the corporate world. Hundreds of others had long careers in government service at one level or another.[66]

None of which is to say that racism disappeared after the Tuskegee Airmen helped desegregate the military. Countless enlisted men had experiences like those of mechanic William Surcey, whose work had earned him a Bronze Star overseas. Surcey asked for a discharge as soon as the Germans surrendered; he wanted to return to the college studies he had interrupted in the spring of 1941. Surcey returned home in 1945 and made his way to a base in Atlanta. "I was feeling pretty good about being discharged," he said. "I went into the office, and here's a lieutenant colonel. So he said to me, 'Well, you all can go home and pick cotton now.' So I looked at him. I said, 'I don't understand you, sir.' He said it again. I said, 'I don't understand you, sir.' He didn't say anything else."[67]

TAAF's leader had an interesting postwar career. Noel Parrish's Air Command and Staff School thesis attracted so much attention that he was chosen for the second class of the Air War College, a program for colonels thought to be on the fast track to the general ranks. Parrish transferred to Air Force headquarters at the Pentagon in 1948, made general in 1954, and transferred again into a highly visible NATO posting in Europe. After returning to the Pentagon, he took on public relations responsibilities and found himself in the middle of Air Force debates regarding the use of nuclear weapons. This position, he said, mainly consisted of "trying to play down the notion that we were just enthusiastically preparing to blow up the planet because that seemed to be the easiest way to fight a war."[68]

Parrish never lost the intellectual curiosity that had attracted him to pilot instruction in the first place. Parrish retired from the Air Force in 1964 and returned to Rice University for graduate study in history. He wrote a master's thesis and PhD dissertation on aspects of U.S. atomic weaponry policy and taught military history for several years at Trinity University in San Antonio, not far from Randolph Field. He died in 1987.[69]

True integration did not develop in the Air Force as quickly as policy makers in 1948 might have hoped. Fighting forces and service groups were desegregated during the Korea conflict, and on-base living and recreational facilities had already been integrated, at least on paper. But blacks continued to find opportunities limited in the Air Force. As late as 1954, the year of the *Brown* decision, African Americans made up only 7.6 percent of the entire enlisted force although they comprised 10 percent of the nation's total population. The number of blacks in the Air Force did not correspond with that of blacks in the total population until 1971, and in that year black officers in the Air Force made up only 1.8 percent of the total officer corps—an increase from 1941 levels, but not a significant enough change. Throughout the period, moreover, black airmen complained that the Air Force as an institution did not do enough to combat off-base racial discrimination.[70]

Much of the integrationist momentum produced in the Truman administration was wasted. The Air Force was slow to produce proactive policies that showed an appreciation for the intensity of blacks' frustrations in the service. The service treaded water through the Eisenhower years, but policy makers in the Kennedy and Johnson administrations did initiate equal-opportunity programs that pushed the service closer to the goal of fully equal treatment and outcome.[71]

An accumulation of petty grievances over job assignments, base housing, and other issues exploded into a full-blown race riot at Travis Air Force Base in California in 1971, and white and black enlisted men and noncommissioned officers battled for four days. The crisis provided an alarm bell to which the service responded with a major expansion of equal opportunity programs, training programs in cross-cultural communication, and a review of racial disparities in the administration of military justice. The Defense Department turned to Lucius Theus, the Tuskegee Airman who had cut his teeth in personnel administration under Benjamin O. Davis Jr. and was now a brigadier general, to administer the programs. They were designed, he said, to modify behavior rather than attitudes. If a racial sensitivity course could change a given white officer or enlisted man's feelings about blacks, all the better. But if the courses only convinced whites that their careers would suffer if they behaved in a racially discriminatory manner, that was good enough for the armed services. Indeed, it was this change in institutional culture that ultimately solidified the progress within the Air Force that had been set in motion by the Tuskegee Airmen a generation earlier.[72]

The successful efforts on the part of the civil rights coalition that led to the creation of the Tuskegee program provided a useful model that activists would replicate in the coming years. The NAACP's assault on Jim Crow through the federal courts proceeded in the years immediately after the war's end and gave the growing movement its most important victories of the period. Other institutions would continue to pressure the federal government to protect black citizens' constitutional privileges and make more opportunities available.

Massive direct action, a new—and arguably the most consequential—tactic of the postwar civil rights movement, emerged from TAAF's environs a decade after the war ended. Black residents of Montgomery continued to resent the kind of treatment Milton Henry had experienced in 1943 on a municipal bus. In December 1955 they organized to protest the indignities that the city's segregation laws had forced them to bear and refused to endure them any longer. The newly formed Montgomery Improvement Association orchestrated a direct-action bus boycott over the next thirteen months that launched the public career of Rev. Martin Luther King Jr. and resulted in a U.S. Supreme Court decision striking down Montgomery's segregation statute. King, his comrades in the newly created Southern Christian Leadership Conference, and a new generation of African American college students organizing under the banners of the Congress of Racial Equality and the Student Nonviolent Coordinating Committee employed the tactics of massive nonviolent resistance in Alabama and beyond to great effect over the coming years.[73]

The experience of the Tuskegee Airmen did not lead directly to these movements, and the Airmen themselves did not participate in all, or even most, of them. Theirs was a conservative revolution when compared with those that came later. But by forcing an instrument of national power to desegregate, by making the federal government take the side of those fighting for racial integration and full opportunity, black Americans in the World War II era handed over to the modern civil rights movement the one lever of power without which it could not have succeeded.

Epilogue
"Let's Make It a Holy Crusade All the Way Around"

Assessing the training program while it was still in existence at TAAF, Col. Noel Parrish observed, "The purpose of the field made it a focal point for one of the major social and governmental problems of the nation. There existed no precedent, no set of customs, no established procedures to guide military men in their efforts to build a functioning military organization in the midst of endless theorizing and uninformed discussion concerning racial characteristics and social proprieties." That such an unusual program could succeed disproved the War Department's 1941 statement of what was at the time conventional wisdom, "The Army is not a sociological laboratory." Gen. Marshall and others at the War Department thought the military could not and should not be expected to solve "a social problem that has perplexed the American people throughout the history of this nation." The AAF's "experiment" at Tuskegee proved them wrong.[1]

"Negro personnel [at TAAF] have proved their value and capacity far beyond the expectations of skeptics, and white personnel of varied backgrounds have developed a good-humored adaptability and an easy-going effectiveness which is sometimes bewildering to visitors," Parrish wrote in 1944. It was possible for the AAF to operate an integrated program and for the program to succeed by the AAF's standards. "Emphasis upon results rather than on methodology, on patient insistence rather than impressive ultimatums, on optimistic effort rather than fretful complaining about minor setbacks have become a tradition at Tuskegee. By such means have the objectives set forth in that direction been attained," Parrish concluded.[2]

The program succeeded for the reasons Parrish outlined and a few others. After the program was created, and especially after Parrish took command of TAAF, it was the quiet and insistent "emphasis on results" that he and Benjamin O. Davis Jr. championed that allowed the Airmen to prove to the AAF that they belonged. Military institutions under civilian control *are* social laboratories, and successful ones must be fundamentally meritocratic. Individuals and groups who can prove themselves able to help the military fight more efficiently and cost-effectively should eventually win acceptance and rise on that basis. It took pressure from outside forces to challenge the racial attitudes of Air Corps leaders before 1941. Wartime conditions combined with continued outside pressure to assure that black Americans were given the chance to prove themselves, and they took full advantage of the opportunity. To the extent that the postwar Air Force was indeed a meritocracy, it became one exactly because the Tuskegee Airmen had forced a change in its institutional culture.

It took most Americans quite a while to realize how significant the Tuskegee Airmen's contributions had been. While the black press covered events at Tuskegee throughout the program's existence, the rest of America knew little of the program, during or after the war. It may not quite have been, as white bomber crew member Larry Fleischer said, "more secret than the atom bomb," but most Americans would not learn of the Tuskegee program until fifty years after the war ended.[3] How historical memory of the Tuskegee Airmen developed and reached a wide audience is fascinating in its own right.

Home Box Office (HBO) produced a fictionalized treatment of the experience titled *The Tuskegee Airmen* that first aired in 1995. The project was the brainchild of Robert W. Williams, a Tuskegee-trained pilot. His wife, Joan, whom he met shortly after he returned home to Southern California after the war, remembered him jotting down memories from his Tuskegee experience in the early 1950s and saying, "There should be a movie about this. That way more people would learn about it." He wrote the original script and worked for decades to get the movie produced. Joan Williams lost track of the number of studio executives who rejected the idea over the years, telling her husband that people were tired of war movies or flatly denying that blacks had flown airplanes in the war. But "he never, never gave up on it," she remembered.[4]

As the fiftieth anniversary of the milestones of World War II approached in the early 1990s, American popular culture rediscovered what was by now being remembered as "The Good War." Hollywood produced a slew of television specials and motion pictures on World War II subjects in the early and mid-1990s, but Williams noticed that in the productions, "all you see is white faces." It was as if black Americans had not fought at all for their country. Fortunately, in the midst of the national rediscovery of the war and its meanings, Williams received a call from an HBO executive: "We understand you have a story, and we'd like to do it." When he took the call, Williams had just been diagnosed with prostate cancer; his doctors gave him five years to live.[5]

From that point, Williams apparently had an experience that few others ever have in Hollywood: He gave up control of his story, but then watched as the production team made exactly the movie he wanted made. They assembled a magnificent cast: Laurence Fishburne played the lead character, a pilot named Hannibal Lee (probably a composite of two actual Airmen, Hannibal Cox and Lee Archer), and was joined by Cuba Gooding Jr., Malcolm Jamal Warner, André Braugher (as B.O. Davis Jr.), and Mekhi Phifer, among others. The film followed a few would-be pilots from their hometowns of Harlem; Ottumwa, Iowa; and points in between to Moton Field and TAAF (where, in one of the many liberties the film took with the historical record, Hannibal Lee piloted an airplane ride for Eleanor Roosevelt), and finally to North Africa and Italy. It explored the competition and camaraderie among the cadets and the relationship between pilot-officers and enlisted support personnel to great effect. (When Hannibal Lee referred to "my own plane," his crew chief responded, "It's not yours, lieutenant, it's mine. I put your name on it so you'd think it's yours.") White bomber pilots who came to Italy with typical white supremacist ideas flew alongside the Red Tails and had their attitudes transformed by the black pilots' superior flying skills. If the film glossed over, conflated, or omitted important historical facts, it was at least emotionally true.[6]

The film's release touched the surviving Tuskegee Airmen and publicized their collective story in a way that they themselves could not. In the early 1970s alumni of the experience then living in Detroit had begun organizing fellow veterans with the explicit goal of preserving and publicizing their shared history. They formed a nonprofit group, Tuskegee Airmen Inc. (TAI), with local chapters and regional groups in 1973. It has since grown into a national organization with thousands of members, fewer than half of whom are original Tuskegee Airmen. Since 1973 TAI has placed hundreds of speakers before public schools and civic groups each year to tell a version of the Tuskegee Airmen story, sponsored local flight programs for minority youth, and raised money for college scholarships. (According to the group, the TAI Scholarship Foundation has provided young men and women with more than $1.2 million in college scholarships since 1978.) But TAI speakers could not hope to reach nearly as many people as a motion picture could.[7]

"I'm glad that it happened when it did," Joan Williams said. "I think that if it had happened at an earlier time, it wouldn't have had the impact." The civil rights movement of the 1960s had made other groups of Americans more aware of the indignities and injustices African Americans had faced throughout their history, she believed. The movement made it possible for Williams's story to make a real impact on whites' understanding of the black experience when it finally appeared. Because the film premiered at a time when more Americans were thinking about the legacies of World War II, its influence was doubly great. HBO first showed the film in 1995 at TAI's 24th annual convention in Atlanta, with a red carpet and all the trappings of a major Hollywood premiere. A caterer prepared vernacular dishes from Alabama, North Africa, and Italy for the soiree, where media coverage was intense. The Tuskegee Airmen, now in their seventies and eighties, became overnight celebrities.[8]

For better or worse, *The Tuskegee Airmen* created and solidified a collective memory of the experience that will never be dislodged. It set in place a narrative that veterans of the experience and interested observers alike all appropriated as their own. People who have never been to Italy now report that white bomber pilots requested escort from the Red Tails as if they had been eyewitnesses to the conversations, because they saw a white character in *The Tuskegee Airmen* do just that. Hundreds of the narratives in the Tuskegee Airmen Oral History Project recorded between 2000 and 2005 followed the film's story arc closely, and the vast majority of the interviewees referenced the film in one way or another; the movie itself became an artifact in the history of the Tuskegee Airmen. Of course, it is impossible to judge to what degree the film influenced these memories, because all of the National Park Service's interviews were recorded after the film made its impact. There is no large body of oral histories with Airmen that were recorded before the film's release, so there is little to compare against the interviews recorded after 2000. It is entirely possible, too, that the film just got the story right—that it accurately captured the collective narrative of the experience as remembered by the people who lived through it.

The reporters in attendance for the film's premiere at the TAI convention covered another milestone. On the evening of August 12, Assistant Secretary of the Air Force Rodney A. Coleman and Air Force Chief of Staff Gen. Ronald R. Fogleman announced at the convention's black-tie banquet that the service was removing the letters of reprimand from the personnel files of men who had been arrested at Freeman Field. They also surprised the sitting TAI president, Roger C. Terry, with the news that the Air Force was setting aside his court-martial conviction and refunding his $150 fine.[9]

Even these decisions were not without controversy, however. The Air Force removed the reprimands only from the records of those who had lodged formal requests to have their records expunged; the ceremony applied to only fifteen of the 104; thirteen others had already had the reprimands removed. Members of the 104 who had already died did not receive posthumous pardons, and many who could have made the request refused to do so on principle. Coleman Young's response to the Air Force's offer to remove his reprimand was, one suspects, a common one. Fellow Detroiter and Freeman Field arrestee Wardell Polk paraphrased Young's response in his own oral history interview: "They can take their 'graciousness' and stick it in their asses!" Polk, too, refused to request a removal. "I think most of us wore that thing as a badge of honor," he said.[10]

The story of the Tuskegee Airmen received national exposure again in December 2006 when William Holton, TAI's historian, dropped a figurative bombshell. With Daniel Haulman, an archivist-historian for the Air Force Historical Research Agency, Holton had uncovered troubling post-mission reports in the agency's archives. The documents seemed to indicate that at least a handful of U.S. Air Force bombers flying under the protection of 332nd fighters had been shot down by German airplanes in the summer of 1944. Holton suspected that a more thorough review of the thousands of post-mission reports he had not yet been able to wade through would reveal additional losses.[11]

Holton and Haulman exposed the "Never lost a bomber" claim for what it was and had been since the end of the war: a myth. They had traced its origins to a May 1945 letter from Col. Buck Taylor, who congratulated B. O. Davis and the 332nd for their perfect record in escort missions. A June 21, 1945, War Department press release stated that as of February of that year, the 332nd "had completed 200 combat missions with the 15th Air Force and had served as escort to heavy bombers without losing a single bomber to enemy fighters." A military public relations official repeated the claim in Gen. Davis's official Air Force biography, and Davis retold it in his 1991 memoir.[12]

By 2006 the phrases "Tuskegee Airmen" and "Never lost a bomber" were all but inseparable, especially among TAI members. Holton's discoveries were more than a year old by this point, and he had privately been telling Tuskegee Airmen to drop the claim from their public presentations since 2004. When newspapers around the country carried an Associated Press story detailing the findings on December 12, they had the effect of bursting a cherished balloon for thousands of black Americans. A follow-up story on the AP wire days later carried the claims of Warren Ludlum, an eighty-three-year old retiree in Old Tappan, New Jersey. Ludlum reported that German fighters had shot down the B-24 he co-piloted on July 25 or 26, 1944, while it was being escorted by Red Tails. Ludlum parachuted to safety but was soon captured and sent to a POW camp. He said he was positive he had flown the mission under the Tuskegee Airmen's escort because at the prison camp he met Starling Penn, a pilot of the 332nd, class of 43-H, who was shot down on the same mission. Holton said that his archival research backed Ludlum's claims.[13]

The mission reports Holton and Haulman cited were all but completely conclusive by themselves. Then again, in 1944 the AAF was sending massive formations with hundreds of bombers, from multiple bomber groups, on missions into Nazi-held territory with hundreds of fighter escorts from multiple fighter groups (including the 332nd) to protect them. These formations spread miles wide. A bomber shot down from one part of a formation might not have been the responsibility of any single fighter group, and Penn might have been escorting bombers far away from Ludlum's when German fighters shot their respective planes down. Historians might never prove decisively that a given plane flying under the direct protection of the Tuskegee Airmen fell under enemy aircraft fire, but it seems indisputable that the "Never lost a bomber" claim is and has always been untenable.

Nonetheless, the reaction from original Tuskegee Airmen and their legions of fans was predictable. One could practically hear aficionados throughout the country protesting, "But they didn't ever lose a bomber! It says so right here on my T-shirt!" "This is outrageous. I think they are trying to destroy our record," responded Carroll Woods, a combat veteran of the 332nd and a classmate of Penn's at TAFS. He asked, "What's the point now?" A letter to the editor of the *Montgomery Advertiser*, the newspaper that broke the story, concurred with Woods: "'Outrageous' is totally correct. . . . This is past history and should remain so. I see no reason to tarnish the records of these black heroes."[14]

Holton protested that he was only trying to set the record straight on behalf of his organization, lest a later historian look at the same documents and conclude that the Tuskegee Airmen had willfully perpetrated a lie. "Over the past 60 years, well-meaning, sincere and highly placed speakers have beguiled audiences" with the "Never lost a bomber" claim, Holton said. Anyone who did so was not lying intentionally, "but rather parroting to the listener information he internalized from past speakers." Holton saw himself as performing an intervention in history, and he was at least successful on the local level. Subsequent letters to the *Montgomery Advertiser* challenged the notion that Holton and Haulman had tarnished anyone's record. "Why would truth tarnish the magnificent record of these courageous men? Consequently, why is image more important than truth?" asked one reader. "Research, regardless of what it shows, will not change the record of their bravery, especially to those whose lives were saved. Even if their accomplishments were less than perfect, the accolades that they have received are well deserved." Another averred, "The Tuskegee Airmen overcame tremendous obstacles to fly in combat against their nation's enemy and for that they should be considered heroic. They do not need their exemplary combat record embellished by myth."[15]

This latter approach to the exposure of the myth was probably the minority opinion among the general public. Unfortunately, in collective memory the Tuskegee Airmen's story was in danger of becoming too precious to withstand critical inquiry. This reality became all too apparent on the January 31, 2007, broadcast of Jon Stewart's "The Daily Show." Speaking on what he called "Black History Month Eve," Larry Wilmore, identified as the fake newscast's "Senior Black Historian," braced himself for February's commemorative period. Wilmore joked that Black History Month served the sole purpose of "making up for centuries of oppression with twenty-eight days of trivia," calling it a time when the American people "bow our heads in solemn reverence for Harriet Tubman and the Tuskegee Airmen." As if on cue, four days later the Coca-Cola Co. ran an advertisement during the television broadcast of Super Bowl XLI. In the advertisement, "Tuskegee 1941" served as one of exactly six moments worth celebrating in the combined history of black Americans and their preferred soft drink. "Tuskegee 1941: Pilots prove heroism has no color," ran the legend next to the image of a Coke bottle. But if the extent of public understanding of the Tuskegee Airmen had progressed from complete ignorance to "Blacks can be great pilots" or "Blacks can be heroic" over the previous sixty years, it had not progressed much at all.[16]

Wilmore's satire struck deep. By the time he spoke, the Tuskegee Airmen had come to represent a feel-good story that Americans of all races and ethnicities could tell themselves during the one month of the year when they were encouraged to think of black history as American history. The oversimplification of their experience threatened to reduce the Tuskegee Airmen to a collective cliché. The "Never lost a bomber" myth packaged their experience neatly and made it safe for mass consumption—just the thing for Black History Month.

That the news of the lost bombers broke shortly before the U.S. Congress honored the Tuskegee Airmen with the Congressional Gold Medal, the highest honor that body can award to civilians, was fortunate. When more than three hundred of the original pilots and members of support crews gathered in the Capitol Rotunda in March 2007 to receive the honor, the emphasis in speeches from President George W. Bush, former Secretary of State Colin Powell, and others was on the Airmen's record in helping their country overcome white supremacy, not on the (mythical) record of the 332nd in combat. "I thank you for what you have done for African-Americans, but more, I thank you for what you have done for America," Powell told them. "You caused America to look into the mirror of its soul, and you showed America that there was nothing a black person couldn't do, there was nothing a human being couldn't do, if given a sense of purpose, if given the opportunity." The Airmen took another bow on the national stage when more than two hundred members attended the inauguration of President Barack Obama as honored guests, providing a poignant link to the historical struggles that had made his election possible.[17]

The question of whether the pilots of the 332nd did or did not lose bombers under their protection is not irrelevant, but it cannot speak to the larger significance of the Tuskegee Airmen's collective experience. Everyone who has considered this question agrees that the combat record of the 332nd was impressive, even if it was not perfect. But the combat record can tell us very little about the 1938–41 lobbying campaign that opened flight training opportunities to African Americans for the first time, or the feud between Tuskegee Institute and the NAACP. It tells us nothing about the creation of a nearly all-black military base at Tuskegee and the culture of achievement that was nurtured there. It cannot teach us about the massive social change of the World War II era of which the Tuskegee Airmen experience was but a part.

The Tuskegee Airmen themselves can teach us about these changes. Their individual stories highlight the social transformation the United States underwent during the war, and they show us how individual men and women made the choices that produced those changes. They can teach us about the differences those transformations made in individual lives and the effects they had on the collective history of the American people. The postwar lives of the four men whose personal stories opened this book demonstrate how these transformations developed. John Roach, Roy Chappell, Milton Henry, and Horace Bohannon established careers and public lives after the war that built on the culture of achievement from which they had gained so much at Tuskegee. Their postwar careers were emblematic of the many directions the civil rights struggle took after the war and demonstrated the possibilities for protest and advancement that the wartime experience had created, but also the limits placed on African American men of their generation.

John Roach graduated from B-25 training in the class of 45-E and was stationed at Godman Field preparing to be deployed to the Pacific when another bomber, the B-29 *Enola Gay,* dropped an atomic weapon on the city of Hiroshima. When Japan surrendered days later, Roach remembered, "You never saw a more upset bunch of young bomber pilots than we were. We just didn't know any better. But that's young kids. I was what? Twenty-and-a-half-years old. We just wanted to get over there and defend the country and at least use our training." Roach did not get to use that training in World War II, but the United States got its money's worth out of his education later on. He left the service in 1946 but was called back to active duty during the Korean and Vietnam Wars, and flew sensitive missions during the Cuban Missile Crisis. He retired from the Air Force as a full colonel.[18]

In 1969 Roach began working for the Federal Aviation Administration (FAA) as an air carrier operations inspector at Logan Airport in Boston, the facility he had visited as a boy. By 1976 he was the chief of the FAA's Boston office, and by 1979 he had risen to deputy regional director, making him responsible for commercial flight standards throughout New England. Not coincidentally, he was at that time the highest-ranking African American in the agency's history. Roach was not a civil rights activist as most would understand that term. He recognized the racial prejudice he faced throughout his career, particularly in the World War II Air Forces, but he "left it to the legal department," as he put it, to deal with those problems and did his best to dispel the notions behind them through his personal conduct. Roach did not march in civil rights protests, and he did not sue anyone for violating his constitutional rights. Instead, he worked hard and made it as difficult as possible for anyone to discriminate against him. In that sense Roach's postwar career was probably representative of the Airmen as a whole. He never accepted inferior treatment and refused to be denied career opportunities because he was black, but he fought his battles with a sense of stoic dignity.[19]

Roach credited his career success to four factors: his family's support, the lessons he learned from growing up in an ethnically diverse neighborhood, the training he received at Tuskegee, and the relationships with people from other backgrounds he was later able to develop in the Air Force. From his instructors at Tuskegee, Roach learned how to apply exacting standards in his flying. He said, "If you did something that was not proper or correct as a Tuskegee Airman, why, right across the country people would be saying, 'See that? Those black guys can't handle that.'" Roach was determined never to give anyone an excuse to say that about him.[20]

What seems to have stuck with Roy Chappell the most from his Tuskegee experience was the pride other black Americans derived from it. Being a Tuskegee Airman and doing well in the role was important to Chappell because it seemed as if the Airmen's success or failure was a matter of life and death for his larger community. His enduring memories of the experience all involved the way others reacted to him as an officer in uniform—be they the black churchwomen on trains who shared their meals with him, black civilians who never let him pay for a drink when he entered a friendly bar, or white strangers who were forced to respect his rank even if they did not honor his humanity. He used the visibility he gained as a Tuskegee Airman in later years to repay the sustaining acts of generosity he had received from black civilians during the war.[21]

Chappell wanted to make a career of the Air Force, but was told bluntly at war's end that African Americans were not welcome in his chosen field of air traffic control. He left the service, moved to Chicago, used his GI Bill benefits to enroll at Roosevelt College, and worked nights at the postal service. He earned a bachelor's degree in psychology and got a job doing what he had decided in the meantime he really wanted to do, which was teaching elementary school. Chappell did that for thirty years.[22]

As president of the Chicago "Dodo" chapter of Tuskegee Airmen Inc., he created the Young Eagles program, which by 2001 had taken more than five thousand inner-city Chicago schoolchildren on their first airplane flights. Before he died in 2002, his fellow Tuskegee Airmen had recognized him with their highest honors, the National President's Award and the Noel Parrish Award. Chappell made it his life's work to widen children's horizons. In the Young Eagles program, he said, "We chat about the opportunities in aviation and try to tell them about staying in school and doing the things they're supposed to do. When the kids come down out of those airplanes after their first flight, oh, it's something else. It's something else, boy. They're so happy. They're not even touching the ground," Chappell said.

"I had one little girl, and she didn't want to fly," he remembered. "She was afraid to fly. And so I took her out and talked to her and walked her around the airplane. Had her touch all the parts of the airplane. Opened up the door, let her look in the airplane and all that. She went up. And when she came back down, I said, 'How do you feel?'" The girl answered, 'I feel like I'm still in heaven.'"[23]

Higher-ups interpreted Milton Henry's challenges to Jim Crow at bases in Alabama and Michigan as conduct unbecoming an officer. He was court-martialed and discharged from the AAF in 1944, at the height of the war. Henry remained defiant six decades later. "My major job wasn't just to fight; it was to declare for human dignity everywhere," he said in 2002. "I just couldn't see letting the government off the hook. If you're engaged in a holy crusade, then let's make it a holy crusade all the way around. The government has to be held up to the standards that it professes."[24]

As compared with the postwar civil rights struggles of other Tuskegee Airmen, Henry took the road less traveled—to say the least. After the war he joined the League for Non-Violent Civil Disobedience to a Segregated Army, for which he canvassed black neighborhoods in Philadelphia. Under the guidance of the league's leaders, A. Philip Randolph and Bayard Rustin, Henry patrolled the streets of the City of Brotherly Love in a sound truck, urging passersby to refuse to register for the Selective Service System. Henry's harangues "sounded like a shocking heresy even to blacks," one listener later recalled.[25]

Henry decided to pursue a legal career and applied to Temple University's law school, but his application was rejected because of the dishonorable discharge. He accompanied a friend to New Haven, Connecticut, for the admissions test to Yale Law School. Henry took the exam on a lark and scored well enough to win not only acceptance but a full scholarship. After graduation he returned to Pennsylvania to take the state bar exam. Because he refused to accede to a restriction on defending civil rights cases, the state bar rejected him.[26]

Henry moved to Pontiac, Michigan, married and had a daughter, and won a seat on the city commission. Dismayed to find that the city's public schools were racially segregated, he filed one of the first school desegregation suits in the urban north. From that point on he would combine a career of political activism, some of it at the very edges of militant violence, with a thriving legal practice.[27]

Henry watched approvingly as a new brand of black activism swept the South in the late 1950s and early 1960s, but found that the push for equal civil rights did not speak to the daily realities of blacks in the northern cities. He rejected the philosophy of nonviolence, advocating greater militancy and a faster pace of change. Henry developed ties to several of the major civil rights figures and organizations of the day, in addition to socialists, radical trade unionists, and black nationalists. At the same time he gravitated toward militant Black Power politics, lending his name and organizing talents to the radical Group on Advanced Leadership (GOAL). GOAL cosponsored a 1963 march in which Martin Luther King Jr. led an estimated crowd of 125,000 through the streets of Detroit. Henry also provided legal advice and bail money to members of the Student Non-violent Coordinating Committee who found themselves in Southern jails because they had challenged Jim Crow.[28]

Concurrently, Henry explored ties with Detroit's Garvey-ite black-nationalist groups and found a kindred spirit in the fiery Nation of Islam minister Malcolm X. Henry was an organizer for the multi-generational 1963 Grassroots Leadership Conference in Detroit at which Malcolm delivered his influential "Message to the Grassroots," a landmark speech in the history of black nationalism in the United States. Henry, who enjoyed tinkering with radios and tape recorders and ran a community radio station in his spare time, recorded the address and distributed it widely. Henry became one of Malcolm X's closest political allies, traveling with him abroad to Egypt, among many other places, and remembered the activist as a man who "saw the humanity in all people…he really was determined to love humanity."[29]

In 1964 Henry ran for a seat in the U.S. Congress on the Freedom Now ticket, hoping to mobilize the black masses as a third-party candidate. John Conyers Jr. trounced him in the election. That same year, according to an FBI informant, Henry delivered a fiery lecture to Detroit's Friday Night Socialist Forum in which he hypothesized "that a well disciplined underground of all black guerillas [sic] could cause pandemonium and in this way let everyone know that the Negro aims to gain his absolute, complete freedom." In 1965 he served as a pallbearer at Malcolm's funeral.[30]

In 1968 Henry renounced integrationist civil rights organizing and black electoral strategies as too incrementalist and changed his name to

Gaidi Obadele. With his brother Richard, who now called himself Imari Abubakari Obadele, he proclaimed the existence of the sovereign Republic of New Africa (RNA) to be carved out of the states of Louisiana, Mississippi, Alabama, Georgia, and South Carolina. The Obadeles demanded $400 billion in reparations from the United States, which would be used to create the new government and repatriate the descendants of slaves who had moved north in the Great Migration. Gaidi Obadele was the republic's first vice president, and Betty Shabazz, Malcolm X's widow, was named second vice president. Imari Obadele assumed the duties of the RNA's Minister of Information and opened a consulate in Jackson, Mississippi.[31]

The Obadele brothers began organizing to hold a plebiscite in the RNA's newly declared lands to let black people know they had a right to self-determination, they said, and offered to open negotiations with the Nixon administration over territorial transfer and reparations. (Strangely enough, they received no response from the White House.) The brothers established the capital of what they called "the still unliberated nation" in Mississippi under the leadership of the more charismatic Imari, but one has to wonder how Milton Henry/Gaidi Obadele would have approached the possibility of returning to Alabama as a conquering RNA official.[32]

Henry had severe second thoughts about militant black nationalism in 1969 when he witnessed at close hand a gun battle between RNA associates and Detroit police at the New Bethel Baptist Church that left the neighborhood looking like "a war zone." Perhaps the Quaker influence of Henry's Philadelphia childhood re-exerted itself. Maybe he remembered the aversion to "bayonets and rifles" that led him to volunteer for the Army Air Corps. Whatever his reason, the "very traumatic experience" at New Bethel led Milton Henry to stop calling himself Gaidi Obadele and disavow militant black nationalism. His brother learned a different lesson from the experience: the RNA needed to raise, arm, and train one hundred thousand troops to defend the republic, he argued. The two drifted apart.[33]

When Henry recorded an oral history interview with the Tuskegee Airmen Oral History Project in 2002, he was still practicing law in Detroit; as an attorney he was perhaps best known for his work on the University of Michigan affirmative action cases that were eventually decided by the U.S. Supreme Court in 2003. At the time he was also Rev. Milton Henry, the pastor of Christ Presbyterian Church in Southfield, Michigan. In the 1970s, while on a drive through the countryside of Ghana, he had happened upon a rural church. Henry read the words of the apostle Paul on the church's sign: "Know ye not but you are not your own, you've been born with a price, even the blood of our Lord Jesus Christ." It was, he later remembered, "an existential moment"—his Christian upbringing apparently reasserting itself. Henry returned home immediately and entered Ashland Theological

Seminary in Ohio. Upon graduation with a master's degree in religious studies, he founded the Metropolitan Jail Ministry in Detroit and founded Christ Presbyterian Church in 1992. When Milton Henry's remarkable life ended in 2006, a perceptive obituary in the *New York Times Magazine* mentioned that his funeral ceremony "included representatives of the Tuskegee Airmen, an honor guard of the Republic of New Africa, and a phalanx of prominent lawyers, judges and clergy. All claimed him."[34]

Horace Bohannon returned to Atlanta and his taxicab after the war. He was interested in maintaining the camaraderie he had so enjoyed as a flight cadet and member of the 332nd, so he tried to join the local American Legion chapter. But "they wanted to have an auxiliary-something for black veterans. You were not a full-fledged member. We didn't like that. Same thing at the VFW." So Bohannon and a few black veteran friends organized the Georgia Veterans League. The president of the Georgia Veterans League was an old friend from Atlanta and a fellow Tuskegee Airman, John Turner. Turner told Bohannon he was wasting his talents in the taxi and set up a meeting for him with Dr. George Mitchell, director of the Southern Regional Council (SRC)'s Veterans Education Program and soon to become executive director of the SRC. Successor to the Commission on Interracial Cooperation, which had been formed in 1919, the SRC was one of the few interracial groups in the South pushing for civil rights reforms in the immediate postwar years. Mitchell was especially keen on consolidating the gains blacks had made during the war in the realm of federal employment. His short-term goal was to pressure the Veterans Administration to hire black veterans as case workers and to cease its shameful treatment of black veterans in the South.[35]

As the head of the SRC's Veteran Services Project, Bohannon traveled throughout the state interviewing comrades about their postwar aspirations. He was not surprised to hear that above all, they wanted "a decent job. They wanted to work. They wanted to make it." Bohannon continued to organize black veterans, but at the SRC he also met liberal whites who encouraged him to join a new veterans group, the interracial American Veterans Committee. He did and formed an Atlanta chapter of the organization. The pattern of Bohannon's activism would hold throughout the rest of his life and was representative of the activism of many African Americans of his generation. He organized blacks to recognize and fight for their collective aspirations; at the same time he sought out alliances with fair-minded whites who could help him change the system from within.[36]

Mitchell and Bohannon considered the work of the Veteran Services Project as having succeeded by 1947, and Mitchell insisted that Bohannon go back to college and earn his degree. Bohannon returned to Lincoln and graduated in 1948. He moved home to Atlanta and worked for a few years as principal of all-black public elementary schools. But he soon found he could make much more money at the Post Office Department, the one federal agency where African Americans faced the least hiring discrimination after the war. (Several Tuskegee Airmen had long postwar careers at the post office.) "It went along pretty good," Bohannon said, "except their whole thing was they wanted a strong back and a weak mind.... They'd bring some white boy in there that didn't know the way to the bathroom, and pretty soon he's the supervisor over you." Disgusted with the glass ceiling at the post office, Bohannon got a job as a juvenile probation officer in Fulton County, Georgia. But he chafed at the segregated and discriminatory conditions in that institution, too, and returned to the post office in the early 1960s as a training officer with responsibility for the entire Southeast region.[37]

From there Bohannon worked his way through the upper ranks of the federal civil service, finally landing in the regional office of the Department of Health, Education, and Welfare (HEW), where he found his life's work. At HEW Bohannon was responsible for working with local authorities to bring the Deep South's segregated school districts, health facilities, and welfare units into compliance with the federal courts' desegregation mandates during a time of tremendous change, the late 1960s and 1970s. "I like it so much," Bohannon remembered telling his boss. "Every day I meet with some different people, and it just tickles me for them to ask me, 'Where are you from, Mr. Bohannon?' And I say, 'I'm from Atlanta, Georgia.'" White Southerners of the time were still certain that desegregation was an effort on the part of northerners to force their values and customs down Southerners' throats, and they certainly were unused to seeing African Americans, much less black Southerners, in positions of authority. "They just knew I was from Flint, Michigan, or somewhere up north, and when I told them that, you could see their face fall!"[38]

The efforts of federal agencies to finally desegregate local school districts and similar institutions, in many cases two decades or more after the U.S. Supreme Court's initial *Brown v. Board of Education* decision, is one of the largely untold success stories of the civil rights era, and Bohannon was at the heart of the struggle. Federalist checks and balances in the U.S. Constitution place a great deal, but not quite a preponderance, of power over issues of education and welfare with local school boards and county welfare agencies. The system allowed white Southerners to continue racially segregationist practices for years after the Supreme Court defined them as unconstitutional. It was up to federal bureaucrats like Bohannon to work with local officials to implement desegregation orders and hold the officials' feet to the fire when they inevitably attempted to backslide. It was important, but largely unheralded, work.

When Bohannon recorded his interview with the Tuskegee Airmen Oral History Project, he was in the mood to reflect on a long and consequential career as a freedom fighter who had accomplished a great deal by working within the system. "Despite the fact that I'm a Georgia-born black boy, I had experiences that promoted me as a person," Bohannon said, and he clearly understood his time at Tuskegee as the turning point in his life. "I have never been in a group as fine as the Tuskegee Airmen. I'm trying to say to you in terms of character, behavior and so forth, I have never seen anything like the Tuskegee Airmen."[39] In other words, as a group of people the Tuskegee Airmen may have been separate for a time, but they were unequaled.

Black Americans won for themselves the opportunity to prove their competence in the prestigious and technologically advanced field of aviation during World War II. The Tuskegee Airmen took advantage of the opportunity, provided a dramatic model of achievement that was difficult to ignore, and hastened the end of the national government's indifference toward Jim Crow. They did not bring the resulting civil rights revolution about by themselves, to be sure, but it is hard to imagine how the transformations that followed could have come about without the example that they set.

Acknowledgments

That the writing of a book is not a solitary endeavor is a cliché in authors' acknowledgments, but it is so unavoidably true in this case that I cannot help writing it again here. Thanks first of all to the narrators of the Tuskegee Airmen Oral History Project.

Directing the research team of the Tuskegee Airmen Oral History Project—Lisa Bratton, Judith Brown, Worth Long, and Bill Mansfield, and our administrative assistant Johnetta Robinson—and having the opportunity to study this subject in such depth with such remarkable people was the thrill of a professional lifetime. I am proud of the body of work we assembled, and I hope the Tuskegee Airmen are as well.

Our partner in that project, Tuskegee Airmen, Inc., provided invaluable assistance in too many ways to mention. I am especially grateful to Hank Sanford, Bill Holton, and Col. Charles McGee of TAI for their having championed the project among TAI's members and for the many personal favors they did for us. We literally could not have managed the project without them. TAI chapters and hundreds of individual members of the organization gave us the gift of their time, their memories, and the contents of their address books. It has truly been an honor to know these men and women.

I am grateful to all of them, but I have to single out Charles "A-Train" Dryden and Theopolis W. "Ted" Johnson, both of Atlanta, for special thanks. I recorded my first interview for the project with A-Train, and over the next eight years I had countless conversations and great laughs with him. (I wish I could share some of the stories behind them here.) May I grow old as gracefully. Before he died in 2006, Ted Johnson compiled one of the most impressive historical documents I have ever seen and used, a database of verifiable participants in the historic Tuskegee Airmen experience. Ted was a real mentor in many ways, and he showed all of us what it means to have a labor of love.

Rep. John Lewis (D-Ga.) procured an earmark for the oral history project that allowed the project to continue its work. I admire Rep. Lewis for many reasons, but I remain especially grateful for this favor.

My colleagues at the National Park Service—including, among many, many others, Bob Blythe, Tony Paredes, Allen Bohnert, Brian Coffey, Tommy Jones, Dan Scheidt, Kirk Cordell, Paul Hatchett, Rick McCollough, Frank Catroppa, Saudia Muwwakkil, Dwight Pitcaithley, Janet McDonnell,

Catherine Farmer Light, Susan Gibson, Christine Biggers, and Deanna Mitchell—made me proud to have been a part of that wonderful national institution if only for a short time. I am especially appreciative for my colleagues in the history department at the University of North Texas who gave me the opportunity to return to academia and direct the university's Oral History Program. My assistants at the UNT Oral History Program, Lisa Fox and Glenn Johnston, and our cast of dedicated students have my deepest gratitude.

Research grants from the University of North Texas and the Franklin and Eleanor Roosevelt Institute made research at far-flung archives possible. I am thankful for the assistance provided by Joe Caver at the Air Force Historical Research Agency and the staffs of the Library of Congress, the National Archives and Records Administration, and the Franklin D. Roosevelt Presidential Library who made my research visits fruitful.

Nancy Toff and Joellyn Ausanka at Oxford University Press helped turn my original manuscript into the book I wanted it to be. In my experience with them, everyone associated with the press has demonstrated why OUP is considered the world's best academic publisher. Two anonymous reviewers offered generous comments and constructive criticism on an early draft of the manuscript that helped me improve the finished product greatly. Thanks also to Eric Rauchway for reading manuscript chapters and making gentle suggestions that helped me polish a few arguments.

I am fortunate to be part of a community of civil rights historians and friends whose ideas have rubbed off on me over the years. In writing this book I have benefited greatly from conversations with Ray Arsenault, Joe Crespino, Emilye Crosby, Pete Daniel, John Dittmer, Brett Gadsden, Wesley Hogan, Hasan Kwame Jeffries, Robyn Spencer, and many others whose names I will realize I should have included here only after the book is published. I have learned so much about the craft of oral history and the many layers of meaning contained in oral history interviews from Don Ritchie, Kathryn Nasstrom, Lu Ann Jones, Cliff Kuhn, Rob Perks, and many other colleagues from the Oral History Association.

Above all, I thank my families—the Moyes, Davises, and Feits—for their rock-solid support and genuine interest in anything I do. Dorothy Davis Moye has been a constant source of inspiration in my life. Joe Moye has never stopped encouraging and supporting me. Bill and Melissa Moye kept me well-fed on research trips to Washington. My brother, Will Moye, has never let my head get too big, and his wife, Sarah, has reined him in whenever he took a little too much pleasure in doing so. I am grateful for both of them. My Davis aunts, uncles, and cousins made me follow the commandment, "Remember who you are and where you come from." Murphy Davis and Ed Loring turned my eyes toward the prize in the first place. Gene and

Barbara Feit provided unconditional love (not an easy thing to give a son-in-law, I would imagine) and more than a little parenting help for a busy working couple, all of which made writing this book easier.

I owe the greatest debt of all to the greatest loves of my life, my wife and best friend, Rachel, and our sons, Luke and Henry. They endured much more time than they should have had to with a husband and father whose head was off in the clouds thinking about the Tuskegee Airmen. I dedicate the book to Luke and Henry, who are already embarking on their own flights of imagination.

Notes

PROLOGUE

1. All direct quotes are from John Roach oral history interview with Todd Moye, Aug. 3, 2001. National Park Service Tuskegee Airmen Oral History Project.

2. See Robert J. Jakeman, *The Divided Skies: Establishing Segregated Flight Training at Tuskegee, Alabama, 1934–1942* (Tuscaloosa: University of Alabama Press, 1992). See also George L. Washington, "The History of Military and Civilian Pilot Training of Negroes at Tuskegee, Alabama, 1939–45" (unpublished manuscript, henceforth abbreviated Washington manuscript), Tuskegee University Special Collections, Tuskegee, Ala. The names of the licensed black pilots appear in Washington, 1–4A.

3. All direct quotes are from Horace A. Bohannon oral history interviews with Worth Long, Jan. 3 and 5, 2001. National Park Service Tuskegee Airmen Oral History Project. See also J. Todd Moye, "'I Never Quit Dreaming About It': Horace Bohannon, the Tuskegee Airmen, and the Dream of Flight," *Atlanta History: A Journal of Georgia and the South* XLVII, Nos. 1 and 2 (2005): 58–71.

4. Brown quoted by Ann Banks, "Doing Battle on Two Fronts," *New York Times,* May 7, 1995.

5. All direct quotes are from Roy Chappell oral history interview with Worth Long, May 16, 2001. National Park Service Tuskegee Airmen Oral History Project.

6. See James C. Warren, *The Tuskegee Airmen Mutiny at Freeman Field* (Vacaville, CA: Conyers, 1996).

7. All direct quotes are from Milton Henry oral history interview with Bill Mansfield, June 11, 2002. National Park Service Tuskegee Airmen Oral History Project.

8. See Lynn M. Homan and Thomas Reilly, *Black Knights: The Story of the Tuskegee Airmen* (Gretna, LA: Pelican Publishing, 2001), 67.

9. The text of King's December 5, 1955, speech at Holt Street Baptist church is available online. See "The Autobiography of Martin Luther King Jr.," www.stanford.edu/group/King/publications/autobiography/chp_7.htm.

10. Throughout this book I refer to all of these men and women, military and civilian, pilots and support crew members, as "Tuskegee Airmen." For more on the Tuskegee Airmen Oral History Project, see J. Todd Moye, "The Tuskegee Airmen Oral History Project and Oral History in the National Park Service," *The Journal of American History* 89/2 (September 2002): 580–87.

CHAPTER I

1. W. Vashon Eagleson oral history interview with William Mansfield, June 15, 2001, Tuskegee Airmen Oral History Project.

2. Harvey Alexander oral history interview with William Mansfield, June 20, 2001. National Park Service Tuskegee Airmen Oral History Project.

3. See Fred Erisman, *Boys' Books, Boys' Dreams, and the Mystique of Flight* (Fort Worth: Texas Christian University Press, 2006), and David T. Courtwright, *Sky as Frontier: Adventure, Aviation, and Empire* (College Station: Texas A&M University

Press, 2005). "Wings for This Man," the propaganda film on the Tuskegee flight program produced by Frank Capra and narrated by Ronald Reagan, is available online. See http://video.google.com/videoplay?docid=-2150770736145060825&q=www.factualfactory.com (accessed July 24, 2007). Arnold quoted by Noel F. Parrish Jr., "The Segregation of Negroes in the Army Air Forces," thesis, Air Command and Staff School, Maxwell Field, Ala., May 1947, 62. Air Force Historical Research Agency (henceforth abbreviated AFHRA).

4. David M. Kennedy, *Freedom from Fear: The American People in Depression and War, 1929–1945* (New York: Oxford University Press, 1999), 764–65.

5. Jane Dailey, *The Age of Jim Crow* (New York: Norton, 2009). See especially Dailey's astute Introduction, xi–li. Lilienthal quoted by William E. Leuchtenburg, *The White House Looks South: Franklin D. Roosevelt, Harry S. Truman, and Lyndon B. Johnson* (Baton Rouge: Louisiana State Press, 2005), 56. See Leuchtenburg, 55–117. See also Harvard Sitkoff, *A New Deal for Blacks: The Emergence of Civil Rights as a National Issue: The Depression Decade* (New York: Oxford University Press, 1978); and Nancy Joan Weiss, *Farewell to the Party of Lincoln: Black Politics in the Age of FDR* (Princeton: Princeton University Press, 1983).

6. For the concept of the long civil rights movement, see Jacquelyn Dowd Hall, "The Long Civil Rights Movement and the Political Uses of the Past," *The Journal of American History* 91/4 (March 2005), 1233–63. For a dissenting viewpoint, see Sundiata Keita Cha-Jua and Clarence Lang, "The 'Long Movement' as Vampire: Temporal and Spatial Fallacies in Recent Black Freedom Studies," *Journal of African American History* 92/2 (Spring 2007): 265–88.

7. U.S. Department of Commerce, Bureau of the Census, *Census of Population: 1940, Volume II Characteristics of the Population, Parts 1 and 2* (Washington: Government Printing Office, 1943), and *Census of Population: 1950, Volume II Characteristics of the Population, Parts 5 and 13* (Washington: Government Printing Office, 1952). Thomas J. Sugrue, *The Origins of the Urban Crisis: Race and Inequality in Postwar Detroit* (Princeton: Princeton University Press, 1996), 23.

8. Kennedy, 768, 775, 777. Walter White, *A Man Called White: The Autobiography of Walter White* (Athens: University of Georgia Press, 1995 [originally published 1948]), 301. Robert J. Norrell, *Reaping the Whirlwind: The Civil Rights Movement in Tuskegee* (New York: Vintage, 1985), 57.

9. "North American Aviation Head Says Colored Men Will be Janitors Only," *Kansas City Call*, March 21, 1941. "White Aircraft Workers Converted on Race Issue," *Chicago Defender*, June 11, 1941. See also James R. Prickett, "Communist Conspiracy or Wage Dispute? The 1941 Strike at North American Aviation," *The Pacific Historical Review*, Vol. 50, No. 2 (May 1981); 215–33.

10. "Defense Handling of Negroes Scored," *New York Times*, June 12, 1941.

11. Randolph quoted by Thomas J. Sugrue, *Sweet Land of Liberty: The Forgotten Struggle for Civil Rights in the North* (New York: Random House, 2008), 32. A. Philip Randolph, letter to Secretary of War Henry L. Stimson, June 4, 1941, National Archives and Records Administration (henceforth abbreviated NARA) Record Group 107 Entry 99, Formerly Top Secret Correspondence of Secretary of War Stimson (Safe File), 1940.45, Box 3.

12. Gail Buckley, *American Patriots: The Story of Blacks in the Military from the Revolution to Desert Storm* (New York: Random House, 2001), 271. Steven F. Lawson, "Debating the Civil Rights Movement: The View from the Nation," in Lawson and Charles Payne, eds., *Debating the Civil Rights Movement, 1945–1968,* 2nd ed. (Lanham, MD: Rowman and Littlefield, 2006), 6.

13. For the experience of blacks in other World War II–era armed services, see for example Melton A. McLaurin, *The Marines of Montford Point: America's First Black Marines* (Chapel Hill: University of North Carolina Press, 2007); Paul Stillwell, *The Golden Thirteen: Recollections of the First Black Naval Officers* (Annapolis, MD: Naval Institute Press, 1993); Dempsey J. Travis, *Views from the Back of the Bus During WWII and Beyond* (Chicago: Urban Research Press, 1995); Phillip McGuire, ed., *Taps for a Jim Crow Army: Letters from Black Soldiers in World War II* (Lexington: University Press of Kentucky, 1983); and Maggi Morehouse, *Fighting in the Jim Crow Army: Black Men and Women Remember World War II* (Lanham, MD: Rowman and Littlefield, 2000).

14. Sherie Mershon and Steven Schlossman, *Foxholes and Color Lines: Desegregating the U.S. Armed Forces* (Baltimore: Johns Hopkins University Press, 1998), 1. "Only White Flyers Will Be Shot Down in Next War," *Chicago Defender,* Aug. 24, 1940.

15. "Aviation: Perpetuating Segregation," *Pittsburgh Courier,* March 29, 1941. For more on the mixed reaction to the announcement of the Tuskegee program, see for instance "Urge Mixed U.S. Army Pilot Training Schools," *Baltimore Afro-American,* March 1, 1941, and "National Airmen's Association Scores Jim Crow Air Corps; Calls Proposal Ridiculous," *New York Age,* Feb. 22, 1941.

16. The Air Corps Act, which includes this language, was enacted on July 2, 1926.

17. Bernard C. Nalty, *Strength for the Fight: A History of African Americans in the Military* (New York: Free Press, 1986), 128–29.

18. U.S. Army War College, "The Use of Negro Manpower in War," 1925. Library, U.S. Army Military History Institute, Carlisle Barracks, Carlisle, Pa. Though classified as a study, this might more accurately be described as a series of memoranda overlain with spurious conclusions and official recommendations.

19. "The Use of Negro Manpower in War," 1. "Famed Biologist Blasts Army 'Doubts' on Ability of Negroes to Fly Bombers," *Chicago Defender,* n.d. NARA Record Group 107, Dec. File 291.2 (Negroes), Box 95.

20. "The Use of Negro Manpower in War," 8.

21. H.E. Ely, "Memorandum for the Chief of Staff Re. The use of negro manpower in war," Oct. 30, 1925. Accompanying document to "The Use of Negro Manpower in War."

22. W.E.B. DuBois, "Close Ranks," *The Crisis,* July 1918. Reprinted in David Levering Lewis, ed., *W.E.B. DuBois: A Reader* (New York: Henry Holt and Co., 1995), 697. DuBois, "Returning Soldiers," *The Crisis,* May 1919.

23. Mershon and Schlossman, 7. David Levering Lewis, *W.E.B. DuBois: Biography of a Race, 1868–1919* (New York: Henry Holt and Co., 1993), 543. "The Use of Negro Manpower in War."

24. "The Use of Negro Manpower in War."

25. Brigadier General George V. Strong, "Memorandum, Subject: Army Air Corps Training Program," Jan. 9, 1940. Lister Hill Papers, Box 109.

26. Rogers quoted by Glenda Elizabeth Gilmore, *Defying Dixie: The Radical Roots of Civil Rights, 1919–1950* (New York: Norton, 2008), 194.

27. Strong, "Memorandum, Subject: Army Air Corps Training Program."

28. Strong, "Memorandum, Subject: Army Air Corps Training Program."

29. Jakeman, chap. 5, passim.

30. Chauncey Spencer oral history interview with Todd Moye, Dec. 18, 2000. National Park Service Tuskegee Airmen Oral History Project. See also Michael Laris, "Freedom Flight," *Washington Post Magazine*, Feb. 16, 2003; and Chauncey Spencer, *Who Is Chauncey Spencer?* (Detroit: Broadside Press, 1975).

31. "166 Schools Picked for Pilot Training," *New York Times*, Sept. 11, 1939. Grove Webster, letter to Roy Wilkins, June 6, 1940, and "The Civilian Pilot Training Program, 1939–1940," NAACP Papers Group II, Box A652.

32. U.S. Bureau of the Census, "Negro Statistical Bulletin No. 3," September 1940. National Association for the Advancement of Colored People Papers Group II, Box A652. See also Washington manuscript.

33. Lawrence P. Scott and William M. Womack Sr., *Double V: The Civil Rights Struggle of the Tuskegee Airmen* (East Lansing: Michigan State University Press, 1998), 82–84, 87.

34. Thompson quoted by Buckley, 257.

35. Marshall quoted by Kennedy, 771.

36. Walter White letters to Franklin D. Roosevelt, July 19, 1937, July 14, 1938, and Sept. 15, 1939. Official File 2538, Box 2, NAACP, 1936–1945, Franklin D. Roosevelt Presidential Library and Museum (henceforth abbreviated FDR Library).

37. Walter White letter to Franklin D. Roosevelt, Nov. 27, 1939. James H. Rowe Jr. Papers Box 23, FDR Library. Scott and Womack, 123–24.

38. Walter White letter to Franklin D. Roosevelt, Nov. 27, 1939; James H. Rowe Jr., "Memorandum For The President," Dec. 27, 1939. Rowe Papers, FDR Library.

39. Walter White letter to Jacob Billikopf, Oct. 9, 1940, and Francis Biddle letter to James H. Rowe, Oct. 21, 1940. FDR Official File 2538, Box 2, NAACP, 1936–1945, FDR Library. White, *A Man Called White*, 198.

40. Donald A. Ritchie, *Reporting from Washington: The History of the Washington Press Corps* (New York: Oxford University Press, 2005), 31; Buckley, 265.

41. James H. Rowe Jr., memorandum to Franklin D. Roosevelt, Oct. 25, 1940. Rowe Papers, Box 23. Scott and Womack, 133–34.

42. William H. Hastie, *On Clipped Wings: The Story of Jim Crow in the Army Air Corps.* (New York: NAACP, 1943), 3–4. AFHRA.

43. For the Coffey School of Aeronautics, Willa Brown, and black aviation in Chicago, see NAACP Papers Group II, Box 89.

44. "History of Tuskegee Army Air Field, Tuskegee, Alabama, from Conception to 6 December, 1941" (1943; revised 1944), 8, 10, 289.28-v.1. AFHRA. "Air Corps to Form a Negro Squadron," *New York Times*, Jan. 17, 1941, and "Army Calls Negro Fliers," *New York Times*, March 22, 1941. See also Jakeman, chap. 8, passim. Homan and Reilly, 39.

45. "Aviation: Perpetuating Segregation," *Pittsburgh Courier*, March 29, 1941. "Negro Flyers," *Chicago Defender*, March 29, 1941. Hastie, *On Clipped Wings*, 4.

46. "N.A.A.C.P. protests War Department plan for segregated air squadron at Tuskegee," NAACP press release, Feb. 14, 1941; Walter White telegram to William H.

Hastie, Jan. 3, 1941; Walter White telegram to F. D. Patterson, Jan. 4, 1940 [sic; 1941]. NAACP Papers Group II, Box B194. "Tuskegee School for Negro Airmen is 'Inadequate,'" *Houston Negro Labor News*, Feb. 22, 1941.

47. Frederick Patterson telegram to Walter White, Jan. 4, 1941. NAACP Papers Group II, Box B194. Roy Wilkins, letter to William H. Hastie, NAACP Papers Group II, Box A652. Patterson quoted in *Atlanta Daily World*, Feb. 1, 1942; copy in "History of Tuskegee Army Air Field, Tuskegee, Alabama, from Conception to 6 December, 1941," 6.

48. Hastie, *On Clipped Wings*, 8–10.

49. Hastie, *On Clipped Wings*, 10.

50. "History of Tuskegee Army Air Field, Tuskegee, Alabama, from Conception to 6 December, 1941," i, 26.

51. F.D. Patterson letter to Robert F. Patterson, Nov. 29, 1941. Lister Hill Papers, Box 188.

52. F.D. Patterson letter to Robert F. Patterson, Nov. 29, 1941.

53. Lister Hill letter to F.D. Patterson, Dec. 1, 1941. Lister Hill Papers, Box 188. "National Defense Contracts and Expenditures." Lister Hill Papers, Box 116. See also Wesley Philips Newton, *Montgomery in the Good War: Portrait of a Southern City, 1939–1946* (Tuscaloosa: University of Alabama Press, 2000).

54. John H. Bankhead letter to George H. Brett, April 28, 1941, and William Varner letter to John H. Bankhead and Lister Hill, April 23, 1941. Records of Headquarters Army Air Forces/Office of the Commanding General. NARA Records of Headquarters Army Air Forces/Office of the Commanding General, Project Files: Air Fields, 1939–1942, Box 1827. For the racial politics of Tuskegee, see also Robert J. Norrell, *Reaping the Whirlwind: The Civil Rights Movement in Tuskegee* (New York: Random House, 1985). For Varner, see Norrell, 40–41.

55. William Varner letter to John H. Bankhead and Lister Hill, April 23, 1941.

56. Transcript, "Telephone conversation between Senator Hill and General Brett, 4/28/41." Records of Headquarters Army Air Forces/Office of the Commanding General. NARA Records of Headquarters Army Air Forces/Office of the Commanding General, Project Files: Air Fields, 1939–1942, Box 1827.

57. Transcript, "Telephone conversation between Senator Hill and General Brett, 4/28/41."

58. W.R. Weaver letter to George H. Brett, April 24, 1941, and George H. Brett letter to W.R. Weaver, April 26, 1941. NARA Records of Headquarters Army Air Forces/Office of the Commanding General, Project Files: Air Fields, 1939–1942, Box 1827.

59. Jakeman, 278–79.

60. "History of Tuskegee Army Air Field, Tuskegee, Alabama, from Conception to 6 December, 1941," n.p. Pompey Hawkins oral history interview with William Mansfield, Feb. 8, 2002; and William A. Walters oral history interview with Todd Moye, May 17, 2002. National Park Service Tuskegee Airmen Oral History Project.

61. Walter White, Feb. 21, 1941, letter to multiple recipients. NAACP Papers Group II, Box A653.

62. U.S. Bureau of the Census, "A Half-Century of Learning: Historical Statistics on Educational Attainment in the United States, 1940 to 2000." www.census.gov/population/socdemo/education/phct41/table4.csv (accessed Dec. 14, 2007).

63. Mohamed Shaik letter to Walter White, March 4, 1941. NAACP Papers Group II, Box A652. Mohamed Shaik oral history interview with Todd Moye, Nov. 9, 2000, National Park Service Tuskegee Airmen Oral History Project.

64. Mac Ross letter to Walter White, Feb. 28, 1941; and L. R. Purnell letter to Walter White, March 13, 1941. NAACP Papers Group II, Box A652.

65. Yancey Williams letter to Walter White, March 17, 1941. NAACP Papers Group II, Box A652. "Barred from Air Corps, Howard Student Sues U.S. War Department," NAACP press release, Jan. 17, 1941, and W. Robert Ming Jr. letter to Thurgood Marshall, Nov. 27, 1940. NAACP Papers Group II, Box B194. "Rejected Pilot Won't Drop Suit," *Pittsburgh Courier,* Jan. 25, 1941.

66. Jakeman, 223–34.

67. Charles Dryden oral history interview with Todd Moye, Sept. 28, 2000. National Park Service Tuskegee Airmen Oral History Project. See also Dryden, *A-Train: Memoirs of a Tuskegee Airman* (Tuscaloosa: University of Alabama Press, 1997). Dryden letters to Walter White, Feb. 25, 1941, and May 21, 1941. NAACP Papers Group II, Box A652.

68. Wilson Vashon Eagleson March 1, 1941, letter to Walter White. NAACP Papers Group II, Box A652; Eagleson interview. See also Jennifer Bailey Woodard, "A Phenomenal Woman," *Indiana Alumni Magazine* (January/February, 1999), http://alumni.indiana.edu/scrapbook/aa/phenom.html and http://alumni.indiana.edu/scrapbook/aa/eagleside.html; and Brad Cook, "Remembering IU's first African-American scholar-athlete," Feb. 9, 2007 (http://homepages.indiana.edu/2007/02–09/story.php?id=1122, accessed Nov. 16, 2007).

69. Eagleson oral history interview.

70. "The Ninety-Ninth Squadron," *Time,* Aug. 3, 1942 (accessed online at www.time.com/time/magazine/article/0,9171,773313,00.html, Nov. 9, 2007). For a sense of the variety of backgrounds the Tuskegee Airmen came from, see the "Roster of Pilot Training Graduates at Tuskegee Army Air Field" compiled by Tuskegee Airman Theopolis "Ted" Johnson, see Lynn M. Homan and Thomas Reilly, *Black Knights: The Story of the Tuskegee Airmen* (Gretna, LA: Pelican, 2001), Appendix.

71. Roy Chappell oral history interview with Worth Long, May 16, 2001. National Park Service Tuskegee Airmen Oral History Project.

72. Twiley Barker oral history interview with William Mansfield, March 8, 2002. National Park Service Tuskegee Airmen Oral History Project.

73. White, *A Man Called White,* 190.

CHAPTER 2

1. Lemuel R. Custis oral history interview with Lisa Bratton, Aug. 17, 2002. National Park Service Tuskegee Airmen Oral History Project.

2. See Norrell, *Reaping the Whirlwind,* chap. 1, passim. The quote appears on p. 13.

3. The rift between Washington and the NAACP has spawned a small mountain's worth of books. See for instance Robert J. Norrell, *Up from History: The Life of Booker T. Washington* (Cambridge: Harvard University Press, 2009).

4. The address is reprinted in Booker T. Washington, *Up from Slavery* (1900: repr., New York: Bantam, 1970), 153–58.

5. Norrell, *Reaping the Whirlwind*, 22–23.

6. Norrell, *Up from History*, 426–27.

7. Norrell, *Reaping the Whirlwind*, 27–29. White, *A Man Called White*, 69–71.

8. Jakeman, 5, 21.

9. Jakeman, 22–25.

10. Jakeman, 29–32.

11. C. Alfred "Chief" Anderson, oral history interview with James C. Hasdorff, June 8–9, 1981, U.S. Air Force Oral History Interview Series, AFHRA.

12. Ibid.

13. Ibid.

14. Ibid.

15. Ibid.

16. Ibid.

17. Washington manuscript, 22–23, 27.

18. Washington manuscript, 41.

19. Washington manuscript, 44, 50, 54; Jakeman, 118–30; Anderson oral history.

20. Jakeman, 139–42.

21. Washington manuscript, 66; Jakeman, 142–44.

22. C. A. Anderson oral history; Washington manuscript, 91.

23. Washington manuscript, 77, 91, 150; Jakeman, 144–49.

24. Washington manuscript, 101–9.

25. Washington manuscript, 109–11, 178.

26. Eleanor Roosevelt, "Flying is Fun," *Collier's Magazine*, April 22, 1939, 15.

27. C. A. Anderson oral history; Jakeman, 245–48.

28. Eleanor Roosevelt, "My Day," prepared for release on March 29, March 31, and April 1, 1941. Eleanor Roosevelt Papers, "My Day" mimeographed copies, Box 1465. See also David Oshinsky, *Polio, An American Story: The Crusade that Mobilized the Nation Against the 20th Century's Most Feared Disease* (New York: Oxford University Press, 2005), 65–66; and Naomi Rogers, "Race and the Politics of Polio: Warm Springs, Tuskegee, and the March of Dimes," *American Journal of Public Health* 97/5 May 2007: 784–96.

29. Eleanor Roosevelt, "My Day," prepared for release on March 29, March 31, and April 1, 1941.

30. Minutes of the meeting of the Julius Rosenwald Fund, March 28, 1941, and "Notes on Fund Interests," June 23, 1941, Eleanor Roosevelt Papers, White House Correspondence, 1933–45, Box 943, FDR Library.

31. Henry C. Bohler oral history interview with Worth Long, Oct. 9, 2001; John Fernandes oral history interview with Tony Paredes, March 13, 2000; Haydel White oral history interview with Worth Long, Sept. 17, 2001; Charles Lang oral history interview with Judith Brown, May 4, 2001. National Park Service Tuskegee Airmen Oral History Project.

32. Jakeman, 242.

33. Hunter quoted by Stanley Sandler, *Segregated Skies: All-Black Combat Squadrons in World War II* (Washington, DC: Smithsonian Institution Press, 1992), 130.

34. Washington manuscript, 181–84.

35. Washington manuscript, 200. Gracie Perry Phillips oral history interview with Worth Long, Sept. 18, 2001; Katie Whitney Williams and Linkwood Williams oral his-

tory interview with Worth Long, March 14, 2001. National Park Service Tuskegee Airmen Oral History Project.

36. Brig. Gen. Noel F. Parrish oral history interview with James C. Hasdorff, June 14, 1974. U.S. Air Force Oral History Interview Series, AFHRA. See also Washington manuscript, 397.

37. Parrish oral history interview.

38. Ibid.

39. Ibid.

40. Ibid.

41. Ibid.; Sandler, 28.

42. Washington manuscript, 128.

43. Parrish letter to "Mother [Lucy L. Parrish]," July 8, 1942. Box 19, Noel F. Parrish Papers. Manuscripts Division, Library of Congress. Parrish oral history interview.

44. Parrish oral history interview.

45. Ibid.

46. Ibid.

47. Washington manuscript, 222, 228, 341.

48. Washington manuscript, 234.

49. Marvin E. Fletcher, *America's First Black General: Benjamin O. Davis, Sr., 1880–1970* (Lawrence: University of Kansas, 1989). Lt. Gen. Benjamin O. Davis Jr. oral history interview with Maj. Alan Gropman, January 1973, 27–28. U.S. Air Force Oral History Interview Series, AFHRA.

50. Benjamin O. Davis Jr., *Benjamin O. Davis, Jr., American: An Autobiography.* (Washington, DC: Smithsonian Institution Press, 1991), 26–28; Davis oral history interview, 37.

51. Davis, 58, 65–67.

52. Washington manuscript, 127. Davis, 65.

53. Parrish oral history interview.

54. Maurice Thomas oral history interview.

55. Alexander Jefferson oral history interview with Worth Long, Aug. 30, 2001. National Park Service Tuskegee Airmen Oral History Project.

56. Ibid. See also Precious Dunn oral history interview with Judith Brown, May 12, 2003; Victor Hancock oral history interview with William Mansfield, Feb. 7, 2001; Walter Palmer oral history interview with William Mansfield, Aug. 24, 2001; and George A. Taylor oral history interview with Worth Long, May 17, 2001. National Park Service Tuskegee Airmen Oral History Project. See also "Macon Countians Hope to Save Chehaw," *Columbus [Ga.] Ledger-Enquirer,* March 27, 1975. Macon County clippings file, Alabama Department of Archives and History.

57. Custis oral history interview.

58. Lewis J. Lynch oral history interview with Bill Mansfield, Oct. 19, 2001. National Park Service Tuskegee Airmen Oral History Project.

59. Ibid.

60. Milton Crenchaw, oral history interview with Worth Long, March 11, 2001. National Park Service Tuskegee Airmen Oral History Project.

61. Ibid.

62. Charles Herbert Flowers II oral history interview with Todd Moye, June 28, 2001. National Park Service Tuskegee Airmen Oral History Project.

63. Ibid.

64. Theophia Lee oral history interview with Todd Moye, June 27, 2001, and Roscoe Draper oral history interview with Lisa Bratton, Jan. 30, 2001. National Park Service Tuskegee Airmen Oral History Project.

65. Charles E. McGee oral history interview with William Mansfield, March 14, 2001. National Park Service Tuskegee Airmen Oral History Project.

66. James Wright oral history interview with William Mansfield, Feb. 20, 2001; Claude Platte oral history interviews with William Mansfield, Sept. 26, 2001, and July 20, 2004; Linkwood Williams oral history interview with Worth Long, March 14, 2001; Alexander Wilkerson, oral history interview with Judith Brown, Feb. 14, 2001; Wendell Lipscomb oral history interview with Lisa Bratton, April 12, 2001; Jack Johnson oral history with Judith Brown, March 15, 2001. Charles S. Johnson Jr. oral history interview with Judith Brown, May 23, 2001. National Park Service Tuskegee Airmen Oral History Project. See also "James Plinton Jr., 81; Broke Color Barriers at U.S. Airlines," *New York Times*, July 14, 1996.

67. Washington manuscript, 272, 288–89, 385.

68. Fannie Gunn Boyd oral history interview with Worth Long, Feb. 6, 2001. National Park Service Tuskegee Airmen Oral History Project.

69. Washington manuscript, 272. Boyd interview.

70. Boyd oral history interview.

71. Washington manuscript, 299–315.

72. Washington manuscript, 308.

73. Twiley Barker, March 8, 2002; Herbert Eugene Carter and Mildred Carter oral history interview with Tony Paredes and Christine Trebellas, March 14, 2000; Herbert Eugene Carter oral history interview with Bob Blythe, March 14, 2000; James Goodwin oral history interview with William Mansfield, Aug. 10, 2001. National Park Service Tuskegee Airmen Oral History Project.

74. Herbert Thorpe oral history interview with William Mansfield, Dec. 8, 2003. National Park Service Tuskegee Airmen Oral History Project.

75. Custis oral history interview.

76. Washington manuscript, 387.

77. See for instance Samuel Broadnax oral history interview with Lisa Bratton, Aug. 21, 2001. National Park Service Tuskegee Airmen Oral History Project.

78. Several of the Tuskegee Airmen remembered variations of the Magoon doggerel. See especially Crawford Dowdell oral history interview with William Mansfield, Dec. 10, 2003, and Roosevelt Lewis oral history interview with Christine Trebellas, March 15, 2000. National Park Service Tuskegee Airmen Oral History Project. I am indebted to Bill Mansfield, a trained folklorist and interviewer for the Tuskegee Airmen Oral History Project, for his insights into the meanings of the Magoon legend.

79. Maj. H.C. Magoon, "Foreword" to "History of the 66th AAF Training Detachment, Moton Field, Tuskegee, Alabama, 1 January 1943 to 31 January 1944." AFHRA.

80. Dowdell oral history interview.

81. Ibid.

82. Washington manuscript, 400–401.

CHAPTER 3

1. Clarence C. Jamison oral history interview with Worth Long, March 22, 2002. National Park Service Tuskegee Airmen Oral History Project.

2. This "Tuskegee experiment" should not be confused with its contemporary, and more notorious, "Tuskegee experiment," the U.S. Public Health Service's Tuskegee Syphilis Study. See James H. Jones, *Bad Blood: The Tuskegee Syphilis Study*, revised edition (New York: Free Press, 1993).

3. Omar D. Blair oral history interview with Todd Moye, May 16, 2002. National Park Service Tuskegee Airmen Oral History Project.

4. See Gilbert Ware, *William H. Hastie: Grace Under Pressure* (New York: Oxford University Press, 1988).

5. Ibid. See chap. 13, passim.

6. Hastie quoted by Ware, 104.

7. Ware, 97; Donald A. Ritchie, *Reporting from Washington*, 31.

8. Truman Gibson oral history with Todd Moye, Aug. 28, 2003. National Park Service Tuskegee Airmen Oral History Project. See also Truman Gibson and Steve Huntley, *Knocking Down Barriers: My Fight for Black America* (Chicago: Northwestern University Press, 2005).

9. Ware, 96–103.

10. Hastie, March 19, 1942, memorandum to the Assistant Secretary of War (Air), NARA Record Group 107, Dec. File 291.2 (Negroes), Box 95.

11. Maj. Gen. George E. Stratemeyer, memorandum to the Air Surgeon, Jan. 11, 1943. NARA Record Group 18, Dec. File 291.2 (Race), Box 103.

12. Hastie, Oct. 19, 1942, memorandum to the Assistant Secretary of War for Air, NARA Record Group 107, Dec. File 291.2 (Negroes), Box 95.

13. Hastie, Feb. 5, 1942, memorandum for the Undersecretary of War, NARA Box 2. See also "Comparison of Intelligence Classifications[,] White and Colored Selectees Inducted June to August, 1941," Tab B to Bryden memorandum.

14. Henry L. Stimson, letter to Dr. Alfred E. Stearns, Jan. 30, 1942. NARA Record Group 107, Entry 99, Formerly Top Secret Correspondence of Secretary of War Stimson, Box 3.

15. Ware, 109, 120–21.

16. Ware, 107–9. See also Spencie Love, *One Blood: The Death and Resurrection of Charles R. Drew* (Chapel Hill: University of North Carolina Press, 1997).

17. Ware, 129.

18. Ware, 130. For "experiment," see Col. St. Clair Street, memorandum for Judge William H. Hastie, Nov. 21, 1941, and Truman Gibson, memorandum to Assistant Secretary for Air Robert A. Lovett, May 18, 1943. NARA Record Group 107, Decimal File 291.2 (Negroes), Box 95.

19. Hastie, memorandum to Robert A. Lovett, March 19, 1942. NARA Record Group 107, Decimal File 291.2 (Negroes), Box 95.

20. Hastie, *On Clipped Wings*, 9.

21. Lovett, memorandum to Hastie, April 29, 1941, and Hastie, memorandum to Lovett, May 2, 1941. NARA Record Group 107, Decimal File 291.2 (Negroes), Box 95.

22. Maj. James A. Ellison, memorandum to Chief of Air Corps, Sept. 19, 1941. NARA Entry 295 Project Files: Air Fields, Box 1827.

23. Hastie, April 23, 1941, memorandum to Robert A. Lovett. NARA Record Group 107, Decimal File 291.2 (Negroes), Box 95.

24. Parrish, "Foreword"; "History of Tuskegee Army Air Field from 7 December 1941 to 31 December 1942," III. AFHRA.

25. "Racial Quota System Bottleneck in Training Flyers, NAACP Claims," *Kansas City Call*, Aug. 21, 1942.

26. "History of Tuskegee Army Air Field from 7 December 1941 to 31 December 1942," 35; "History of Tuskegee Army Air Field from 1 January 1943 to 29 February 1944," 86. AFHRA.

27. "History of Tuskegee Army Air Field from Conception to 6 December 1941," 1–2. AFHRA.

28. "History of Tuskegee Army Air Field from Conception to 6 December 1941," 33–34; "History of Tuskegee Army Air Field from 7 December 1941 to 31 December 1942," 24, 29. Homan and Reilly, 71.

29. "History of Tuskegee Army Air Field from 7 December 1941 to 31 December 1942," 11–13.

30. "History of Tuskegee Army Air Field from Conception to 6 December 1941," 26. Gen. II. II. Arnold, memorandum for the Inspector General, Sept. 30, 1941. NARA Entry 295 Project Files: Air Fields, Box 1827.

31. "History of Tuskegee Army Air Field from Conception to 6 December 1941," 39–41; "History of Tuskegee Army Air Field from 7 December 1941 to 31 December 1942," 14, 94.

32. "Negro Air Unit Quota is Filled," *Montgomery Advertiser*, April 3, 1941, and "Collapse of Morale is Blamed for Failure to Fill Jim Crow Air Unit," *Chicago Defender*, May 3, 1941.

33. Washington manuscript, 218–25. LeRoy Gillead oral history interview with Lisa Bratton, July 15, 2002. National Park Service Tuskegee Airmen Oral History Project.

34. Elmer Jones oral history interview with William Mansfield, Feb. 9, 2001. National Park Service Tuskegee Airmen Oral History Project. "History of the 99th Fighter Squadron, 1 March—17 October 1943." AFHRA. "History of Tuskegee Army Air Field from 7 December 1941 to 31 December 1942," 33. Omar Blair oral history interview.

35. Homan and Reilly, 52. "History of Tuskegee Army Air Field from 7 December 1941 to 31 December 1942," 102.

36. Mildred Hemmons Carter oral history interview with Tony Paredes, March 14, 2000. National Park Service Tuskegee Airmen Oral History Project.

37. Mildred Hemmons Carter oral history interview. See also Herbert Eugene Carter oral history interview with Bob Blythe, March 14, 2000. National Park Service Tuskegee Airmen Oral History Project.

38. Mildred Hemmons Carter oral history interview.

39. "History of Tuskegee Army Air Field from 7 December 1941 to 31 December 1942," 103, 106.

40. Leslie Edwards oral history interview with William Mansfield, April 19, 2001. National Park Service Tuskegee Airmen Oral History Project.

41. Ibid.

42. Ibid.

43. Charles E. McGee oral history interview with Bill Mansfield, March 14, 2001. National Park Service Tuskegee Airmen Oral History Project.

44. Horace Bohannon oral history interview. Charles Kerford oral history interview with William Mansfield, April 4, 2001. National Park Service Tuskegee Airmen Oral History Project. Again, I am indebted to Bill Mansfield for sharing his insights into this chapter of Tuskegee Airmen folklore.

45. George Abercrombie oral history interview with Worth Long, Oct. 9, 2001. National Park Service Tuskegee Airmen Oral History Project.

46. Robert A. Margo, *Race and Schooling in the South, 1880–1950: An Economic History* (Chicago: University of Chicago Press, 1994), 81. See Sugrue, *Sweet Land of Liberty.* "History of Tuskegee Army Air Field from 1 January 1943 to 29 February 1944," 84.

47. "History of Tuskegee Army Air Field from 7 December 1941 to 31 December 1942," 15.

48. E.S. Adams, Oct. 16, 1940 memorandum.Frank Murray Dixon Papers, Alabama Department of Archives and History, Container SG12275.

49. Gillead interview. Col. Frederick H. V. von Kimble, memorandum to Commanding General, Southeast Army Air Forces Training Command, May 13, 1942. Dixon Papers, Container SG12275.

50. Von Kimble memorandum to Commanding General, Southeast Army Air Forces Training Command, May 13, 1942.

51. Maj. Gen. George E. Stratemeyer, memorandum to Commanding General, Army Air Forces Flying Training Command, May 18, 1942. Dixon Papers, Container SG12275. Charles W. Dryden oral history interview. Francis Horne oral history interview with William Mansfield, July 17, 2001. National Park Service Tuskegee Airmen Oral History Project.

52. Parrish oral history interview.

53. Ibid. Washington manuscript, 393.

54. Truman Gibson, April 4, 1942, memorandum; Virgil Peterson, April 24, 1942, memorandum; William H. Hastie, May 7, 1942, memorandum.Dixon Papers, Container SG12275. "History of Tuskegee Army Air Field from 7 December 1941 to 31 December 1942," 37–40. Parrish oral history interview.

55. Philip Doddridge memo, May 18, 1942. Dixon Papers, Container SG12275.

56. *California Eagle,* April 9, 1942. Appendix to "History of Tuskegee Army Air Field from 7 December 1941 to 31 December 1942." Maj. Gen. William Bryden, memorandum for the Undersecretary of War, Feb. 16, 1942. NARA Record Group 107 Dec. File 291.2 (Negroes), Box 2.

57. Fred Hoehler letter to Arthur W. Page, Nov. 22, 1942; Gov. Frank Dixon letter to R.H. Powell, Dec. 1, 1942; R.H. Powell letter to Gov. Frank Dixon, Nov. 30, 1942.

Dixon Papers, Container SG12275. "History of Tuskegee Army Air Field from 1 January 1943 to 29 February 1944," 15–16.

58. Col. Noel C. Parrish, "Foreword" to "History of Tuskegee Army Air Field from Conception to 6 December 1941."

59. John W. Rogers oral history interview with Lisa Bratton, Sept. 18, 2003. See also Harvey Sanford oral history interview with Todd Moye, July 31, 2001. National Park Service Tuskegee Airmen Oral History Project. Buckley, 260.

60. Richard B. Collins memorandum to Walter White, Sept. 26, 1942; Walter White, letter to Dr. Eugene H. Dibble, Oct. 3, 1942; Theodore O. Spaulding letter to Walter White, Sept. 23, 1942. NAACP Papers Group II, Box 194.

61. Robert L. Carter oral history interview with Lisa Bratton, Oct. 14, 2004. National Park Service Tuskegee Airmen Oral History Project.

62. Ibid.

63. Parrish oral history interview. Buckley, 287.

64. Hastie, Jan. 5, 1943, memorandum for the Secretary of War through the Under Secretary of War. NARA Record Group 107 Dec. File 291.2 (Negroes), Box 95.

65. Ibid.

66. Truman Gibson oral history with Todd Moye, Aug. 28, 2003. National Park Service Tuskegee Airmen Oral History Project. See also Truman Gibson and Steve Huntley, *Knocking Down Barriers: My Fight for Black America* (Chicago: Northwestern University Press, 2005), 79, and chap. 9, passim. Gen. George E. Stratemeyer, Jan. 12, 1943, memorandum for the Assistant Secretary of War. NARA Record Group 107 Dec. File 291.2 (Negroes), Box 95.

67. Hastie, *On Clipped Wings.*

68. Ibid.

69. Ibid.

70. "Blame Command For Low Morale At Tuskegee Base," *Pittsburgh Courier*, Feb. 20, 1943. Appendix to "History of Tuskegee Army Air Field from 1 January 1943 to 29 February 1944."

71. Charles M. Bowden, Letter to the Editor, *Chicago Defender*, March 13, 1943. Appendix to "History of Tuskegee Army Air Field from 1 January 1943 to 29 February 1944."

72. "History of Tuskegee Army Air Field from 1 January 1943 to 29 February 1944," 37.

73. "History of the 99th Fighter Squadron, 1 March—17 October 1943." AFHRA.

74. Chappell oral history interview.

75. Ibid.

76. Ibid.

77. "History of Tuskegee Army Air Field from Conception to 6 December 1941," 15; "History of Tuskegee Army Air Field from 7 December 1941 to 31 December 1942," 8–10; "History of Tuskegee Army Air Field from 1 January 1943 to 29 February 1944," 1–4.

78. "History of Tuskegee Army Air Field from 7 December 1941 to 31 December 1942," 34.

79. "History of Tuskegee Army Air Field from 7 December 1941 to 31 December 1942," 75.

80. "History of Tuskegee Army Air Field from January 1, 1943 to 29 February 1944," 56.

81. See for instance "Does America Need Aviators?" *Pittsburgh Courier*, Aug. 2, 1942. "History of Tuskegee Army Air Field from January 1, 1943 to 29 February 1944," 73–79.

82. William H. Hastie, July 18, 1942, memorandum to Commanding General, AAF Training Command. NARA Record Group 107 Dec. File 2191.2 (Race), Box 104.

83. Col. L. O. Ryan, Oct. 21, 1944, memorandum to Commanding General, AAF Training Command. NARA Record Group 107 Dec. File 291.2 (Race), Box 104.

84. "History of Tuskegee Army Air Field from 7 December 1941 to December 1942," 118. "Etta Moten Sings for Aviation Cadets," *Kansas City Call*, March 5, 1942.

85. "History of Tuskegee Army Air Field from January 1, 1943 to 29 February 1944," 99.

86. Yvonne Plummer Terrelongue oral history interview with William Mansfield, March 16, 2003. National Park Service Tuskegee Airmen Oral History Project.

87. Davis, 90–91. Dryden, 94, 100.

88. Jamison oral history interview.

89. Davis, 89–92.

CHAPTER 4

1. Dryden, *A-Train*, 108, 112.

2. "History of the 99th Fighter Squadron, 1 March–17 October 1943." AFHRA. Bernard Proctor oral history interview with Lisa Bratton, Feb. 5, 2001. National Park Service Tuskegee Airmen Oral History Project.

3. "History of the 99th Fighter Squadron, 1 March–17 October 1943." Dryden, 119–20.

4. George Bolling oral history interview with Lisa Bratton, Aug. 22, 2001. William Surcey oral history interview with William Mansfield, Feb. 24, 2001. National Park Service Tuskegee Airmen Oral History Project. Watson quoted by Homan and Reilly, 85.

5. George Bolling oral history interview with Lisa Bratton, Aug. 22, 2001. Bernard Proctor oral history interview with Lisa Bratton, June 4, 2001. Dryden, 137–39. Louis Purnell oral history interview with William Mansfield, Feb. 5, 2001. National Park Service Tuskegee Airmen Oral History Project. See also "Pantelleria, 1943," *Air Force Magazine*, June 2002, 64– 68.

6. Dryden, 125–26; Homan and Reilly, 87–89.

7. Dryden oral history interview.

8. Ibid.

9. Bolling oral history interview.

10. Watson quoted by Homan and Reilly, 103–4.

11. Davis quoted by Gibson, 124. See "Statement by Lieutenant Colonel Benjamin Oliver Davis Jr., at Press Conference, Friday, Sept. 10, 1943." Box 3, Truman K. Gibson Papers. Manuscript Division, Library of Congress.

12. "Experiment Proved?" *Time*, Sept. 20, 1943. Accessed online at www.time.com/time/magazine/article/0,9171,774586,000.html.

13. Letters to the Editor, *Time*, Oct. 18, 1943. Accessed online at www.time.com/time/magazine/article/0.9171,777986,00.html.

14. Gibson, 125; Davis, 103; Homan and Reilly, 101–2.

15. Mershon and Schlossman, 62; Gibson, 124–26.

16. Davis quoted by Gibson, 126.

17. Davis, 107.

18. "History of the 99th Fighter Squadron, 1 March–17 October 1943"; "History of the 99th Fighter Squadron, 1 November 1943–January 1944." AFHRA.

19. Proctor Feb. 5, 2001, interview.

20. White, *A Man Called White*, 255.

21. Ibid, 255–56.

22. "History of the 99th Fighter Squadron, 1 Feb–30 April 1944." AFHRA. Proctor Feb. 5, 2001, oral history interview. Homan and Reilly, 111, 115.

23. "Sweet Victories," *Time*, Feb. 14, 1944. Accessed online at www.time.com/time/magazine/article/0,9171,885395,00.html. "Negroes Praised as Air Fighters," *New York Times*, June 25, 1944.

24. William Campbell oral history interview with Lisa Bratton, Jan. 21, 2001. National Park Service Tuskegee Airmen Oral History Project. Homan and Reilly, 168.

25. Lucius Theus oral history interview with William Mansfield, June 5, 2001. National Park Service Tuskegee Airmen Oral History Project.

26. See "Scandal at Selfridge," *Time*, May 17, 1943; "Colman's Court," *Time*, Sept. 13, 1943; "Colman's Court," *Time*, Sept. 27, 1943; and "Selfridge Justice," *Time*, Oct. 18. Accessed online at www.time.com/time/magazine/article/0,9171,851683,00.html, www.time.com/time/magazine/article/0,9171,791104,00.html, www.time.com/time/magazine/article/0,9171,850348,00.html, and www.time.com/time/magazine/article/0,9171,778055,00.html, respectively.

27. Campbell oral history interview.

28. Sugrue, *Origins*, 23, 29. Sugrue, *Sweet Land of Liberty*, 66–68. Dominic J. Capeci Jr., ed., *Detroit and the Good War: The World War II Letters of Mayor Edward Jeffries and Friends* (Lexington: University Press of Kentucky, 1996), 16. See also Robert Shogan and Tom Craig, *The Detroit Race Riot: A Study in Violence* (Philadelphia: Chilton Books, 1964). Alexander Jefferson and Lewis Carlson, *Red Tail Captured, Red Tail Free* (New York: Fordham University Press, 2005), 32.

29. Alexander Jefferson oral history with Worth Long, Aug. 30, 2001. National Park Service Tuskegee Airmen Oral History Project. See also Jefferson and Carlson.

30. Jefferson and Carlson, 32, 34.

31. Milton Henry, letter to E. Washington Rhodes, Sept. 1, 1943. NAACP Papers Group II, Box B150: Soldier Complaints.

32. Ibid. Leroy Bowman, oral history interview with William Mansfield, March 21, 2003. National Park Service, Tuskegee Airmen Oral History Project.

33. William Hastie, petition on behalf of Robert L. Carter to Secretary of War Stimson, ca. 1944. NAACP Papers Group II, Box 149: Soldier Complaints. See also Robert L. Carter, *A Matter of Law: A Memoir of Struggle in the Cause of Equal Rights* (New York: New Press, 2005); and the concise Robert L. Carter oral history interview with Lisa Bratton, Oct. 14, 2004. National Park Service Tuskegee Airmen Oral History Project.

34. Hastie petition to Secretary of War Stimson.

35. Patricia Sullivan, "Judge Carter and the *Brown* Decision," *OAH Newsletter*, Feb. 2004, www.oah.org/pubs/nl/2004feb/sullivan.html.

36. Jefferson and Carlson, 34–35. Dryden, 173.

37. Dryden, 176. Jefferson and Carlson, 36.

38. Dryden, 176.

39. Dryden, 3–6, 178–83. Dryden oral history interview.

40. Watson quoted by Gerald Astor, *The Right to Fight: A History of African Americans in the Military* (New York: Da Capo Press, 2001) 234–35. See also Dryden, 192. Spann Watson oral history interview with Lisa Bratton, March 12, 2001. National Park Service Tuskegee Airmen Oral History Project.

41. Edmund Wilkinson oral history interview with Worth Long, March 12, 2001. National Park Service Tuskegee Airmen Oral History Project.

42. Wilkinson oral history interview. See also George Watson Sr. oral history interview with Lisa Bratton, Feb. 8, 2001. National Park Service Tuskegee Airmen Oral History Project.

43. Wilkinson oral history interview. See also Davis, 114.

44. Wilkinson oral history interview.

45. Woodrow Crockett oral history interview with Bill Mansfield, March 15, 2001. National Park Service Tuskegee Airmen Oral History Project.

46. Homan and Reilly, 130. "History of the 332nd Fighter Group for December 1944." AFHRA.

47. Jefferson and Carlson, 52–55.

48. Jefferson and Carlson, 60.

49. Jefferson and Carlson, 64–65.

50. Jefferson and Carlson, 76.

51. Larry Fleischer oral history interview with Todd Moye, April 24, 2001. National Park Service Tuskegee Airmen Oral History Project.

52. Fleischer oral history interview. George G. Barnett oral history interview with Todd Moye, Jan. 12, 2001. National Park Service Tuskegee Airmen Oral History Project.

53. Fleischer oral history interview. His account is corroborated by oral history interviews with crewmembers Barnett, Francis X. Connolly, and Michael Preputnik.

54. Fleischer oral history interview.

55. Fleischer oral history interview. Francis X. Connolly oral history interview with Lisa Bratton, Jan. 31, 2001. National Park Service Tuskegee Airmen Oral History Project.

56. Fleischer and Barnett oral history interviews.

57. Ibid.

58. "History of the 332nd Fighter Group for December 1944." AFHRA. Louis Purnell, "The Flight of the Bumblebee," *Air & Space Magazine*, October–November 1989, 39.

59. Wilkinson oral history interview.

60. Ibid.

61. "99th Fighter Squadron War Diary, December 1943–January 1944;" "Medical History of the 332nd Fighter Group, 13 October–March 1945." AFHRA.

62. Surcey oral history interview.

63. All direct quotes are from Charles E. McGee interview with William Mansfield, March 14, 2001. National Park Service Tuskegee Airmen Oral History Project.

64. Roscoe Brown oral history interview with Lisa Bratton, March 1, 2001. National Park Service Tuskegee Airmen Oral History Project.

65. "Doing Battle on Two Fronts."

66. Brown oral history interview. Buckley, 294.

67. See for instance oral history interviews with Omar Blair, Woodrow Crockett, and George Watson.

68. I rely here on the statistics compiled by Tuskegee Airmen, Inc., an alumni group. See http://tuskegeeairmen.org/uploads/stats.pdf.

69. White, *A Man Called White*, 365–66. See also Gaynelle Barksdale, "Graduate Theses of Atlanta University, 1931–1941," Robert W. Woodruff Library, Atlanta University Center, http://digitalcommons.auctr.edu/cgi/viewcontent.cgi?article=1006&context=lib_tdindex.

70. War Department Bureau of Public Relations, "Colonel Benjamin O. Davis Assumes Command of 477th Composite Group," for June 21, 1945, release. Box 160, NAACP Papers Group II. "Negroes Praised as Air Fighters."

71. From Jefferson's oral history interview: "'Whites to the right, niggers to the left.' He didn't say 'niggers,' he said 'Negroes to the left,' but I knew what he meant. Back to the so-called good old days, back to the United States. 'Whites to the right, Negroes to the left.'" In Jefferson's memoir, he has the private using the word "nigger." See Jefferson and Carlson, 106–7.

CHAPTER 5

1. John S. Lyons, letter to NAACP headquarters, Dec.14, 1943. NAACP Papers Group II, Box B150: Soldier Complaints. Pvt. William Bryant, letter to NAACP headquarters, ca. Aug. 17, 1943; and Pvt. George Brisco, letter to Walter White, Jan. 18, 1943. NAACP Papers Group II, Box 149: Soldier Complaints. B.W. Davenport, memorandum for the Commanding General, Army Air Forces, March 10, 1943. NARA Record Group 18, decimal file 291.2 (Race), Box 103.

2. Acting Adjutant Gen. H.B. Lewis, letter to Roy Wilkins, Nov. 4, 1942. NARA Record Group 107 Dec. File 291.2 (Negroes), Box 95.

3. Truman Gibson, memorandum to Assistant Secretary for Air Robert A. Lovett, May 18, 1943. NARA Record Group 107 Dec. File 291.2 (Negroes), Box 95.

4. Alan L. Gropman, *The Air Force Integrates, 1945–1964*, 2nd ed. (Washington, DC: Smithsonian Institution Press, 1998), 10.

5. Gropman, 10–11.

6. Ibid. James C. Warren, *The Tuskegee Airmen Mutiny at Freeman Field* (Vacaville, CA: Conyers, 1995), 137.

7. Gropman, 10–11. LeRoy Gillead oral history interview with Lisa Bratton, July 15, 2002. National Park Service Tuskegee Airmen Oral History Project.

8. Leslie S. Perry, memorandum to Robert P. Patterson, April 24, 1945. NAACP Papers Group II, Box 2.

9. Warren, 25, 28.

10. White, letter to Secretary of War Stimson, April 19, 1945; Perry memorandum to Patterson, April 24, 1945. Alexander Jefferson, a pilot of the 332nd, recalled Hunter's speech almost exactly as White reported it. See Warren 20–21. Col. Max F. Schneider, memorandum for Gen. Hunter, March 29, 1944. NARA Record Group 107, Decimal File 291.2 (Race), Box 104.

11. Ibid. Warren, 26.

12. Warren, 23. Schneider memorandum.

13. John J. McCloy, memorandum for the Secretary of War, June 4, 1945. NARA Record Group 107 Dec. File 291.2 (Negroes), Box 95. Florence Kibble and Esther P. Burns, letter to Eleanor Roosevelt, Feb. 18, 1944. NARA Record Group 107, Decimal File 291.2 (Race), Box 104.

14. Arnold, memorandum for Chiefs of All Headquarters Offices, May 2, 1944. NARA Record Group 107, Decimal File 291.2 (Race), Box 104.

15. Schneider memorandum.

16. Gropman, 11.

17. White letter to Secretary of War Stimson, April 19, 1945.

18. Perry memorandum to Patterson, April 24, 1945.

19. Robert Payton et al., letter to the Inspector General, Sept. 24, 1944. NARA Record Group 107, Decimal File 291.2 (Race), Box 104.

20. Chappell oral history interview. James C. Warren oral history interview with Lisa Bratton, Jan. 18, 2001. National Park Service Tuskegee Airmen Oral History Project.

21. War Department M.I.D. investigation of Coleman A. Young, Oct. 10, 1944. NARA Record Group 107, Reports of Racial Situation, Box 261. Warren oral history interview.

22. Brig. Gen. A. Hornsby, report to Commanding General, Central Flying Training Command, n.d. NARA Record Group 107, Decimal File 291.2 (Race), Box 104.

23. Warren oral history interview.

24. Col. John E. Harris, memorandum for the Air Inspector, May 29, 1944. NARA Record Group 107, Decimal File 291.2 (Race), Box 104.

25. Perry, memorandum to Patterson, April 24, 1945. Hastie memorandum to Arnold, July 18, 1942. NARA Record Group 18, Tuskegee Army Air Field, Box 1826. Walter White, letter to Secretary of War Stimson, April 19, 1945. NAACP Papers Group II, Box 2.

26. Perry, memorandum to Patterson, April 24, 1945.

27. Perry, memorandum to Patterson, April 24, 1945 Warren, 29. Warren oral history interview. F. Trubee Davison, memorandum to Commanding General, First Air Force, Dec. 8, 1942; B.W. Davenport, memorandum to the Commanding General, Army Air Forces, March 10, 1943. NARA Record Group 18, Decimal file 291.2 (Race), Box 103.

28. Walter White, letter to Secretary of War Stimson, April 19, 1945. NAACP Papers Group II, Box 2. Warren, 3, 131, 134.

29. Col. John E. Harris, Memorandum for the Air Inspector, April 14 and 20, 1945. AFHRA L68.7061–67.

30. Warren, 6–12.

31. Walter White, letter to Secretary of War Stimson, April 19, 1945; Leslie S. Perry, memorandum to Robert P. Patterson, April 24, 1945. NAACP Papers Group II, Box 2.

32. Perry memorandum to Patterson, April 24, 1945.

33. Gillead oral history interview.

34. Inspector General's Report, April 14 and 20, 1945. Warren, 3.

35. Theodore O. Mason oral history interview with Judith Brown, Dec. 14, 2001. National Park Service Tuskegee Airmen Oral History Project.

36. Warren, 34. Gillead oral history interview.

37. Gillead oral history interview.

38. Quentin P. Smith oral history interview with William Mansfield, July 21, 2002. National Park Service Tuskegee Airmen Oral History Project.

39. LeRoy Battle oral history interview with Judith Brown, Feb. 14, 2001. Haydel White oral history interview with Worth Long, Sept. 17, 2001. National Park Service Tuskegee Airmen Oral History Project.

40. Hiram Little oral history interview with Lisa Bratton, Dec. 28, 2000. National Park Service Tuskegee Airmen Oral History Project.

41. Ibid.

42. Ibid.

43. Ibid.

44. Ibid.

45. Inspector General's Report, April 14 and 20, 1945.

46. Perry, memorandum to Patterson, April 24, 1945.

47. Roger C. Terry oral history interview with Lisa Bratton, Feb. 28, 2002. National Park Service Tuskegee Airmen Oral History Project.

48. Ibid.

49. Mitchell Higginbotham oral history interview with Judith Brown, May 11, 2002; and Wardell Polk oral history interview with Worth Long, June 11, 2002. National Park Service Tuskegee Airmen Oral History Project.

50. Warren, 94, 98.

51. Warren, 90, 136–37. Fitzroy Newsum oral history interview with Todd Moye, May 17, 2002. National Park Service Tuskegee Airmen Oral History Project.

52. William T. Coleman Jr., letter to Leslie Perry, April 27, 1945; White letter to Secretary of War Stimson, April 19, 1945. NAACP Papers Group II, Box 2. See also Coleman's video interview with the National Visionary Leadership Project, at www.visionaryproject.com/colemanwilliam.

53. Warren, 154, 156–59.

54. Warren, 168.

55. Warren, 176–80.

56. Terry oral history interview.

57. Ibid. "Theodore Berry, 94, Civil Rights Pioneer, Dies," *New York Times*, Oct. 17, 2000.

58. Warren, 100–2.

59. Terry oral history interview.

60. Ibid.

61. Ibid.

62. Warren, 186.

63. Terry oral history interview.

64. Gropman, 21.

65. Gropman, 20.

66. Warren, 120.

67. Scott and Womack, 273, 276–77.

68. Dryden, 207, 234, 237.

CHAPTER 6

1. See Willie Ruff, *A Call to Assembly: The Autobiography of a Musical Storyteller* (New York: Viking, 1991), chapters 18–21, passim. The quote appears on p. 157.

2. Dryden oral history interview. Mershon and Schlossman, 153.

3. Lawson, 81; Buckley, 265. For the experience of blacks in the other services, see for example Melton A. McLaurin, *The Marines of Montford Point: America's First Black Marines* (Chapel Hill: University of North Carolina Press, 2007); Paul Stillwell, *The Golden Thirteen: Recollections of the First Black Naval Officers* (Annapolis: Naval Institute Press, 1993); Dempsey J. Travis, *Views from the Back of the Bus During WWII and Beyond* (Chicago: Urban Research Press, 1995); Phillip McGuire, ed., *Taps for a Jim Crow Army: Letters from Black Soldiers in World War II* (Lexington: University Press of Kentucky, 1983); and Maggi Morehouse, *Fighting in the Jim Crow Army: Black Men and Women Remember World War II* (Lanham, MD: Rowman and Littlefield, 2000).

4. Parrish oral history interview with James C. Hasdorff, June 14, 1974. Office of Air Force History, U.S. Air Force Historical Research Agency, Maxwell Field, Alabama.

5. Noel F. Parrish Jr., "The Segregation of Negroes in the Army Air Forces," thesis, Air Command and Staff School, Maxwell Field, Alabama, May 1947, 54. AFHRA.

6. Parrish oral history interview.

7. Ibid. Parrish thesis, 19.

8. Parrish thesis, 43.

9. Gropman, xii, 4. Parrish thesis, 42.

10. Gibson and Huntley, 105–7.

11. Gibson and Huntley, 107–8.

12. Gibson and Huntley, 119–20, 204.

13. Gibson oral history interview. Gibson and Huntley, 199.

14. Gibson oral history interview.

15. Gropman, 23–27. Mershon and Schlossman, 154.

16. Gropman, 28.

17. Gropman, 29–32.

18. Parrish quoted by Gropman, 32, 33.

19. Gropman, 38–40.

20. Buckley, 336–37; Parrish thesis, 36.

21. Gropman, 63–64; Gardner, 116.

22. Parrish thesis, 73. Parrish oral history, 143.

23. Egerton, 361–62. See also Berman, 44–46.

24. Scott and Womack, 271–72; Egerton, 362–63; Gardner, 18; Walter White, *A Man Called White*, 330–31. Truman quoted by Nalty, 237.

25. Steven F. Lawson, "Preface" and "Introduction: Setting the Agenda of the Civil Rights Movement," in Lawson, ed., *To Secure These Rights: The Report of President Harry S. Truman's Committee on Civil Rights* (Boston: Bedford/St. Martin's, 2004), iv, v, 13, 29–30. All quoted passages refer to Lawson's edition. The full text of the report is also available online from the Truman Presidential Library, www.trumanlibrary.org/civil-rights/srights1.htm.

26. For the 1948 presidential election, see Berman, 79–136; Kari Frederickson, *The Dixiecrat Revolt and the End of the Solid South, 1932–1968* (Chapel Hill: University of North Carolina Press, 2000); Patricia Sullivan, *Days of Hope: Race and Democracy in the New Deal Era* (Chapel Hill: University of North Carolina Press, 1996), 249–75; and Timothy N. Thurber, *The Politics of Equality: Hubert H. Humphrey and the African American Freedom Struggle* (New York: Columbia University Press, 1999), 52–66.

27. Lawson, 21–24; Berman, 66–70.

28. Lawson, 26; Gardner, 28–32, 41.

29. Berman, 65–66. See also Carol Anderson, *Eyes off the Prize: The United Nations and the African American Struggle for Human Rights, 1944–1955* (Cambridge: Cambridge University Press, 2003); Mary L. Dudziak, *Cold War Civil Rights: Race and the Image of American Democracy* (Princeton: Princeton University Press, 2000); and Penny Von Eschen, *Race Against Empire: Black Americans and Anticolonialism, 1937–1957* (Ithaca, NY: Cornell University Press, 1997).

30. Lawson, 22. Gunnar Myrdal, *An American Dilemma: The Negro Problem and Modern Democracy* (New York: Harper, 1944).

31. Lawson, 53.

32. Lawson, 134, 176–77. For the importance of the Morgan case, see Raymond Arsenault, *Freedom Riders: 1961 and the Struggle for Racial Justice* (New York: Oxford University Press, 2006).

33. Berman, 81–84.

34. Berman, 98–100, 117–20.

35. Gardner, 112.

36. Gropman, 63, 65–68, 85; Gardner, 115.

37. Parrish thesis, 22.

38. See Dryden, *A-Train*, chap.11, passim.

39. Scott and Womack, 274. Robert L. Carter memorandum to Roy Wilkins and Thurgood Marshall, March 10, 1949.NAACP Papers Group II, Box 192.

40. Ibid.

41. Scott and Womack, 288. Dryden oral history interview. Lewis Lynch oral history interview with William Mansfield, Oct. 19, 2001. National Park Service Tuskegee Airmen Oral History Project.

42. Dryden oral history interview.

43. Harry T. Stewart oral history interview with Worth Long, June 4, 2001. National Park Service Tuskegee Airmen Oral History Project.

44. Stewart interview. James H. Harvey III oral history interview with Todd Moye, May 13, 2002. National Park Service Tuskegee Airmen Oral History Project. See also Harvey Alexander interview.

45. Harvey oral history interview.

46. Harvey and Stewart oral history interviews. Alva Temple oral history interview with Worth Long, June 4, 2001. National Park Service Tuskegee Airmen Oral History Project.

47. Harvey oral history interview.

48. Gardner, 120.

49. William Gray oral history interview with Todd Moye, April 23, 2001. National Park Service Tuskegee Airmen Oral History Project.

50. Lucius Theus oral history interview with William Mansfield, June 5, 2001. National Park Service Tuskegee Airmen Oral History Project.

51. Theopolis W. ("Ted") Johnson oral history interview with Todd Moye, Nov. 9, 2000. National Park Service Tuskegee Airmen Oral History Project.

52. Warren oral history interview.

53. Ibid.

54. Ibid.

55. See for instance Walter White, letter to North West [sic] Airline, Dec. 6, 1945. Lloyd S. Hathcock, letter to Walter White, Jan. 7, 1945. NAACP Papers Group II, Box A8.

56. Linus C. Glotzbach, letter to Walter White, Dec. 31, 1945. NAACP Papers Group II, Box A8.

57. See "James Plinton Jr., 81; Broke Color Barriers at U.S. Airlines," *New York Times*, July 14, 1996; and "New Faces," *Time*, Sept. 2, 1957 (accessed online, www.time.com/time/magazine/article/0,9171,809846,00.htmlBuckley, 294.

58. Dryden oral history interview; McGee oral history interview.

59. Buckley, 360–62.

60. See James R. McGovern, *Black Eagle: General Daniel "Chappie" James, Jr.* (University: University of Alabama Press, 1985); and J. Alfred Phelps, *Chappie: America's First Black Four Star General: The Life and Times of Daniel James Jr.* (Novato, CA: Presidio Press, 1991). See also "General Daniel 'Chappie' James Jr.," Air Force Link www.af.mil/history/person.asp?dec=1970–1980&pid=123006480; and "Daniel ('Chappie') James Jr.," American Airpower Biography www.airpower.maxwell.af.mil/airchronicles/cc/james.html.

61. Lynch oral history interview.

62. Gropman, 56. G.L. Washington manuscript.

63. Gropman, 56.

64. Lynch oral history interview.

65. See for instance "The New Black Power of Coleman Young," *New York Times*, Dec. 16, 1979.

66. Roscoe Brown oral history interview. John B. Turner oral history interview with William Mansfield, April 4, 2002. National Park Service Tuskegee Airmen Oral History Project.

67. William Surcey oral history interview with William Mansfield, Feb. 24, 2001. National Park Service Tuskegee Airmen Oral History Project.

68. Parrish oral history.

69. In addition to the 1974 oral history interview, see Noel F. Parrish oral history interview with Angell, Goldberg, and Hildreth, May 22–23, 1961; and Parrish oral history interview with Vivian M. White August 6–10, 1980. Air Force Historical Research Agency.

70. Gropman, 166–67.

71. Gropman, 155.

72. Gropman, 159–63; Theus oral history interview.

73. For the Montgomery Improvement Association and bus boycott see, for instance, Adam Fairclough, *Martin Luther King, Jr.* (Athens: University of Georgia Press, 1995), chap. 2, passim; Taylor Branch, *Parting the Waters: America in the King Years, 1954–63* (New York: Touchstone, 1988), chap. 5, passim; J. Mills Thornton, *Dividing Lines: Municipal Politics and the Struggle for Civil Rights in Montgomery, Birmingham, and Selma* (Tuscaloosa: University of Alabama Press, 2002), chap. 2, passim; and Jo Ann Robinson with David J. Garrow, *The Montgomery Bus Boycott and the Women Who Started It* (Knoxville: University of Tennessee Press, 1987).

EPILOGUE

1. Noel Parrish, "Forward [*sic*]," from "History of Tuskegee Army Air Field, Tuskegee, Alabama, from Conception to 6 December 1941" (1943; revised 1944), 289.28-v.1. U.S. Air Force Historical Research Agency. Marshall quoted in Kennedy, 771.

2. Parrish, "Forward."

3. Fleischer oral history interview.

4. Joan Williams oral history interview with Lisa Bratton, April 11, 2002. National Park Service Tuskegee Airmen Oral History Project. *The Tuskegee Airmen,* directed by Robert Markowitz (1995; New York, NY: HBO Films).

5. Joan Williams interview.

6. Markowitz, *The Tuskegee Airmen.*

7. For early efforts to organize TAI, see "Black Ex-Pilots Recall Bias in WWII," *New York Times,* Aug. 14, 1972; and "Black Pilots Recall Exploits of World War II," *New York Times,* Nov. 15, 1976. The East Coast chapter of TAI went so far as to produce a pamphlet titled "The Tuskegee Airmen Story (A Speech Guide)" to standardize the story Tuskegee Airmen shared with audiences. It includes the following: "[T]heir most distinctive achievement was that not one friendly bomber was lost to enemy aircraft attacks during 200 escort missions. This success was unique because no other fighter unit with nearly as many missions could make the same claim." Copy in author's possession. For the record, the author is donating a portion of the proceeds from this book to the Tuskegee Airmen Scholarship Foundation.

8. Joan Williams oral history interview.

9. "Record of black pilots amended; Air Force rescinds WWII reprimand," *Atlanta Journal-Constitution,* Aug. 13, 1995. "Roger 'Bill' Terry dies at 87; member of WWII Tuskegee Airmen," *Los Angeles Times,* June 14, 2009.

10. "Record of black pilots amended; Air Force rescinds WWII reprimand." Wardell Polk oral history interview with Worth Long, June 11, 2002. Tuskegee Airmen Oral History Project.

11. "Air Force data dispute lore of Tuskegee pilots," *Dallas Morning News,* Dec. 12, 2006.

12. War Department Bureau of Public Relations, "Colonel Benjamin O. Davis Assumes Command of 477th Composite Group," June 21, 1945. Box 160, NAACP

Papers Group II. Full disclosure: I have repeated the claim in print, although I attempted to acknowledge the claim without endorsing its accuracy. See J. Todd Moye, "The Tuskegee Airmen Oral History Project and Oral History in the National Park Service," *Journal of American History* 89/2 (September 2002): 580–87.

13. "Air Force data dispute lore of Tuskegee pilots;" "WWII bomber pilot: Shot down while escorted by Tuskegee Airmen," *Fort Worth Star-Telegram*, Dec. 15, 2006.

14. "Tuskegee Airman's [sic] record disputed," *Montgomery Advertiser*, Dec. 10, 2006; "Sunday Soundoff: Researchers seeking to tarnish record," *Montgomery Advertiser*, Dec. 17, 2006.

15. "Tuskegee Airman's [sic] record disputed," *Montgomery Advertiser*, Dec. 10, 2006; "Letters to the Editor," *Montgomery Advertiser*, Dec. 26, 2006, and Dec. 28, 2006.

16. *The Daily Show*, Comedy Central, Jan. 31, 2007. A print version of the Coca-Cola ad appeared in the *New York Times*, Feb. 1, 2007. See also Fergus M. Bordewich, "History's Tangled Threads," *New York Times*, Feb. 2, 2007.

17. See "A Top Honor for Soaring Achievements," *Washington Post*, March 29, 2007; "Tuskegee Airmen Receive a Nation's Salute," *Washington Post*, March 30, 2007; "Inauguration is a Culmination for Black Airmen," *New York Times*, Dec. 10, 2008; and "Black Airmen, Frail but Proud, Salute Another Pioneer," *New York Times*, Jan. 20, 2009.

18. John Roach oral history interview with Todd Moye, Aug. 3, 2001. National Park Service Tuskegee Airmen Oral History Project.

19. Ibid.

20. Ibid.

21. Roy Chappell oral history interview with Worth Long, May 16, 2001. National Park Service Tuskegee Airmen Oral History Project.

22. Ibid.

23. Ibid.

24. Milton Henry oral history interview with Bill Mansfield, June 11, 2002. National Park Service Tuskegee Airmen Oral History Project. See also Milton Henry interview with Nick Salvatore, April 14, 2000. C.L. Franklin Oral History Project, Bentley Historical Library, University of Michigan.

25. Nick Salvatore, *Singing in a Strange Land: C.L. Franklin, the Black Church, and the Transformation of America* (New York: Little, Brown and Co., 2005), 231–32.

26. Henry oral history interview with Bill Mansfield; Salvatore, *Singing in a Strange Land*, 231–32; Francis Wilkinson, "Segregationist Dreamer: Milton Henry, b. 1919," *New York Times Magazine*, Dec. 31, 2006.

27. Wilkinson, "Segregationist Dreamer."

28. Peniel E. Joseph, "Dashikis and Democracy: Black Studies, Student Activism, and the Black Power Movement," *The Journal of African American History* 88/2 (Spring 2003): 190; and Joseph, *Waiting 'Til the Midnight Hour: A Narrative History of Black Power in America* (New York: Henry Holt), 56. Henry oral history interview with Salvatore.

29. Joseph, *Waiting 'Til the Midnight Hour*, 57, 89. See also Wilkinson. Henry oral history interview with Salvatore.

30. Joseph, 108. Salvatore, *Singing in a Strange Land*, 242–43, 256–63.

31. See Robin D.G. Kelley, *Freedom Dreams: The Black Radical Imagination* (Boston: Beacon Press), 124–27; Timothy B. Tyson, *Radio Free Dixie: Robert F. Williams and the Roots of Black Power* (Chapel Hill: University of North Carolina Press, 1999); and Donald Cunningen, "Bringing the Revolution Down Home: The Republic of New Africa in Mississippi," *Sociological Spectrum* 19/1 (January-March 1999): 63–92.

32. Cunningen, "Bringing the Revolution Down Home."

33. Salvatore, *Singing in a Strange Land*, 294, 299–300.

34. Henry oral history interview with Salvatore; Herb Boyd, "Civil rights attorney and activist, Milton Henry, passes," *New York Amsterdam News*, Sept. 28–Oct. 4, 2006; Jennifer Phillips, "Milton Henry, Committed Activist," *Philadelphia Tribune*, Oct. 1, 2006; Wilkinson, "Segregationist Dreamer."

35. For Mitchell and the SRC, see Leslie W. Dunbar, "The Southern Regional Council," *Annals of the American Academy of Political and Social Science*, Vol. 357, The Negro Protest (January 1965): 108–12; Steve Suitts, "The Southern Regional Council and the Roots of Rural Change," *Southern Cultures* 13/3 (1991): 5–12; Sullivan, *Days of Hope*; and Egerton, *Speak Now Against the Day*. Horace Bohannon interview with Worth Long, Feb. 5, 2001. See also John Turner oral history interview with William Mansfield, April 4, 2002.

36. Bohannon quoted in Jennifer E. Brooks, *Defining the Peace: World War II Veterans, Race, and the Remaking of Southern Political Tradition* (Chapel Hill: University of North Carolina Press, 2004), 17. See also Brooks, "Winning the Peace: Georgia Veterans and the Struggle to Define the Political Legacy of World War II," *The Journal of Southern History* 66/3 (August 2000): 565–604.

37. Horace Bohannon interview with Worth Long, Feb. 5, 2001.

38. Ibid. See also Kathryn Nasstrom, *Everybody's Grandmother and Nobody's Fool: Frances Freeborn Pauley and the Struggle for Racial Justice* (Ithaca, NY: Cornell University Press, 2000), chap. 5, passim.

39. Horace Bohannon interview with Worth Long, Feb. 5, 2001.

A NOTE ON SOURCES

1. For more on the Tuskegee Airmen Oral History Project, see J. Todd Moye, "The Tuskegee Airmen Oral History Project and Oral History in the National Park Service," *The Journal of American History* 89/2 (September 2002): 580–87.

2. Alessandro Portelli, "What Makes Oral History Different," *The Oral History Reader, Second Edition*, ed. Robert Perks and Alistair Thomson (New York: Routledge, 2007): 32–42. See Portelli's quotes on 33, 36.

A Note on Sources

In 1998 the U.S. National Park Service (NPS) began developing Tuskegee Airmen National Historic Site at Moton Field in Alabama, working in partnership with Tuskegee Airmen Inc. (TAI) and Tuskegee University. As part of its efforts to document the historic experience and build opportunities for visitor education, NPS set aside part of a congressional appropriation for an oral history project to record the memories of the surviving participants. NPS hired me as the director of the Tuskegee Airmen Oral History Project in 2000. Between late 2000 and summer 2005 a staff of four historians/oral history interviewers—Lisa Bratton, Judith Brown, Worth Long, and Bill Mansfield—and I recorded more than eight hundred interviews with a wide cross-section of veterans of the experience. They included pilots and support personnel who trained at Tuskegee and elsewhere, men and women who had been combat veterans and desk jockeys, secretaries and parachute packers, doctors and lawyers, and even members of the all-white bomber crews who flew alongside the Airmen in combat. It would be impossible to convey the full depth and variety of the oral histories in a short space here, but it should go without saying that the interviews, which are now archived at the newly opened Tuskegee Airmen National Historic Site, serve as the essential core of my effort to tell this story.[1]

TAI provided the Tuskegee Airmen Oral History Project with the names and contact information for hundreds of men and women who could be verified as having participated in the experience. This saved the oral history project literally hundreds, perhaps thousands, of man-hours. Word of mouth also led to interviewees, as did our publicity efforts, but we found the vast majority of our narrators via TAI. I should mention that everyone associated with TAI insisted that the oral history project would only succeed if we interviewed support personnel as well as pilots, and they worked with us to that end.

Of the five interviewers on the oral history project staff (including me), two had been trained as academic historians, two as folklorists, and one in the academic field of African American studies. Two were African American, three were white; two were women and three were men; one was himself a military veteran and another had an encyclopedic knowledge of military aircraft. Each brought a unique background, set of concerns, and ideas about the important questions to ask in each interview, and I feel sure that the diversity of the staff ranks added immensely to the quality of the finished product. Project interviewers traveled to interviewees' homes to record the interviews and, for the most part, followed the life history style of interviewing. As a group we did our best to adhere to the Oral History Association's "Evaluation Guidelines," an indispensable collection of best practices and ethical principles. We tried to ask open-ended questions and allow interviewees to set the terms for discussion to the degree possible. Though we went into each interview with a list of topics we wanted to cover— some of them tailored to individual narrators, but most common to all the interviews— we found that the most important questions we asked in any interview were not the perfectly worded ones we had prepared beforehand, but the follow-up questions that helped a given interviewee elaborate on or explain a point.

Interviews averaged somewhere around ninety minutes in length, although some were much shorter and others lasted hours. A professional transcriptionist transcribed each interview, and most were edited by both the interviewer and interviewee. Interviewees were given the right to edit and/or delete what appeared in final transcripts, but it was unusual for an interviewee to change anything other than grammar. For several reasons, the most important of which were the advanced age of the population we were trying to reach and the fickle nature of the federal budget process, the oral history staff had to prioritize speed over accuracy. In other words, we made an effort to interview as many people as we possibly could with the money we had available and then edited interview transcripts with the time we had left. As a result, strict grammarian constructionists who have the chance to review some of the transcripts will have reason to find fault with our work. But I still would not change any of the decisions I made then.

I share the Italian oral historian Alessandro Portelli's conviction that "written and oral sources are not mutually exclusive," and that oral history sources explain "less about events than about their meaning." I have used the Tuskegee Airmen oral histories as sources in a few different ways for the purposes of this book—most noticeably, to complement, round out, or challenge the archival record, or to explore topics left out of the archival record. Oral history can be a wonderful companion to archival evidence for authors of narrative social history such as this, but it cannot be a substitute. Where information from oral histories contradicted written information from primary and/or secondary sources, I have so noted in the text or the endnotes.[2]

Moreover, oral history can provide historians much more than just background color or "filler" for the gaps in written sources. My basic understanding of this historic experience flows from the narratives that our interviewees constructed, and I have tried to structure the narrative of the book in a way that allows the Tuskegee Airmen themselves to introduce the major themes of this shared history in their own words. I have tried to remain faithful to what I will call (for lack of a better term) the collective worldview of our narrators as they expressed it in the interviews. The oral histories are the best sources we have for their collective ability to communicate what it was like to experience life in the black Air Force. For the purposes of my book, this is what makes the interviews most valuable—but a folklorist, military historian, scholar of memory studies, or scholar from another discipline could find in the collection a valuable trove of information for different purposes. (And I hope that many others will take advantage of the resource.)

Transcribing the spoken word into written text is much more art form than science, as is transforming transcript into narrative prose. In processing transcripts, the staff of the Tuskegee Airmen Oral History Project strove to edit for the narrator's intended meaning, and we gave interviewees the chance to edit the transcripts themselves before archiving them. Therefore, a given transcript might not be a perfect, verbatim representation of what a narrator said on tape, but it should (at least in theory) reflect the meaning the interviewee intended to convey without distorting what was actually said in the recording. In condensing the transcripts for use here, I have followed the same rule of thumb: edit for intended meaning. In cases I have combined sentences from separate parts of a given interview or, in fewer cases, rearranged words in sentences for clarity's sake. In the instances where I have put words in narrators' mouths, the added words are enclosed in brackets.

The following is a short, representative example of how I have managed the process of editing a transcript for use in this book. This section of Lisa Bratton's interview with Lemuel R. Custis is exactly as it appeared in the finalized Tuskegee Airmen Oral History Project transcript, which had been edited by both Bratton and Custis:

BRATTON: What was your first impression of Tuskegee?

CUSTIS: In what way?

BRATTON: When you first arrived at the train station, if you went down by train, when you first saw it. What do you remember thinking?

CUSTIS: Well, I had mixed feelings or mixed emotions because we had gone down on the train. Uncle Sam had sent us down on a train, and that was my first experience in the Deep South, and it was the first time they pulled a curtain on the old boy. [He refers to the practice of drawing a curtain around African Americans in the dining car of trains below the Mason-Dixon Line.] I really then understood I was black. I just *thought* I was before, but [chuckles] I knew I was after that. That's when they pulled the curtain. I had never seen that before. I had heard through the grapevine that they did this to some people and so forth. As a black person you hear these things from elderly people or people that had come from the South, but it had never happened to me, so it was quite an experience to have that happen.

But I must say this: and I'll never forget how nice the porters were to me, helped me survive that trip. As I said, again, having that curtain pulled on you, and you feel—you wonder what's going on, how to handle it. But they said, "We'll take care of you. We'll see that you get the food if you don't want to go [to the dining car]," because even I went up to get the food, which Uncle Sam was providing, they pulled the curtain on you in the dining car. You know that.

BRATTON: Mm-hm.

CUSTIS: So they said, "If you want to go up there, we'll take care of you. If you don't, you can stay in the compartment and we'll bring the food back." So they were very nice. I woke up one or two mornings—I guess the next morning or something—in Chehaw, Alabama. [Laughs] And so that was the train stop, at Chehaw, Alabama, for Tuskegee. And so they had a jeep there to meet me. I was the only one getting off there at Chehaw at that time.

Interested readers may compare this version to the one that appears at the opening of Chapter 2.

Bibliography

ARCHIVES
Air Force Historical Research Agency, Maxwell Field, Montgomery, Alabama
Air Force Oral History Collection
C. Alfred "Chief" Anderson, oral history interview with James C. Hasdorff, June 8–9, 1981.
Benjamin O. Davis Jr., oral history interview with Alan Gropman, January 1973.
Noel F. Parrish, oral history interview with Angell, Goldberg, and Hildreth, May 22–23, 1961.
Noel F.Parrish, oral history interview with James C. Hasdorff, June 14, 1974.
Noel F.Parrish, oral history interview with Vivian M. White, August 6–10, 1980.

Archival Materials
William H. Hastie, "On Clipped Wings: The Story of Jim Crow in the Army Air Corps" (pamphlet).
Histories of 66th AAF Flying Detachment, Corps of Aviation Cadets, Moton Field, and Tuskegee Army Air Field.
Noel F. Parrish Jr., "The Segregation of Negroes in the Army Air Forces." Thesis, Air Command and Staff School, Maxwell Field, Alabama, May 1947.
"The Preflight Schools in World War II." U.S. Air Force Historical Study no. 90.
Squadron and Group histories and war diaries.

Alabama Department of Archives and History, Montgomery, Alabama
Gov. Frank Murray Dixon Papers
Macon County subject files

Hoole Special Collections Library, University of Alabama, Tuscaloosa, Alabama
Lister Hill Papers

Library of Congress, Washington, D.C.
Manuscripts Division
Truman K. Gibson Papers
National Association for the Advancement of Colored People Papers
Noel F. Parrish Papers

Prints and Photographs Division
Toni Frissell Collection
National Association for the Advancement of Colored People Collection

National Archives and Records Administration, Washington, D.C.
Records of the Army Air Forces. Record Group 18
Records of the Assistant Secretary of War for Air. Record Group 107
Records of Headquarters U.S. Air Force. Record Group 341
Records of the Office of the Secretary of the Air Force. Record Group 340
Records of the Office of the Secretary of War. Record Group 107

Records of the Office of the Assistant Secretary of War, Civil Aide to the Secretary. Record Group 107
Records of the Under Secretary of War. Record Group 107

Franklin D. Roosevelt Presidential Library and Archives, Hyde Park, N.Y.
Francis Biddle Papers
James H. Rowe Jr. Papers
Official File
Eleanor Roosevelt Papers

Tuskegee Airmen National Historic Site, National Park Service, Tuskegee, Alabama
Tuskegee Airmen Oral History Project Interviews
George Abercrombie, oral history interview with Worth Long, October 9, 2001.
Harvey Alexander, oral history interview with William Mansfield, June 20, 2001.
Twiley Barker, oral history interview with William Mansfield, March 8, 2002.
George G. Barnett, oral history interview with Todd Moye, January 12, 2001.
LeRoy Battle, oral history interview with Judith Brown, February 14, 2001.
Omar D. Blair, oral history interview with Todd Moye, May 16, 2002.
Horace A. Bohannon, oral history interviews with Worth Long, January 3 and 5, 2001.
Henry C. Bohler, oral history interview with Worth Long, October 9, 2001.
George Bolling, oral history interview with Lisa Bratton, August 22, 2001.
Leroy Bowman, oral history interview with William Mansfield, March 21, 2003.
Fannie Gunn Boyd, oral history interview with Worth Long, February 6, 2001.
Samuel Broadnax, oral history interview with Lisa Bratton, August 21, 2001.
Roscoe Brown, oral history interview with Lisa Bratton, March 1, 2001.
William Campbell, oral history interview with Lisa Bratton, January 21, 2001.
Herbert Eugene Carter, oral history interview with Bob Blythe, March 14, 2000.
Herbert Eugene Carter and Mildred Carter, oral history interview with Tony Paredes
    and Christine Trebellas, March 14, 2000.
Mildred Hemmons Carter, oral history interview with Tony Paredes, March 14, 2000.
Robert L. Carter, oral history interview with Lisa Bratton, October 14, 2004.
Roy Chappell, oral history interview with Worth Long, May 16, 2001.
Francis X. Connolly, oral history interview with Lisa Bratton, January 31, 2001.
Milton Crenchaw, oral history interview with Worth Long, March 11, 2001.
Woodrow Crockett, oral history interview with Bill Mansfield, March 15, 2001.
Lemuel R. Custis, oral history interview with Lisa Bratton, August 17, 2002.
Crawford Dowdell, oral history interview with William Mansfield, December 10,
    2003.
Roscoe Draper, oral history interview with Lisa Bratton, January 30, 2001.
Precious Dunn, oral history interview with Judith Brown, May 12, 2003.
Charles W. Dryden, oral history interview with Todd Moye, September 28, 2000.
W. Vashon Eagleson, oral history interview with William Mansfield, June 15, 2001.
Leslie Edwards, oral history interview with William Mansfield, April 19, 2001.
John Fernandes, oral history interview with Tony Paredes, March 13, 2000.
Larry Fleischer, oral history interview with Todd Moye, April 24, 2001.
Charles Herbert Flowers II, oral history interview with Todd Moye, June 28, 2001.

Truman Gibson, oral history interview with Todd Moye, August 28, 2003.

LeRoy Gillead, oral history interview with Lisa Bratton, July 15, 2002.

James Goodwin, oral history interview with William Mansfield, August 10, 2001.

William Gray, oral history interview with Todd Moye, April 23, 2001.

Victor Hancock, oral history interview with William Mansfield, February 7, 2001.

James H. Harvey III, oral history interview with Todd Moye, May 13, 2002.

Pompey Hawkins, oral history interview with William Mansfield, February 8, 2002.

Milton Henry, oral history interview with William Mansfield, June 11, 2002.

Mitchell Higginbotham, oral history interview with Judith Brown, May 11, 2002.

Francis Horne, oral history interview with William Mansfield, July 17, 2001.

Clarence C. Jamison, oral history interview with Worth Long, March 22, 2002.

Alexander Jefferson, oral history interview with Worth Long, August 30, 2001.

Charles S. Johnson Jr., oral history interview with Judith Brown, May 23, 2001.

Jack Johnson, oral history interview with Judith Brown, March 15, 2001.

Theopolis W. ("Ted") Johnson, oral history interview with Todd Moye, November 9, 2000.

Elmer Jones, oral history interview with William Mansfield, February 9, 2001.

Charles Kerford, oral history interview with William Mansfield, April 4, 2001.

Charles Lang, oral history interview with Judith Brown, May 4, 2001.

Theophia Lee, oral history interview with Todd Moye, June 27, 2001.

Roosevelt Lewis, oral history interview with Christine Trebellas, March 15, 2000.

Wendell Lipscomb, oral history interview with Lisa Bratton, April 12, 2001.

Hiram Little, oral history interview with Lisa Bratton, December 28, 2000.

Lewis Lynch, oral history interview with William Mansfield, October 19, 2001.

Theodore O. Mason, oral history interview with Judith Brown, December 14, 2001.

Charles E. McGee, oral history interview with William Mansfield, March 14, 2001.

Fitzroy Newsum, oral history interview with Todd Moye, May 17, 2002.

Walter Palmer, oral history interview with William Mansfield, August 24, 2001.

Gracie Perry Phillips, oral history interview with Worth Long, September 18, 2001.

Claude Platte, oral history interviews with William Mansfield, September 26, 2001, and July 20, 2004.

Wardell Polk, oral history interview with Worth Long, June 11, 2002.

Michael Preputnik, oral history interview with William Mansfield, August 16, 2002.

Bernard Proctor, oral history interviews with Lisa Bratton, February 5, 2001, and June 4, 2001.

Louis Purnell, oral history interview with William Mansfield, February 5, 2001.

John Roach, oral history interview with Todd Moye, August 3, 2001.

John W. Rogers, oral history interview with Lisa Bratton, September 18, 2003.

Harvey Sanford, oral history interview with Todd Moye, July 31, 2001.

Mohamed Shaik, oral history interview with Todd Moye, November 9, 2000.

Quentin P. Smith, oral history interview with William Mansfield, July 21, 2002.

Chauncey Spencer, oral history interview with Todd Moye, December 18, 2000.

Harry T. Stewart, oral history interview with Worth Long, June 4, 2001.

William Surcey, oral history interview with William Mansfield, February 24, 2001.

George A. Taylor, oral history interview with Worth Long, May 17, 2001.

Alva Temple, oral history interview with Worth Long, June 4, 2001.
Yvonne Terrelongue, oral history interview with William Mansfield, March 16, 2003.
Roger C. Terry, oral history interview with Lisa Bratton, February 28, 2002.
Lucius Theus, oral history interview with William Mansfield, June 5, 2001.
Maurice Thomas, oral history interview with Judith Brown, October 4, 2001.
Herbert Thorpe, oral history interview with William Mansfield, December 8, 2003.
John B. Turner, oral history interview with William Mansfield, April 4, 2002.
William A. Walters, oral history interview with Todd Moye, May 17, 2002.
James C. Warren, oral history interview with Lisa Bratton, January 18, 2001.
George Watson Sr., oral history interview with Lisa Bratton, February 8, 2001.
Spann Watson, oral history interview with Lisa Bratton, March 12, 2001.
Haydel White, oral history interview with Worth Long, September 17, 2001.
Alexander Wilkerson, oral history interview with Judith Brown, February 14, 2001.
Edmund Wilkinson, oral history interview with Worth Long, March 12, 2001.
Katie Whitney Williams, oral history interview with Worth Long, March 14, 2001.
Linkwood Williams, oral history interview with Worth Long, March 14, 2001.
James Wright, oral history interview with William Mansfield, February 20, 2001.

Tuskegee University Special Collections, Tuskegee, Alabama
George L. Washington, "The History of Military and Civilian Pilot Training of
Negroes at Tuskegee, Alabama, 1939–45" (unpublished manuscript).

U.S. Army Military History Institute, Carlisle Barracks, Carlisle, Pa.
U.S. Army War College, "The Use of Negro Manpower in War," 1925.

NEWSPAPERS

Atlanta Daily World	*Kansas City Call*
Atlanta Journal-Constitution	*Montgomery Advertiser*
(Baltimore) *Afro-American*	*New York Age*
(Los Angeles) *California Eagle*	*New York Amsterdam News*
Chicago Defender	*New York Times*
Columbus (Ga.) Ledger-Enquirer	*Philadelphia Tribune*
Dallas Morning News	*Pittsburgh Courier*
Fort Worth Star-Telegram	*Washington Post*
Houston Negro Labor News	

BOOKS, ARTICLES, THESES, AND DISSERTATIONS

Altschuler, Glenn, and Stuart Blumin. *The GI Bill: A New Deal for Veterans.*
   New York: Oxford University Press, 2009.
Ambrose, Stephen E. *The Wild Blue: The Men and Boys Who Flew the B-24s over
   Germany.* New York: Simon & Schuster, 2001.
Anderson, Carol. *Eyes off the Prize: The United Nations and the African American
   Struggle for Human Rights, 1944–1955.* Cambridge: Cambridge University
   Press, 2003.

Anderson, Jervis. *A. Philip Randolph: A Biographical Portrait.* New York: Harcourt Brace Jovanovich, 1974.

Arsenault, Raymond. *Freedom Riders: 1961 and the Struggle for Racial Justice.* New York: Oxford University Press, 2006.

Astor, Gerald. *The Right to Fight: A History of African Americans in the Military.* New York: Da Capo Press, 2001.

Barbeau, Arthur, and Florette Henri. *The Unknown Soldiers: Black American Troops in World War I.* Philadelphia: Temple University Press, 1974.

Bates, Beth Tompkins. *Pullman Porters and the Rise of Protest Politics in Black America, 1925–1945.* Chapel Hill: University of North Carolina Press, 2000.

Berman, William C. *The Politics of Civil Rights in the Truman Administration.* Columbus: Ohio State University Press, 1970.

Bird, Kai. *The Chairman: John J. McCloy, the Making of the American Establishment.* New York: Simon & Schuster, 1992.

Branch, Taylor. *Parting the Waters: America in the King Years, 1954–63.* New York: Touchstone, 1988.

Brooks, Jennifer E. *Defining the Peace: World War II Veterans, Race, and the Remaking of Southern Political Tradition.* Chapel Hill: University of North Carolina Press, 2004.

———. "Winning the Peace: Georgia Veterans and the Struggle to Define the Political Legacy of World War II." *The Journal of Southern History* 66/3 (August 2000): 565–604.

Buni, Andrew. *Robert L. Vann and the Pittsburgh Courier: Politics and Black Journalism.* Pittsburgh: University of Pittsburgh Press, 1974.

Bussey, Charles. *Firefight at Yechon.* McLean, Va.: Brassey's, 1991.

Capeci, Dominic J. Jr. *Layered Violence: The Detroit Rioters of 1943.* Jackson: University Press of Mississippi, 1991.

Carter, Robert L. *A Matter of Law: A Memoir of Struggle in the Cause of Equal Rights.* New York: New Press, 2005.

Cell, John W. *The Highest Stage of White Supremacy: The Origins of Segregation in South Africa and the American South.* Cambridge: Cambridge University Press, 1982.

Cha-Jua, Sundiata Keita, and Clarence Lang. "The 'Long Movement' as Vampire: Temporal and Spatial Fallacies in Recent Black Freedom Studies," *Journal of African American History* 92/2 (Spring 2007): 265–88.

Cook, Brad. "Remembering IU's first African-American scholar-athlete." Feb. 9, 2007. http://homepages.indiana.edu/2007/02–09/story.php?id=1122.

Corn, Joseph J. *The Winged Gospel: America's Romance with Aviation, 1900–1950.* New York: Oxford University Press, 1983.

Courtwright, David T. *Sky as Frontier: Adventure, Aviation, and Empire.* College Station: Texas A&M University Press, 2005.

Cunningen, Donald. "Bringing the Revolution Down Home: The Republic of New Africa in Mississippi," *Sociological Spectrum* 19 (1999): 63–92.

Dailey, Jane. *The Age of Jim Crow.* New York: Norton, 2009.

Dalfiume, Richard M. *Desegregation of the U.S. Armed Forces: Fighting on Two Fronts, 1939–1953.* Columbia: University of Missouri Press, 1969.

———. "The Fahy Committee and Desegregation of the Armed Forces," *The Historian* 31/1 (November 1968): 1–20.

Daniel, Pete. "Black Power in the 1920s: The Case of Tuskegee Veterans Hospital," *Journal of Southern History* 36 (August 1970): 368–88.

Davis, Benjamin O. Jr. *Benjamin O. Davis, Jr., American: An Autobiography.* Washington, D.C.: Smithsonian Institution Press, 1991.

Dryden, Charles W. *A-Train: Memoirs of a Tuskegee Airman.* Tuscaloosa: University of Alabama Press, 1997.

Dudziak, Mary L. *Cold War Civil Rights: Race and the Image of American Democracy.* Princeton: Princeton University Press, 2000.

Dunbar, Leslie W. "The Southern Regional Council." *Annals of the American Academy of Political and Social Science,* Vol. 357, The Negro Protest (January 1965): 108–12.

Egerton, John. *Speak Now Against the Day: The Generation Before the Civil Rights Movement in the South.* Chapel Hill: University of North Carolina Press, 1995.

Erisman, Fred. *Boys' Books, Boys' Dreams, and the Mystique of Flight.* Fort Worth: Texas Christian University Press, 2006.

Fairclough, Adam. *Martin Luther King, Jr.* Athens: University of Georgia Press, 1995.

Finkle, Lee. "The Conservative Aims of Militant Rhetoric: Black Power During World War II." *Journal of American History* 60 (December 1973): 692–713.

Fletcher, Marvin. *America's First Black General: Benjamin O. Davis, Sr., 1880–1970.* Lawrence: University Press of Kansas, 1989.

Francis, Charles E. *The Tuskegee Airmen.* Boston: Bruce Humphries, 1955.

Frederickson, Kari. *The Dixiecrat Revolt and the End of the Solid South, 1932–1968.* Chapel Hill: University of North Carolina Press, 2000.

Gardner, Michael R. *Harry Truman and Civil Rights: Moral Courage and Political Risks.* Carbondale: Southern Illinois University Press, 2002.

Garfinkel, Herbert. *When Negroes March: The March on Washington Movement in the Organizational Politics for FEPC.* Glencoe, Ill.: Free Press, 1959.

Gibson, Truman, and Steve Huntley. *Knocking Down Barriers: My Fight for Black America.* Chicago: Northwestern University Press, 2005.

Gill, Gerald R. "Afro-American Opposition to the United States' Wars of the Twentieth Century: Dissent, Discontent, and Disinterest." PhD diss., Howard University, 1985.

Gillmore, Glenda Elizabeth. *Defying Dixie: The Radical Roots of Civil Rights, 1919–1950.* New York: Norton, 2008.

Greer, Thomas H. "Army Air Doctrinal Roots, 1917–1918," *Military Affairs* 20/4 (Winter 1956): 202–16.

Gropman, Alan L. *The Air Force Integrates, 1945–1964,* 2nd ed. Washington, D.C.: Smithsonian Institution Press, 1998.

Hall, Jacquelyn Dowd. "The Long Civil Rights Movement and the Political Uses of the Past." *The Journal of American History* 91/4 (March 2005): 1233–63.

Hardesty, Von, and Dominick Pisano. *Black Wings: The American Black in Aviation.* Washington, D.C.: Smithsonian Institution Press, 1984.

Harlan, Louis. *Booker T. Washington: The Making of a Black Leader, 1856–1901.* New York: Oxford University Press, 1972.

————. *Booker T. Washington: The Wizard of Tuskegee, 1901–1915.* New York: Oxford University Press, 1983.

Hastie, William H. *On Clipped Wings: The Story of Jim Crow in the Army Air Corps.* New York: National Association for the Advancement of Colored People, 1943.

Holway, John. *Red Tails, Black Wings.* Las Cruces, N.M.: Yucca Tree Press, 1997.

Homan, Lynn M., and Thomas Reilly, *Black Knights: The Story of the Tuskegee Airmen.* Gretna, La.: Pelican, 2001.

Jackson, Walter A. *Gunnar Myrdal and America's Conscience: Social Engineering and Racial Liberalism, 1938–1987.* Chapel Hill: University of North Carolina Press, 1990.

Jakeman, Robert J. *The Divided Skies: Establishing Segregated Flight Training at Tuskegee, Alabama, 1934–1942.* Tuscaloosa: University of Alabama Press, 1992.

Jefferson, Alexander, and Lewis Carlson. *Red Tail Captured, Red Tail Free: The Memoirs of a Tuskegee Airman and POW.* New York: Fordham University Press, 2005.

Jones, James H. *Bad Blood: The Tuskegee Syphilis Study,* rev. ed. New York: Free Press, 1993.

Joseph, Peniel E. "Dashikis and Democracy: Black Studies, Student Activism, and the Black Power Movement." *The Journal of African American History* 88/2 (Spring 2003): 182–203.

————. *Waiting 'Til the Midnight Hour: A Narrative History of Black Power in America.* New York: Henry Holt, 2006.

Kelley, Robin D. G. *Freedom Dreams: The Black Radical Imagination.* Boston: Beacon Press, 2002.

Kennedy, David M. *Freedom from Fear: The American People in Depression and War, 1929–1945.* New York: Oxford University Press, 1999.

Kirby, John B. *Black Americans in the Roosevelt Era: Liberalism and Race.* Knoxville: University of Tennessee Press, 1980.

Laris, Michael. "Freedom Flight." *Washington Post Magazine,* Feb. 16, 2003.

Lawson, Steven F., and Charles Payne, eds. *Debating the Civil Rights Movement, 1945–1968,* 2nd ed. Lanham, Md.: Rowman and Littlefield, 2006.

Lawson, Steven F., ed. *To Secure These Rights: The Report of President Harry S. Truman's Committee on Civil Rights.* Boston: Bedford/St. Martin's, 2004.

Lee, Ulysses. *The United States Army in World War II, Special Studies: The Employment of Negro Troops.* Washington, D.C.: Office of the Chief of Military History, 1966.

Leuchtenburg, William E. *The White House Looks South: Franklin D. Roosevelt, Harry S. Truman, and Lyndon B. Johnson.* Baton Rouge: Louisiana State Press, 2005.

Lewis, David Levering. *W.E.B. DuBois: Biography of a Race, 1868–1919.* New York: Henry Holt, 1993.

————, ed. *W.E.B. DuBois: A Reader.* New York: Henry Holt, 1995.

Lindbergh, Charles A. "Aviation, Geography, and Race." *Reader's Digest,* November 1939, 64–67.

Love, Spencie. *One Blood: The Death and Resurrection of Charles R. Drew.* Chapel Hill: University of North Carolina Press, 1997.

MacGregor, Morris J. *The Integration of the Armed Forces, 1940–1965.* Washington, D.C.: U.S. Army Center of Military History, 1981.

Margo, Robert A. *Race and Schooling in the South, 1880–1950: An Economic History.* Chicago: University of Chicago Press, 1994.

McCoy, Donald R., and Richard T. Ruetten. *Quest and Response: Minority Rights and the Truman Administration.* Lawrence: University Press of Kansas, 1973.

McGovern, James R. *Black Eagle: General Daniel "Chappie" James, Jr.* Tuscaloosa: University of Alabama Press, 1985.

McGuire, Phillip. *He, Too, Spoke for Democracy: Judge Hastie, World War II, and the Black Soldier.* New York: Greenwood Press, 1988.

———, ed. *Taps for a Jim Crow Army: Letters from Black Soldiers in World War II.* Lexington: University Press of Kentucky, 1993.

McLaurin, Melton A. *The Marines of Montford Point: America's First Black Marines.* Chapel Hill: University of North Carolina Press, 2007.

Mershon, Sherie, and Steven Schlossman. *Foxholes and Color Lines: Desegregating the U.S. Armed Forces.* Baltimore: Johns Hopkins University Press, 1988.

Mettler, Suzanne. *Soldiers to Citizens: The G.I. Bill and the Making of the Greatest Generation.* New York: Oxford University Press, 2005.

Moore, Brenda L. *To Serve My Country, to Serve My Race: The Story of the Only African-American WACS Stationed Overseas During World War II.* New York: New York University Press, 1998.

Morehouse, Maggi. *Fighting in the Jim Crow Army: Black Men and Women Remember World War II.* Lanham, Md.: Rowman and Littlefield, 2000.

Morris, Aldon D. *The Origins of the Civil Rights Movement.* New York: Free Press, 1984.

Moskos, Charles C. Jr. "Racial Integration in the Armed Forces." *American Journal of Sociology* 72/2 (September 1966): 132–48.

———. "Success Story: Blacks in the Army." *The Atlantic,* May 1986, 64–72.

Moye, J. Todd. "'I Never *Quit* Dreaming About It': Horace Bohannon, the Tuskegee Airmen, and the Dream of Flight," *Atlanta History: A Journal of Georgia and the South* 47/1–2 (2005), 58–71.

———. "The Tuskegee Airmen Oral History Project and Oral History in the National Park Service." *Journal of American History* 89/2 (September 2002), 580–87.

Myrdal, Gunnar. *An American Dilemma: The Negro Problem and Modern Democracy.* New York: Harper, 1944.

Nalty, Bernard C. *Strength for the Fight: A History of Black Americans in the Military.* New York: Free Press, 1986.

———. *The Right to Fight: African American Marines in World War II.* Washington, D.C.: History and Museums Division, Headquarters, U.S. Marine Corps, 1995.

———, ed. *Winged Shield, Winged Sword, 1907–1950: A History of the United States Air Force.* Honolulu: University Press of the Pacific, 2003.

Nasstrom, Kathryn. *Everybody's Grandmother and Nobody's Fool: Frances Freeborn Pauley and the Struggle for Racial Justice.* Ithaca, N.Y.: Cornell University Press, 2000.

Newton, Wesley Phillips. *Montgomery in the Good War: Portrait of a Southern City, 1939–1946.* Tuscaloosa: University of Alabama Press, 2000.

———. "Patriots of Color: An Alabama Family in the Good War," *Alabama Heritage* 69 (Summer 2003): 24–31.

Norrell, Robert J. *Reaping the Whirlwind: The Civil Rights Movement in Tuskegee.* New York: Knopf, 1985.

———. *Up from History: The Life of Booker T. Washington.* Cambridge: Harvard University Press, 2009.

O'Neill, William L. *A Democracy at War: America's Fight at Home and Abroad in World War II.* New York: Free Press, 1993.

Oshinsky, David. *Polio, An American Story: The Crusade that Mobilized the Nation Against the 20th Century's Most Feared Disease.* New York: Oxford University Press, 2005.

Osur, Alan M. *Blacks in the Army Air Forces During World War II.* Washington, D.C.: Office of Air Force History, 1977.

Paszek, Lawrence J. "Negroes and the Air Force, 1939–1949." *Military Affairs* 31 (March 1967): 1–9.

Perata, David D. *Those Pullman Blues: An Oral History of the African-American Railroad Attendant.* New York: Twayne, 1996.

Percy, William Alexander. "Jim Crow and Uncle Sam: The Tuskegee Flying Units and the U.S. Army Air Forces in Europe During World War II." *The Journal of Military History* 67/3 (2003): 773–810.

Pfeffer, Paula F. *A. Philip Randolph, Pioneer of the Civil Rights Movement.* Baton Rouge: Louisiana State Press, 1990.

Phelps, J. Alfred. *Chappie: America's First Black Four-Star General.* Novato, Calif.: Presidio Press, 1991.

Plummer, Brenda Gayle. *Rising Wind: Black Americans and U.S. Foreign Affairs, 1935–1960.* Chapel Hill: University of North Carolina Press, 1996.

Polenberg, Richard. *War and Society: The United States, 1941–1945.* Philadelphia: Lippincott, 1972.

Portelli, Alessandro. "What Makes Oral History Different." *The Oral History Reader,* 2nd ed. Edited by Robert Perks and Alistair Thomson. New York: Routledge, 2007.

Powell, Colin. *My American Journey.* New York: Ballantine, 1996.

Prickett, James R. "Communist Conspiracy or Wage Dispute? The 1941 Strike at North American Aviation." *The Pacific Historical Review,* 50/2 (May 1981): 215–33.

Purnell, Louis. "The Flight of the Bumblebee," *Air and Space Magazine,* October-November 1989, 33–40.

Reed, Merl E. *Seedtime for the Modern Civil Rights Movement: The President's Committee on Fair Employment Practice, 1941–1946.* Baton Rouge: Louisiana State University Press, 1991.

Ritchie, Donald A. *Reporting from Washington: The History of the Washington Press Corps.* New York: Oxford University Press, 2005.

Robinson, Jo Ann, with David J. Garrow. *The Montgomery Bus Boycott and the Women Who Started It.* Knoxville: University of Tennessee Press, 1987.

Rogers, Naomi. "Race and the Politics of Polio: Warm Springs, Tuskegee, and the March of Dimes," *American Journal of Public Health* 97/5 (May 2007): 784–96.

Roosevelt, Eleanor. "Abolish Jim Crow!" *New Threshold* 1/2 (August 1943):4, 34.

———. "Flying is Fun." *Collier's Magazine,* April 22, 1939, 15.

Ruff, Willie. *A Call to Assembly: The Autobiography of a Musical Storyteller.* New York: Viking, 1991.

Salvatore, Nick. *Singing in a Strange Land: C. L. Franklin, the Black Church, and the Transformation of America*. New York: Little, Brown, 2005.

Sandler, Stanley. *Segregated Skies: All-Black Combat Squadrons in World War II*. Washington, D.C.: Smithsonian Institution Press, 1992.

Scott, Emmett. *History of the American Negro in the World War*. Chicago: Homewood Press, 1919.

Scott, Lawrence P., and William M. Womack Sr., *Double V: The Civil Rights Struggle of the Tuskegee Airmen*. East Lansing: Michigan State University Press, 1998.

Shogan, Robert, and Tom Craig. *The Detroit Race Riot: A Study in Violence*. Philadelphia: Chilton Books, 1964.

Sitkoff, Harvard. "Harry Truman and the Election of 1948: The Coming of Age of Civil Rights in American Politics." *Journal of Southern History* 37/4 (November 1971): 597–616.

———. *A New Deal for Blacks. The Emergence of Civil Rights as a National Issue: The Depression Decade*. New York: Oxford University Press, 1978.

———. "Racial Militancy and Interracial Violence in the Second World War." *Journal of American History* 58/3 (December 1971): 661–81.

Smith, Charlene E. McGee. *Tuskegee Airman: The Biography of Charles E. McGee, Air Force Fighter Combat Record Holder*. Boston: Branden Publishing, 1999.

Smith, Graham. *When Jim Crow Met John Bull*. New York: St. Martin's, 1987.

Spencer, Chauncey. *Who is Chauncey Spencer?* Detroit: Broadside Press, 1975.

Stillman, Richard J. *Integration of the Negro in the U.S. Armed Forces*. New York: Praeger, 1968.

Stillwell, Paul. *The Golden Thirteen*. Annapolis, Md.: Naval Institute Press, 1993.

Sugrue, Thomas J. *The Origins of the Urban Crisis: Race and Inequality in Postwar Detroit*. Princeton: Princeton University Press, 1996.

———. *Sweet Land of Liberty: The Forgotten Struggle for Civil Rights in the North*. New York: Random House, 2008.

Suitts, Steve. "The Southern Regional Council and the Roots of Rural Change." *Southern Cultures* 13/3 (1991): 5–12.

Sullivan, Patricia. *Days of Hope: Race and Democracy in the New Deal Era*. Chapel Hill: University of North Carolina Press, 1999.

———. "Judge Carter and the *Brown* Decision," *OAH Newsletter*, February 2004. www.oah.org/pubs/nl/2004feb/sullivan.html.

Takaki, Ronald. *Double Victory: A Multicultural History of America in World War II*. Boston: Back Bay Books, 2001.

Thornton, J. Mills. *Dividing Lines: Municipal Politics and the Struggle for Civil Rights in Montgomery, Birmingham, and Selma*. Tuscaloosa: University of Alabama Press, 2002.

Thurber, Timothy N. *The Politics of Equality: Hubert H. Humphrey and the African American Freedom Struggle*. New York: Columbia University Press, 1999.

Travis, Dempsey J. *Views from the Back of the Bus During WWII and Beyond*. Chicago: Urban Research Press, 1995.

Tyson, Timothy B. *Radio Free Dixie: Robert F. Williams and the Roots of Black Power*. Chapel Hill: University of North Carolina Press, 1999.

U.S. Bureau of the Budget. *The United States at War*. Washington, D.C.: United States Government Printing Office, 1946.

U.S. Department of Commerce, Bureau of the Census. *Census of Population: 1940, Volume II Characteristics of the Population, Parts 1 and 2*. Washington, D.C.: Government Printing Office, 1943.

———. *Census of Population: 1950, Volume II Characteristics of the Population, Parts 5 and 13*. Washington, D.C.: Government Printing Office, 1952.

Von Eschen, Penny. *Race Against Empire: Black Americans and Anticolonialism, 1937–1957*. Ithaca, N.Y.: Cornell University Press, 1997.

Ware, Gilbert. *William Hastie: Grace Under Pressure*. New York: Oxford University Press, 1984.

Warren, James C. *The Tuskegee Airmen Mutiny at Freeman Field*. Vacaville, Calif.: Conyers, 1996.

Washington, Booker T. *Up from Slavery*. Reprint of 1900 ed. New York: Bantam, 1970.

Weiss, Nancy Joan. *Farewell to the Party of Lincoln: Black Politics in the Age of FDR*. Princeton: Princeton University Press, 1983.

White, Walter. *A Man Called White: The Autobiography of Walter White*. Reprint of 1948 ed. Athens: University of Georgia Press, 1995.

———. *A Rising Wind*. Garden City, N.Y.: Doubleday, 1945.

Wilkins, Roy, and Tom Matthews. *Standing Fast: The Autobiography of Roy Wilkins*. New York: Viking, 1982.

Wilkinson, Francis. "Segregationist Dreamer: Milton Henry, b. 1919," *New York Times Magazine*, Dec. 31, 2006.

Woodard, Jennifer Bailey. "A Phenomenal Woman." *Indiana Alumni Magazine* (January/February 1999). http://alumni.indiana.edu/scrapbook/aa/phenom.html and http://alumni.indiana.edu/scrapbook/aa/eagleside.html.

Wolk, Herman S. "Pantelleria, 1943." *Air Force Magazine*, June 2002, 64–68.

Yarmolinsky, Adam. *The Military Establishment: Its Impact on American Society*. New York: Harper & Row, 1971.

Index

Moton, Robert R., 43–44
Mussolini, Benito, 121
Myrdahl, Gunnar, 147, 155

Nation of Islam, 181
National Association for the
    Advancement of Colored People
    (NAACP), 2, 8, 16–17, 25, 26–27,
    29–30, 42, 56, 71, 77, 91, 107–8, 123,
    131–32, 141, 154–55, 159, 168–70;
    conflict with Tuskegee Institute, 31–35;
    investigations into treatment of blacks
    in AAF, 131–32, 134–35, 140–42; Legal
    Defense Fund, 109; National Legal
    Committee, 37–38, 71. *See also* DuBois,
    W.E.B.; Hastie, William H.; White,
    Walter; Wilkins, Roy
National Council of Negro Women, 158
National Negro Press Association, 92
National Military Establishment, 152
National Park Service, U.S., 12, 174
National Security Act of 1947, 152
Navy, U.S., 22, 75, 146, 157, 158
New Bethel Baptist Church, 182
Newsum, Fitzroy ("Buck"), 140
92nd Infantry Division, 20, 22, 149
96th Air Service Group, 89, 96, 108,
    111, 121
96th Article of War, 110
99th Pursuit Squadron, 30, 49, 57, 77,
    80, 84, 91, 93, 94, 106–7, 113, 123–26,
    149; assigned to combat overseas,
    96–98; in combat, 98–103, 104–5
1940 presidential election, 26–28
1948 presidential election, 154, 157–58
Nippert, Louis, 150
Nkrumah, Kwame, 11
Norfolk Journal and Guide, 166–67
North American Air Defense Command
    (NORAD), 166
North American Aviation Co., 16
North Carolina A&T College, 24
North Carolina College for Negroes, 38
North Carolina Mutual Insurance Co., 5
Northwest Air Lines, 164–65

Obadele, Gaidi. *See* Henry,
    Milton
Obadele, Imari Abubukari, 182
Obama, Barack H., 177
On Clipped Wings, 91–92
100th Fighter Squadron, 68, 77, 105, 112,
    120–21, 144
Oscoda Field, Mich., 108, 111
Oued N'Ja, Morocco, 98

P-39 (aircraft), 107
P-40 (aircraft), 97, 99
P-47 (aircraft), 6, 161
P-51 (aircraft), 112, 119, 121, 161
Pannell, Ulysses S., 58
Pantelleria, 99–100, 102
Parrish, Noel C., 53–57, 59–60, 67–68,
    86–87, 90, 92, 94, 158, 160, 168, 171;
    advocates full racial integration in
    postwar Air Force, 146–48, 150–52;
    assumes command of TAAF, 88–89,
    95
*Participation of Troops in the Post-War
    Military Establishment*, 150
Patterson, Frederick D., 25, 30–34, 41,
    44–45, 48, 50, 166–67
Patterson, Robert P., 32, 91
Penn, Starling, 175–6
Perry, Gracie, 53
Perry, Leslie S., 134
Pets Aviation School, 46
Philadelphia, Pa., 9–10, 46
Pittsburgh Courier, 12, 16, 19, 23, 25, 27,
    30, 92, 166–67
Platte, Claude, 64
Ploesti oil fields, 118–19
Plinton, James O., 63, 165
Plummer, Matthew, 64
Polk, P. K., 96
Polk, Wardell, 139, 174
Post Office Department, 184
Powell, Colin, 177
Powell, Richard H., Jr., 88
President's Commission on Civil Rights
    (PCCR), 153–57

Proctor, Bernard, 98, 103
Purnell, Louis R., 37, 99, 116

Rainey, Octave, 37
Ramitelli Airfield, Italy, 112, 115–16, 120, 160
Ramsey, James, 133
Randolph, A. Philip, 16–18, 25, 28, 139, 157, 180
Randolph Field, Tex., 54, 67, 73, 162, 167–68
Rapid City, S.D., 132
Reagan, Ronald, 14
Reed, G.A., 63
Republic of New Africa, 182
Richards-Gebaur Air Force Base, Mo., 165
Roach, John, 1–3, 6, 12, 178–79
Roberts, George S. ("Spanky"), 58, 60, 101, 105
Robeson, Paul, 96
Robinson, Hilyard R., 35
Rogers, J. A., 23
Rogers, J. D., 133, 138, 141
Rogers, John W., 89
Rommell, J. E., 99
Roosevelt, Eleanor, 8, 15, 27, 50–53, 127, 173
Roosevelt, Franklin D., 15–16, 18, 23, 26–27, 53, 58, 71
Roosevelt, Theodore, 43
Rosenberg, Frank, 49
Rosenwald Fund, 50–52
Rosenwald, Julius, 50
Ross, Mac, 37, 58
Rowe, James H., Jr., 27–28
Royal Air Force, 11, 23, 25
Royal Canadian Air Force, 25
Ruff, Willie, 145
Rustin, Bayard, 180

San Diego, Calif., 16
Segregation, 6–7, 10–11, 56, 120; at AAF bases during World War II, 123; of officers' clubs, 7–9, 125–26, 129–30,

132–35. *See also* Jim Crow; Tuskegee Army Air Field, segregation on base; Freeman Field "mutiny"
Selfridge Field, Mich., 78, 83, 105–9, 110, 126–28, 134
Selway, Robert R., 8–9, 95, 106, 124, 126, 128–29, 131–35, 137–40, 143, 149–50, 159, 163
766th Air Force Band, 145
777th Bombardment Squadron, 114
79th Fighter Group, 103–5, 113
Seymour, Ind., 132
Shabazz, Betty, 182
Shaik, Mohamed, 37
Shelton, Forrest, 47, 63
Sheppard Field, Tex., 7, 82–83
Shull, Lynwood L., 153
Sicily invasion, 100–101
Sioux Falls AAF Technical Training School, Iowa, 123
64th Article of War, 8, 135–36
66th Army Air Corps Primary Flight School, 53, 63. *See also* Moton Field
617th Medium Bombardment Squadron, 82
618th Medium Bombardment Squadron, 138
Slade, William H., 58
Sloan, James, 28
Smith, Luke S., 55–56
Smith, Quentin P., 136
Smith, William T., 57, 68
Southall, Clarence G., 129
Southern Christian Leadership Conference, 170
Spaatz, Carl, 102, 152–53
Spaulding, "Pokey," 5
Spencer, Chauncey, 24
SS *Josiah Bartlett*, 111–12
Stalag Luft III (German POW camp), 114, 122
Stalag Luft VIIA (German POW camp), 122
Stanley, Robert H., 43–44